Graph Machine Learning

Learning

Take graph data to the next level by applying
machine learning techniques and algorithms

Claudio Stamile

Aldo Marzullo

Enrico Deusebio

MW00836872

BIRMINGHAM—MUMBAI

Graph Machine Learning

Copyright © 2021 Packt Publishing

All rights reserved. No part of this book may be reproduced, stored in a retrieval system, or transmitted in any form or by any means, without the prior written permission of the publisher, except in the case of brief quotations embedded in critical articles or reviews.

Every effort has been made in the preparation of this book to ensure the accuracy of the information presented. However, the information contained in this book is sold without warranty, either express or implied. Neither the authors, nor Packt Publishing or its dealers and distributors, will be held liable for any damages caused or alleged to have been caused directly or indirectly by this book.

Packt Publishing has endeavored to provide trademark information about all of the companies and products mentioned in this book by the appropriate use of capitals. However, Packt Publishing cannot guarantee the accuracy of this information.

Group Product Manager: Kunal Parikh
Publishing Product Manager: Devika Battike
Senior Editor: Roshan Kumar
Content Development Editor: Sean Lobo
Technical Editor: Sonam Pandey
Copy Editor: Safis Editing
Project Coordinator: Aparna Ravikumar Nair
Proofreader: Safis Editing
Indexer: Vinayak Purushotham
Production Designer: Joshua Misquitta

First published: May 2021

Production reference: 1270521

Published by Packt Publishing Ltd.
Livery Place
35 Livery Street
Birmingham
B3 2PB, UK.

ISBN 978-1-80020-449-2

www.packt.com

Alla memoria di mio Zio, Franchino Avolio. Alle ruote delle bici troppo sgonfie, all'infanzia che mi ha regalato.

In memory of my uncle, Franchino Avolio. To the wheels of bikes that are too flat, to the childhood he gave me.

– Claudio Stamile

To my family, my roots.

– Aldo Marzullo

To Lili, for always reminding me with your 'learning' process how wonderful the human brain and life are.

– Enrico Deusebio

Contributors

About the authors

Claudio Stamile received an M.Sc. degree in computer science from the University of Calabria (Cosenza, Italy) in September 2013 and, in September 2017, he received his joint Ph.D. from KU Leuven (Leuven, Belgium) and Université Claude Bernard Lyon 1 (Lyon, France). During his career, he has developed a solid background in artificial intelligence, graph theory, and machine learning, with a focus on the biomedical field. He is currently a senior data scientist in CGnal, a consulting firm fully committed to helping its top-tier clients implement data-driven strategies and build AI-powered solutions to promote efficiency and support new business models.

Aldo Marzullo received an M.Sc. degree in computer science from the University of Calabria (Cosenza, Italy) in September 2016. During his studies, he developed a solid background in several areas, including algorithm design, graph theory, and machine learning. In January 2020, he received his joint Ph.D. from the University of Calabria and Université Claude Bernard Lyon 1 (Lyon, France), with a thesis entitled *Deep Learning and Graph Theory for Brain Connectivity Analysis in Multiple Sclerosis*. He is currently a postdoctoral researcher at the University of Calabria and collaborates with several international institutions.

Enrico Deusebio is currently the chief operating officer at CGnal, a consulting firm that helps its top-tier clients implement data-driven strategies and build AI-powered solutions. He has been working with data and large-scale simulations using high-performance facilities and large-scale computing centers for over 10 years, both in an academic and industrial context. He has collaborated and worked with top-tier universities, such as the University of Cambridge, the University of Turin, and the Royal Institute of Technology (KTH) in Stockholm, where he obtained a Ph.D. in 2014. He also holds B.Sc. and M.Sc. degrees in aerospace engineering from Politecnico di Torino.

About the reviewers

Kacper Kubara is a technical co-founder of Artemo and a data engineer at Annual Insight, and is currently pursuing a postgraduate degree in AI at the University of Amsterdam. Despite the focus of his research being graph representation learning, he is also interested in the tools and methods that help to bridge the gap between the AI industry and academia.

Tural Gulmammadov has been leading a group of data scientists and machine learning engineers at Oracle to tackle applied machine learning problems from various industries. He is dedicated to and motivated by the applications of graph theory and discrete mathematics in machine learning over distributed computational environments. He is a cognitive science, statistics, and psychology enthusiast, as well as a chess player, painter, seasonal horse rider, and paddler.

Table of Contents

Section 2 – Machine Learning on Graphs

3

Unsupervised Graph Learning

4

Supervised Graph Learning

5

Problems with Machine Learning on Graphs

Section 3 – Advanced Applications of Graph Machine Learning

6

Social Network Graphs

7

Text Analytics and Natural Language Processing Using Graphs

Preface

Graph Machine Learning provides a new set of tools for processing network data and leveraging the power of the relationship between entities that can be used for predictive, modeling, and analytics tasks.

You will start with a brief introduction to graph theory and Graph Machine Learning, learning to understand their potential. As you proceed, you will become well versed with the main machine learning models for graph representation learning: their purpose, how they work, and how they can be implemented in a wide range of supervised and unsupervised learning applications. You'll then build a complete machine learning pipeline, including data processing, model training, and prediction, in order to exploit the full potential of graph data. Moving on, you will cover real-world scenarios, such as extracting data from social networks, text analytics, and natural language processing using graphs and financial transaction systems on graphs. Finally, you will learn how to build and scale out data-driven applications for graph analytics to store, query, and process network information, before progressing to explore the latest trends on graphs.

By the end of this machine learning book, you will have learned the essential concepts of graph theory and all the algorithms and techniques used to build successful machine learning applications.

Who this book is for

This book is for data analysts, graph developers, graph analysts, and graph professionals who want to leverage the information embedded in the connections and relations between data points, unravel hidden structures, and exploit topological information to boost their analysis and models' performance. The book will also be useful for data scientists and machine learning developers who want to build machine learning-driven graph databases. A beginner-level understanding of graph databases and graph data is required. An intermediate-level working knowledge of Python programming and machine learning is also expected to make the most out of this book.

What this book covers

Chapter 1, Getting Started with Graphs, introduces the basic concepts of graph theory using the NetworkX Python library.

Chapter 2, Graph Machine Learning, introduces the main concepts of graph machine learning and graph embedding techniques.

Chapter 3, Unsupervised Graph Learning, covers recent unsupervised graph embedding methods.

Chapter 4, Supervised Graph Learning, covers recent supervised graph embedding methods.

Chapter 5, Problems with Machine Learning on Graphs, introduces the most common machine learning tasks on graphs.

Chapter 6, Social Network Analysis, shows an application of machine learning algorithms on social network data.

Chapter 7, Text Analytics and Natural Language Processing Using Graphs, shows the application of machine learning algorithms to natural language processing tasks.

Chapter 8, Graph Analysis for Credit Card Transactions, shows the application of machine learning algorithms to credit card fraud detection.

Chapter 9, Building a Data-Driven Graph-Powered Application, introduces some technologies and techniques that are useful for dealing with large graphs.

Chapter 10, Novel Trends on Graphs, introduces some novel trends (algorithms and applications) in graph machine learning.

To get the most out of this book

A Jupyter or a Google Colab notebook is sufficient to cover all the examples. For some chapters, Neo4j and Gephi are also required.

Software/Hardware covered in the book	OS Requirements
Python	Windows, macOS X, and Linux (any)
Neo4j	Windows, macOS X, and Linux (any)
Gephi	Windows, macOS X, and Linux (any)
Google Colab or Jupyter Notebook	Windows, macOS X, and Linux (any)

If you are using the digital version of this book, we advise you to type the code yourself or access the code via the GitHub repository (link available in the next section). Doing so will help you avoid any potential errors related to the copying and pasting of code.

Download the example code files

You can download the example code files for this book from GitHub at `https://github.com/PacktPublishing/Graph-Machine-Learning`. In case there's an update to the code, it will be updated on the existing GitHub repository.

We also have other code bundles from our rich catalog of books and videos available at `https://github.com/PacktPublishing/`. Check them out!

Download the color images

We also provide a PDF file that has color images of the screenshots/diagrams used in this book. You can download it here: `https://static.packt-cdn.com/downloads/9781800204492_ColorImages.pdf`.

Conventions used

There are a number of text conventions used throughout this book.

`Code in text`: Indicates code words in text, database table names, folder names, filenames, file extensions, pathnames, dummy URLs, user input, and Twitter handles. Here is an example: "Mount the downloaded `WebStorm-10*.dmg` disk image file as another disk in your system."

A block of code is set as follows:

```
html, body, #map {
  height: 100%;
  margin: 0;
  padding: 0
}
```

When we wish to draw your attention to a particular part of a code block, the relevant lines or items are set in bold:

```
Jupyter==1.0.0
networkx==2.5
matplotlib==3.2.2
node2vec==0.3.3
karateclub==1.0.19
scipy==1.6.2
```

Any command-line input or output is written as follows:

```
$ mkdir css
$ cd css
```

Bold: Indicates a new term, an important word, or words that you see on screen. For example, words in menus or dialog boxes appear in the text like this. Here is an example: "Select **System info** from the **Administration** panel."

> **Tips or important notes**
> Appear like this.

Get in touch

Feedback from our readers is always welcome.

General feedback: If you have questions about any aspect of this book, mention the book title in the subject of your message and email us at customercare@packtpub.com.

Errata: Although we have taken every care to ensure the accuracy of our content, mistakes do happen. If you have found a mistake in this book, we would be grateful if you would report this to us. Please visit www.packtpub.com/support/errata, selecting your book, clicking on the Errata Submission Form link, and entering the details.

Piracy: If you come across any illegal copies of our works in any form on the internet, we would be grateful if you would provide us with the location address or website name. Please contact us at copyright@packt.com with a link to the material.

If you are interested in becoming an author: If there is a topic that you have expertise in, and you are interested in either writing or contributing to a book, please visit authors.packtpub.com.

Reviews

Please leave a review. Once you have read and used this book, why not leave a review on the site that you purchased it from? Potential readers can then see and use your unbiased opinion to make purchase decisions, we at Packt can understand what you think about our products, and our authors can see your feedback on their book. Thank you!

For more information about Packt, please visit `packt.com`.

Section 1 – Introduction to Graph Machine Learning

In this section, the reader will get a brief introduction to graph machine learning, showing the potential of graphs combined with the right machine learning algorithms. Moreover, a general overview of graph theory and Python libraries is provided in order to allow the reader to deal with (that is, create, modify, and plot) graph data structures.

This section comprises the following chapters:

- *Chapter 1, Getting Started with Graphs*
- *Chapter 2, Graph Machine Learning*

1
Getting Started with Graphs

Graphs are mathematical structures that are used for describing relations between entities and are used almost everywhere. For example, social networks are graphs, where users are connected depending on whether one user "*follows*" the updates of another user. They can be used for representing maps, where cities are linked through streets. Graphs can describe biological structures, web pages, and even the progression of neurodegenerative diseases.

Graph theory, the study of graphs, has received major interest for years, leading people to develop algorithms, identify properties, and define mathematical models to better understand complex behaviors.

This chapter will review some of the concepts behind graph-structured data. Theoretical notions will be presented, together with examples to help you understand some of the more general concepts and put them into practice. In this chapter, we will introduce and use some of the most widely used libraries for the creation, manipulation, and study of the structure dynamics and functions of complex networks, specifically looking at the Python `networkx` library.

The following topics will be covered in this chapter:

- Introduction to graphs with `networkx`
- Plotting graphs
- Graph properties
- Benchmarks and repositories
- Dealing with large graphs

Technical requirements

We will be using Jupyter Notebooks with *Python 3.8* for all of our exercises. In the following code snippet, we show a list of Python libraries that will be installed for this chapter using `pip` (for example, run `pip install networkx==2.5` on the command line, and so on):

```
Jupyter==1.0.0
networkx==2.5
snap-stanford==5.0.0
matplotlib==3.2.2
pandas==1.1.3
scipy==1.6.2
```

In this book, the following Python commands will be referred to:

- `import networkx as nx`
- `import pandas as pd`
- `import numpy as np`

For more complex data visualization tasks, Gephi (`https://gephi.org/`) is also required. The installation manual is available here: `https://gephi.org/users/install/`. All code files relevant to this chapter are available at `https://github.com/PacktPublishing/Graph-Machine-Learning/tree/main/Chapter01`.

Introduction to graphs with networkx

In this section, we will give a general introduction to graph theory. Moreover, in order to merge theoretical concepts with their practical implementation, we will enrich our explanation with code snippets in Python, using `networkx`.

A **simple undirected graph** (or simply, a graph) G is defined as a couple $G=(V,E)$, where $V=\{v_1, .., v_n\}$ is a set of nodes (also called **vertices**) and $E=\{\{v_k,v_w\} .., \{v_i,v_j\}\}$ is a set of two-sets (set of two elements) of edges (also called **links**), representing the connection between two nodes belonging to V.

It is important to underline that since each element of E is a two-set, there is no order between each edge. To provide more detail, $\{v_k,v_w\}$ and $\{v_w,v_k\}$ represent the same edge.

We now provide definitions for some basic properties of graphs and nodes, as follows:

- The **order** of a graph is the number of its vertices $|V|$. The **size** of a graph is the number of its edges $|E|$.

- The **degree** of a vertex is the number of edges that are adjacent to it. The **neighbors** of a vertex v in a graph G is a subset of vertex V' induced by all vertices adjacent to v.

- The **neighborhood graph** (also known as an ego graph) of a vertex v in a graph G is a subgraph of G, composed of the vertices adjacent to v and all edges connecting vertices adjacent to v.

An example of what a graph looks like can be seen in the following screenshot:

V = [Paris, Milan, Dublin, Rome]

E = [{Milan, Dublin}, {Milan, Paris}, {Paris, Dublin}, {Milan, Rome}]

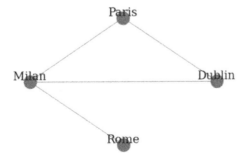

Figure 1.1 – Example of a graph

According to this representation, since there is no direction, an edge from **Milan** to **Paris** is equal to an edge from **Paris** to **Milan**. Thus, it is possible to move in the two directions without any constraint. If we analyze the properties of the graph depicted in *Figure 1.1*, we can see that it has *order* and *size* equal to 4 (there are, in total, four vertices and four edges). The **Paris** and **Dublin** vertices have degree 2, **Milan** has degree 3, and **Rome** has degree 1. The neighbors for each node are shown in the following list:

- Paris = {Milan, Dublin}
- Milan = {Paris, Dublin, Rome}
- Dublin = {Paris, Milan}
- Rome = {Milan}

The same graph can be represented in networkx, as follows:

```
import networkx as nx
G = nx.Graph()
V = {'Dublin', 'Paris', 'Milan', 'Rome'}
E = [('Milan','Dublin'), ('Milan','Paris'), ('Paris','Dublin'),
('Milan','Rome')]
G.add_nodes_from(V)
G.add_edges_from(E)
```

Since by default, the nx.Graph() command generates an undirected graph, we do not need to specify both directions of each edge. In networkx, nodes can be any hashable object: strings, classes, or even other networkx graphs. Let's now compute some properties of the graph we previously generated.

All the nodes and edges of the graph can be obtained by running the following code:

```
print(f"V = {G.nodes}")
print(f"E = {G.edges}")
```

Here is the output of the previous commands:

```
V = ['Rome', 'Dublin', 'Milan', 'Paris']
E = [('Rome', 'Milan'), ('Dublin', 'Milan'), ('Dublin',
'Paris'), ('Milan', 'Paris')]
```

We can also compute the graph order, the graph size, and the degree and neighbors for each of the nodes, using the following commands:

```
print(f"Graph Order: {G.number_of_nodes()}")
print(f"Graph Size: {G.number_of_edges()}")
print(f"Degree for nodes: { {v: G.degree(v) for v in G.nodes}
}")
print(f"Neighbors for nodes: { {v: list(G.neighbors(v)) for v
in G.nodes} }")
```

The result will be the following:

```
Graph Order: 4
Graph Size: 4
Degree for nodes: {'Rome': 1, 'Paris': 2, 'Dublin':2, 'Milan':
3}
Neighbors for nodes: {'Rome': ['Milan'], 'Paris': ['Milan',
'Dublin'], 'Dublin': ['Milan', 'Paris'], 'Milan': ['Dublin',
'Paris', 'Rome']}
```

Finally, we can also compute an ego graph of a specific node for the graph G, as follows:

```
ego_graph_milan = nx.ego_graph(G, "Milan")
print(f"Nodes: {ego_graph_milan.nodes}")
print(f"Edges: {ego_graph_milan.edges}")
```

The result will be the following:

```
Nodes: ['Paris', 'Milan', 'Dublin', 'Rome']
Edges: [('Paris', 'Milan'), ('Paris', 'Dublin'), ('Milan',
'Dublin'), ('Milan', 'Rome')]
```

The original graph can be also modified by adding new nodes and/or edges, as follows:

```
#Add new nodes and edges
new_nodes = {'London', 'Madrid'}
new_edges = [('London','Rome'), ('Madrid','Paris')]
G.add_nodes_from(new_nodes)
G.add_edges_from(new_edges)
print(f"V = {G.nodes}")
print(f"E = {G.edges}")
```

This would output the following lines:

```
V = ['Rome', 'Dublin', 'Milan', 'Paris', 'London', 'Madrid']
E = [('Rome', 'Milan'), ('Rome', 'London'), ('Dublin',
'Milan'), ('Dublin', 'Paris'), ('Milan', 'Paris'), ('Paris',
'Madrid')]
```

Removal of nodes can be done by running the following code:

```
node_remove = {'London', 'Madrid'}
G.remove_nodes_from(node_remove)
print(f"V = {G.nodes}")
print(f"E = {G.edges}")
```

This is the result of the preceding commands:

```
V = ['Rome', 'Dublin', 'Milan', 'Paris']
E = [('Rome', 'Milan'), ('Dublin', 'Milan'), ('Dublin',
'Paris'), ('Milan', 'Paris')]
```

As expected, all the edges that contain the removed nodes are automatically deleted from the edge list.

Also, edges can be removed by running the following code:

```
node_edges = [('Milan','Dublin'), ('Milan','Paris')]
G.remove_edges_from(node_edges)
print(f"V = {G.nodes}")
print(f"E = {G.edges}")
```

The final result will be as follows:

```
V = ['Dublin', 'Paris', 'Milan', 'Rome']
E = [('Dublin', 'Paris'), ('Milan', 'Rome')]
```

The networkx library also allows us to remove a single node or a single edge from a graph G by using the following commands: G.remove_node('Dublin') and G.remove_edge('Dublin', 'Paris').

Types of graphs

In the previous section, we described how to create and modify simple undirected graphs. Here, we will show how we can extend this basic data structure in order to encapsulate more information, thanks to the introduction of **directed graphs** (**digraphs**), weighted graphs, and multigraphs.

Digraphs

A digraph G is defined as a couple $G=(V, E)$, where $V=\{V_1, .., V_n\}$ is a set of nodes and $E=\{(V_k,V_w) .., (V_i,V_j)\}$ is a set of ordered couples representing the connection between two nodes belonging to V.

Since each element of E is an ordered couple, it enforces the direction of the connection. The edge (V_k,V_w) means *the node* V_k *goes into* V_w. This is different from (V_w,V_k) since it means *the node* V_w *goes to* V_k. The starting node V_w is called the *head*, while the ending node is called the *tail*.

Due to the presence of edge direction, the definition of node degree needs to be extended.

Indegree and outdegree

For a vertex v, the number of head ends adjacent to v is called the **indegree** (indicated by $deg^-(v)$ of v, while the number of tail ends adjacent to v is its **outdegree** (indicated by $deg^+(v)$).

An example of what a digraph looks like is available in the following screenshot:

V = [Paris, Milan, Dublin, Rome]

E = [(Milan, Dublin), (Paris , Milan), (Paris, Dublin), (Milan, Rome)]

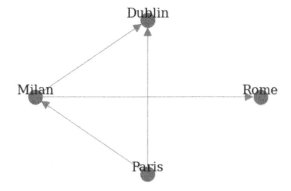

Figure 1.2 – Example of a digraph

The direction of the edge is visible from the arrow—for example, **Milan** -> **Dublin** means from **Milan** to **Dublin**. **Dublin** has $deg^-(v) = 2$ and $deg^+(v) = 0$, **Paris** has $deg^-(v) = 0$ and $deg^+(v) = 2$, **Milan** has $deg^-(v) = 1$ and $deg^+(v) = 2$, and **Rome** has $deg^-(v) = 1$ and $deg^+(v) = 0$.

The same graph can be represented in `networkx`, as follows:

```
G = nx.DiGraph()
V = {'Dublin', 'Paris', 'Milan', 'Rome'}
E = [('Milan','Dublin'), ('Paris','Milan'), ('Paris','Dublin'),
('Milan','Rome')]
G.add_nodes_from(V)
G.add_edges_from(E)
```

The definition is the same as that used for simple undirected graphs; the only difference is in the `networkx` classes that are used to instantiate the object. For digraphs, the `nx.DiGraph()` class is used.

`Indegree` and `Outdegree` can be computed using the following commands:

```
print(f"Indegree for nodes: { {v: G.in_degree(v) for v in
G.nodes} }")
print(f"Outdegree for nodes: { {v: G.out_degree(v) for v in
G.nodes} }")
```

The results will be as follows:

```
Indegree for nodes: {'Rome': 1, 'Paris': 0, 'Dublin': 2,
'Milan': 1}
Outdegree for nodes: {'Rome': 0, 'Paris': 2, 'Dublin': 0,
'Milan': 2}
```

As for the undirected graphs, `G.add_nodes_from()`, `G.add_edges_from()`, `G.remove_nodes_from()`, and `G.remove_edges_from()` functions can be used to modify a given graph G.

Multigraph

We will now introduce the multigraph object, which is a generalization of the graph definition that allows multiple edges to have the same pair of start and end nodes.

A **multigraph G** is defined as $G=(V, E)$, where V is a set of nodes and E is a multi-set (a set allowing multiple instances for each of its elements) of edges.

A multigraph is called a **directed multigraph** if *E* is a multi-set of ordered couples; otherwise, if *E* is a multi-set of two-sets, then it is called an **undirected multigraph**.

An example of a directed multigraph is available in the following screenshot:

V = [Paris, Milan, Dublin, Rome]

E = [(Milan, Dublin), (Milan, Dublin), (Paris , Milan), (Paris, Dublin), (Milan, Rome), (Milan, Rome)]

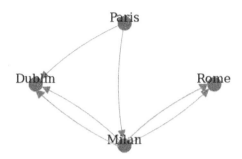

Figure 1.3 – Example of a multigraph

In the following code snippet, we show how to use networkx in order to create a directed or an undirected multigraph:

```
directed_multi_graph = nx.MultiDiGraph()
undirected_multi_graph = nx.MultiGraph()
V = {'Dublin', 'Paris', 'Milan', 'Rome'}
E = [('Milan','Dublin'), ('Milan','Dublin'), ('Paris','Milan'),
('Paris','Dublin'), ('Milan','Rome'), ('Milan','Rome')]
directed_multi_graph.add_nodes_from(V)
undirected_multi_graph.add_nodes_from(V)
directed_multi_graph.add_edges_from(E)
undirected_multi_graph.add_edges_from(E)
```

The only difference between a directed and an undirected multigraph is in the first two lines, where two different objects are created: nx.MultiDiGraph() is used to create a directed multigraph, while nx.MultiGraph() is used to build an undirected multigraph. The function used to add nodes and edges is the same for both objects.

Weighted graphs

We will now introduce directed, undirected, and multi-weighted graphs.

An **edge-weighted graph** (or simply, a weighted graph) G is defined as $G=(V, E, w)$ where V is a set of nodes, E is a set of edges, and w: E $\rightarrow \mathbb{R}$ is the weighted function that assigns at each edge e $\in$ E a weight expressed as a real number.

A **node-weighted graph** G is defined as $G=(V, E, w)$, where V is a set of nodes, E is a set of edges, and w: V $\rightarrow \mathbb{R}$ is the weighted function that assigns at each node v $\in$ V a weight expressed as a real number.

Please keep the following points in mind:

- If E is a set of ordered couples, then we call it a **directed weighted graph**.
- If E is a set of two-sets, then we call it an **undirected weighted graph**.
- If E is a multi-set, we will call it a **weighted multigraph** (**directed weighted multigraph**).
- If E is a multi-set of ordered couples, it is an **undirected weighted multigraph**.

An example of a directed edge-weighted graph is available in the following screenshot:

V = [Paris, Milan, Dublin, Rome]

E = [(Milan, Dublin, 19), (Paris , Milan, 8), (Paris, Dublin, 11), (Milan, Rome, 5)]

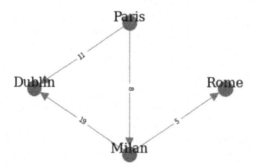

Figure 1.4 – Example of a directed edge-weighted graph

From *Figure 1.4*, it is easy to see how the presence of weights on graphs helps to add useful information to the data structures. Indeed, we can imagine the edge weight as a "cost" to reach a node from another node. For example, reaching **Dublin** from **Milan** has a "cost" of 19, while reaching **Dublin** from **Paris** has a "cost" of 11.

In `networkx`, a directed weighted graph can be generated as follows:

```
G = nx.DiGraph()
V = {'Dublin', 'Paris', 'Milan', 'Rome'}
E = [('Milan','Dublin', 19), ('Paris','Milan', 8),
('Paris','Dublin', 11), ('Milan','Rome', 5)]
G.add_nodes_from(V)
G.add_weighted_edges_from(E)
```

Bipartite graphs

We will now introduce another type of graph that will be used in this section: multipartite graphs. Bi- and tripartite graphs—and, more generally, kth-partite graphs—are graphs whose vertices can be partitioned in two, three, or more k-th sets of nodes, respectively. Edges are only allowed across different sets and are not allowed within nodes belonging to the same set. In most cases, nodes belonging to different sets are also characterized by particular node types. In *Chapters 7, Text Analytics and Natural Language Processing Using Graphs,* and *Chapter 8, Graphs Analysis for Credit Cards Transaction,* we will deal with some practical examples of graph-based applications and you will see how multipartite graphs can indeed arise in several contexts—for example, in the following scenarios:

- When processing documents and structuring the information in a bipartite graph of documents and entities that appear in the documents

- When dealing with transactional data, in order to encode the relations between the buyers and the merchants

A bipartite graph can be easily created in `networkx` with the following code:

```
import pandas as pd
import numpy as np
n_nodes = 10
n_edges = 12
bottom_nodes = [ith for ith in range(n_nodes) if ith % 2 ==0]
 top_nodes = [ith for ith in range(n_nodes) if ith % 2 ==1]
iter_edges = zip(
    np.random.choice(bottom_nodes, n_edges),
    np.random.choice(top_nodes, n_edges))
edges = pd.DataFrame([
    {"source": a, "target": b} for a, b in iter_edges])
B = nx.Graph()
```

```
B.add_nodes_from(bottom_nodes, bipartite=0)
B.add_nodes_from(top_nodes, bipartite=1)
B.add_edges_from([tuple(x) for x in edges.values])
```

The network can also be conveniently plotted using the `bipartite_layout` utility function of `networkx`, as illustrated in the following code snippet:

```
from networkx.drawing.layout import bipartite_layout
pos = bipartite_layout(B, bottom_nodes)
nx.draw_networkx(B, pos=pos)
```

The `bipatite_layout` function produces a graph, as shown in the following screenshot:

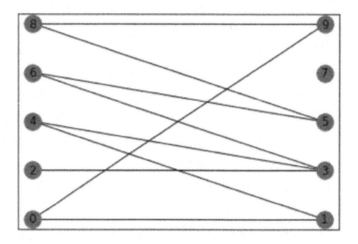

Figure 1.5 – Example of a bipartite graph

Graph representations

As described in the previous sections, with `networkx`, we can actually define and manipulate a graph by using node and edge objects. In different use cases, such a representation would not be as easy to handle. In this section, we will show two ways to perform a compact representation of a graph data structure—namely, an adjacency matrix and an edge list.

Adjacency matrix

The **adjacency matrix** M of a graph $G=(V,E)$ is a square matrix $(|V| \times |V|)$ matrix such that its element M_{ij} is 1 when there is an edge from node i to node j, and 0 when there is no edge. In the following screenshot, we show a simple example where the adjacency matrix of different types of graphs is displayed:

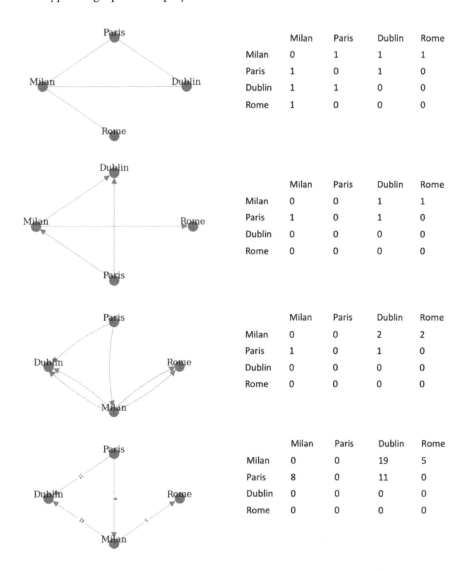

Figure 1.6 – Adjacency matrix for an undirected graph, a digraph, a multigraph, and a weighted graph

It is easy to see that adjacency matrices for undirected graphs are always symmetric, since no direction is defined for the edge. The symmetry instead is not guaranteed for the adjacency matrix of a digraph due to the presence of constraints in the direction of the edges. For a multigraph, we can instead have values greater than 1 since multiple edges can be used to connect the same couple of nodes. For a weighted graph, the value in a specific cell is equal to the weight of the edge connecting the two nodes.

In networkx, the adjacency matrix for a given graph can be computed in two different ways. If G is the networkx of *Figure 1.6*, we can compute its adjacency matrix as follows:

```
nx.to_pandas_adjacency(G) #adjacency matrix as pd DataFrame
nt.to_numpy_matrix(G) #adjacency matrix as numpy matrix
```

For the first and second line, we get the following results respectively:

	Rome	Dublin	Milan	Paris
Rome	0.0	0.0	0.0	0.0
Dublin	0.0	0.0	0.0	0.0
Milan	1.0	1.0	0.0	0.0
Paris	0.0	1.0	1.0	0.0

```
[[0. 0. 0. 0.]
 [0. 0. 0. 0.]
 [1. 1. 0. 0.]
 [0. 1. 1. 0.]]
```

Since a numpy matrix cannot represent the name of the nodes, the order of the element in the adjacency matrix is the one defined in the G.nodes list.

Edge list

As well as an adjacency matrix, an edge list is another compact way to represent graphs. The idea behind this format is to represent a graph as a list of edges.

The **edge list** L of a graph $G=(V,E)$ is a list of size $|E|$ matrix such that its element L_i is a couple representing the tail and the end node of the edge i. An example of the edge list for each type of graph is available in the following screenshot:

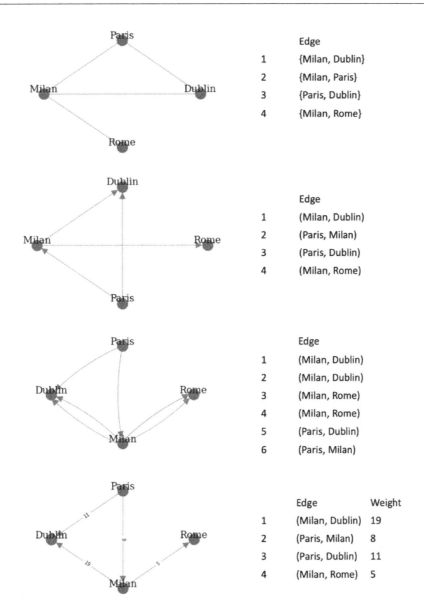

Figure 1.7 – Edge list for an undirected graph, a digraph, a multigraph, and a weighted graph

In the following code snippet, we show how to compute in `networkx` the edge list of the simple undirected graph *G* available in *Figure 1.7*:

```
print(nx.to_pandas_edgelist(G))
```

By running the preceding command, we get the following result:

	source	target
0	Milan	Dublin
1	Milan	Rome
2	Paris	Milan
3	Paris	Dublin

Other representation methods, which we will not discuss in detail, are also available in `networkx`. Some examples are `nx.to_dict_of_dicts(G)` and `nx.to_numpy_array(G)`, among others.

Plotting graphs

As we have seen in previous sections, graphs are intuitive data structures represented graphically. Nodes can be plotted as simple circles, while edges are lines connecting two nodes.

Despite their simplicity, it could be quite difficult to make a clear representation when the number of edges and nodes increases. The source of this complexity is mainly related to the position (space/Cartesian coordinates) to assign to each node in the final plot. Indeed, it could be unfeasible to manually assign to a graph with hundreds of nodes the specific position of each node in the final plot.

In this section, we will see how we can plot graphs without specifying coordinates for each node. We will exploit two different solutions: `networkx` and Gephi.

networkx

`networkx` offers a simple interface to plot graph objects through the `nx.draw` library. In the following code snippet, we show how to use the library in order to plot graphs:

```
def draw_graph(G, nodes_position, weight):
        nx.draw(G, pos_ position, with_labels=True, font_size=15,
node_size=400, edge_color='gray', arrowsize=30)
            if plot_weight:
            edge_labels=nx.get_edge_attributes(G,'weight')
            nx.draw_networkx_edge_labels(G, pos_ position, edge_
 labels=edge_labels)
```

Here, `nodes_position` is a dictionary where the keys are the nodes and the value assigned to each key is an array of length 2, with the Cartesian coordinate used for plotting the specific node.

The `nx.draw` function will plot the whole graph by putting its nodes in the given positions. The `with_labels` option will plot its name on top of each node with the specific `font_size` value. `node_size` and `edge_color` will respectively specify the size of the circle, representing the node and the color of the edges. Finally, `arrowsize` will define the size of the arrow for directed edges. This option will be used when the graph to be plotted is a digraph.

In the following code example, we show how to use the `draw_graph` function previously defined in order to plot a graph:

```
G = nx.Graph()
V = {'Paris', 'Dublin','Milan', 'Rome'}
E = [('Paris','Dublin', 11), ('Paris','Milan', 8),
        ('Milan','Rome', 5), ('Milan','Dublin', 19)]
G.add_nodes_from(V)
G.add_weighted_edges_from(E)
node_position = {"Paris": [0,0], "Dublin": [0,1], "Milan":
[1,0], "Rome": [1,1]}
draw_graph(G, node_position, True)
```

The result of the plot is available to view in the following screenshot:

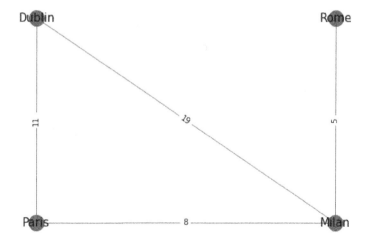

Figure 1.8 – Result of the plotting function

The method previously described is simple but unfeasible to use in a real scenario since the node_position value could be difficult to decide. In order to solve this issue, networkx offers a different function to automatically compute the position of each node according to different layouts. In *Figure 1.9*, we show a series of plots of an undirected graph, obtained using the different layouts available in networkx. In order to use them in the function we proposed, we simply need to assign node_position to the result of the layout we want to use—for example, node_position = nx.circular_ layout(G). The plots can be seen in the following screenshot:

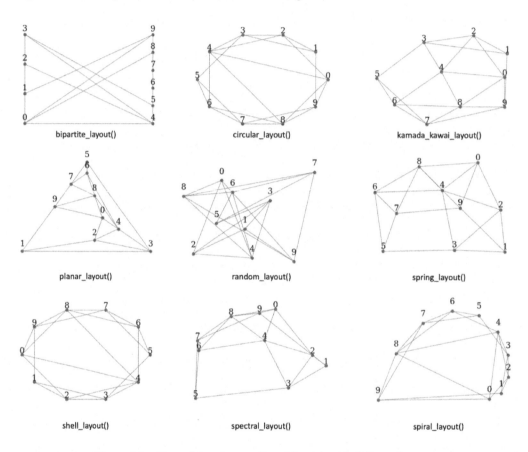

Figure 1.9 – Plots of the same undirected graph with different layouts

networkx is a great tool for easily manipulating and analyzing graphs, but it does not offer good functionalities in order to perform complex and good-looking plots of graphs. In the next section, we will investigate another tool to perform complex graph visualization: Gephi.

Gephi

In this section, we will show how **Gephi** (an open source network analysis and visualization software) can be used for performing complex, fancy plots of graphs. For all the examples showed in this section, we will use the `Les Miserables.gexf` sample (a weighted undirected graph), which can be selected in the **Welcome** window when the application starts.

The main interface of Gephi is shown in *Figure 1.10*. It can be divided into four main areas, as follows:

1. **Graph**: This section shows the final plot of the graph. The image is automatically updated each time a filter or a specific layout is applied.

2. **Appearance**: Here, it is possible to specify the appearance of nodes and edges.

3. **Layout**: In this section, it is possible to select the layout (as in `networkx`) to adjust the node position in the graph. Different algorithms, from a simple random position generator to a more complex Yifan Hu algorithm, are available.

4. **Filters & Statistics**: In this set area, two main functions are available, outlined as follows:

    a. **Filters**: In this tab, it is possible to filter and visualize specific subregions of the graph according to a set property computed using the **Statistics** tab.

    b. **Statistics**: This tab contains a list of available graph metrics that can be computed on the graph using the **Run** button. Once metrics are computed, they can be used as properties to specify the edges' and nodes' appearance (such as node and edge size and color) or to filter a specific subregion of the graph.

You can see the main interface of Gephi in the following screenshot:

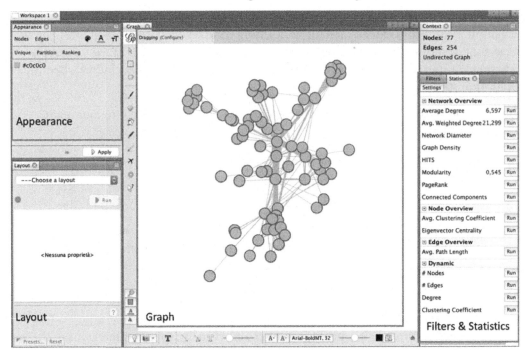

Figure 1.10 – Gephi main window

Our exploration of Gephi starts with the application of different layouts to the graph. As previously described, in `networkx` the layouts allow us to assign to each node a specific position in the final plot. In Gephi 1.2, different layouts are available. In order to apply a specific layout, we have to select from the **Layout** area one of the available layouts, and then click on the **Run** button that appears after the selection.

The graph representation, visible in the **Graph** area, will be automatically updated according to the new coordinates defined by the layout. It should be noted that some layouts are parametric, hence the final graph plot can significantly change according to the parameters used. In the following screenshot, we propose several examples for the application of three different layouts:

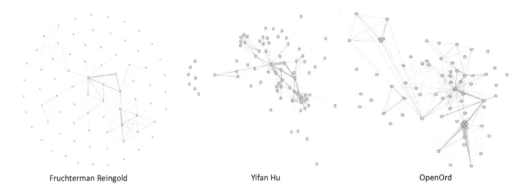

Fruchterman Reingold   Yifan Hu   OpenOrd

Figure 1.11 – Plot of the same graph with different layout

We will now introduce the available options in the **Appearance** menu visible in *Figure 1.10*. In this section, it is possible to specify the style to be applied to edges and nodes. The style to be applied can be static or can be dynamically defined by specific properties of the nodes/edges. We can change the color and the size of the nodes by selecting the **Nodes** option in the menu.

In order to change the color, we have to select the color palette icon and decide, using the specific button, if we want to assign a **Unique** color, a **Partition** (discrete values), or a **Ranking** (range of values) of colors. For **Partition** and **Ranking**, it is possible to select from the drop-down menu a specific **Graph** property to use as reference for the color range. Only the properties computed by clicking **Run** in the **Statistics** area are available in the drop-down menu. The same procedure can be used in order to set the size of the nodes. By selecting the concentric circles icon, it is possible to set a **Unique** size to all the nodes or to specify a **Ranking** of size according to a specific property.

As for the nodes, it is also possible to change the style of the edges by selecting the **Edges** option in the menu. We can then select to assign a **Unique** color, a **Partition** (discrete values), or a **Ranking** (range of values) of colors. For **Partition** and **Ranking**, the reference value to build the color scale is defined by a specific **Graph** property that can be selected from the drop-down menu.

It is important to remember that in order to apply a specific style to the graph, the **Apply** button should be clicked. As a result, the graph plot will be updated according to the style defined. In the following screenshot, we show an example where the color of the nodes is given by the **Modularity Class** value and the size of each node is given by its degree, while the color of each edge is defined by the edge weight:

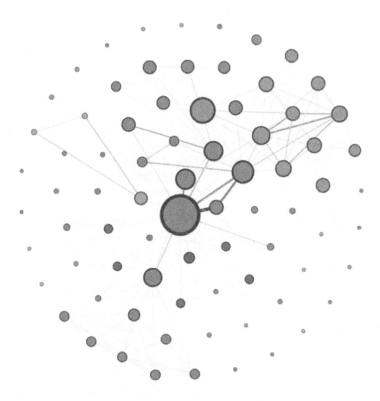

Figure 1.12 – Example of graph plot changing nodes' and edges' appearance

Another important section that needs to be described is **Filters & Statistics**. In this menu, it is possible to compute some statistics based on graph metrics.

Finally, we conclude our discussion on Gephi by introducing the functionalities available in the **Statistics** menu, visible in the right panel in *Figure 1.10*. Through this menu, it is possible to compute different statistics on the input graph. Those statistics can be easily used to set some properties of the final plot, such as nodes'/edges' color and size, or to filter the original graph to plot just a specific subset of it. In order to compute a specific statistic, the user then needs to explicitly select one of the metrics available in the menu and click on the **Run** button (*Figure 1.10*, right panel).

Moreover, the user can select a subregion of the graph, using the options available in the **Filters** tab of the **Statistics** menu, visible in the right panel in *Figure 1.10*. An example of filtering a graph can be seen in *Figure 1.13*. To provide more details of this, we build and apply to the graph a filter, using the **Degree** property. The result of the filters is a subset of the original graph, where only the nodes (and their edges) having the specific range of values for the degree property are visible.

This is illustrated in the following screenshot:

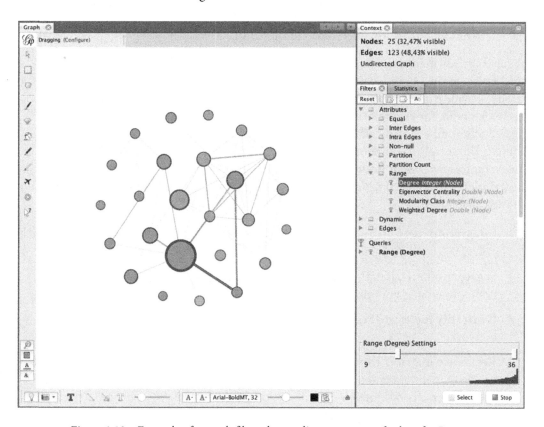

Figure 1.13 – Example of a graph filtered according to a range of values for Degree

Of course, Gephi allows us to perform more complex visualization tasks and contains a lot of functionalities that cannot be fully covered in this book. Some good references to better investigate all the features available in Gephi are the official Gephi guide (https:// gephi.org/users/) or the *Gephi Cookbook* book by Packt Publishing.

Graph properties

As we have already learned, a *graph* is a mathematical model that is used for describing relations between entities. However, each complex network presents intrinsic properties. Such properties can be measured by particular metrics, and each measure may characterize one or several local and global aspects of the graph.

In a graph for a social network such as Twitter, for example, users (represented by the *nodes* of the graph) are connected to each other. However, there are users that are more connected than others (influencers). On the Reddit social graph, users with similar characteristics tend to group into communities.

We have already mentioned some of the *basic features* of graphs, such as the *number of nodes and edges* in a graph, which constitute the size of the graph itself. Those properties already provide a good description of the structure of a network. Think about the Facebook graph, for example: it can be described in terms of the number of nodes and edges. Such numbers easily allow it to be distinguished from a much smaller network (for example, the social structure of an office) but fail to characterize more complex dynamics (for example, how *similar* nodes are connected). To this end, more advanced graph-derived **metrics** can be considered, which can be grouped into four main categories, outlined as follows:

- **Integration metrics**: These measure how nodes tend to be interconnected with each other.

- **Segregation metrics**: These quantify the presence of groups of interconnected nodes, known as communities or modules, within a network.

- **Centrality metrics**: These assess the importance of individual nodes inside a network.

- **Resilience metrics**: These can be thought of as a measure of how much a network is able to maintain and adapt its operational performance when facing failures or other adverse conditions.

Those metrics are defined as **global** when expressing a measure of an overall network. On the other hand, **local** metrics measure values of individual network elements (nodes or edges). In weighted graphs, each property may or may not account for the *edge weights*, leading to **weighted and unweighted metrics**.

In the following section, we describe some of the most commonly used metrics that measure global and local properties. For simplicity, unless specified differently in the text, we illustrate the global unweighted version of the metric. In several cases, this is obtained by averaging the local unweighted properties of the node.

Integration metrics

In this section, some of the most frequently used integration metrics will be described.

Distance, path, and shortest path

The concept of **distance** in a graph is often related to the number of edges to traverse in order to reach a target node from a given source node.

In particular, consider a source node i and a target node j. The set of edges connecting node i to node j is called a **path**. When studying complex networks, we are often interested in finding the **shortest path** between two nodes. A shortest path between a source node i and a target node j is the path having the lowest number of edges compared to all the possible paths between i and j. The **diameter** of a network is the number of edges contained in the longest shortest path among all possible shortest paths.

Take a look at the following screenshot. There are different paths to reach **Tokyo** from **Dublin**. However, one of them is the shortest (the edges on the shortest path are highlighted):

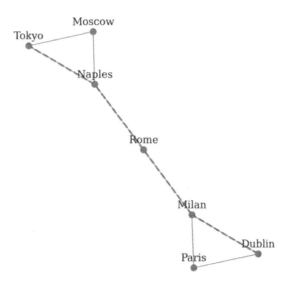

Figure 1.14 – The shortest path between two nodes

The `shortest_path` function of the `networkx` Python library enables users to quickly compute the shortest path between two nodes in a graph. Consider the following code, in which a seven-node graph is created by using `networkx`:

```
G = nx.Graph()
nodes = {1:'Dublin',2:'Paris',3:'Milan',4:'Rome',5:'Naples',
         6:'Moscow',7:'Tokyo'}
G.add_nodes_from(nodes.keys())
G.add_edges_from([(1,2),(1,3),(2,3),(3,4),(4,5),(5,6),(6,7),(7
,5)])
```

The shortest path between a source node (for example, `'Dublin'`, identified by the key 1) and a target node (for example, `'Tokyo'`, identified by the key 7) can be obtained as follows:

```
path = nx.shortest_path(G,source=1,target=7)
```

This should output the following:

```
[1,3,4,5,6]
```

Here, `[1,3,4,5,7]` are the nodes contained in the shortest path between `'Tokyo'` and `'Dublin'`.

Characteristic path length

The **characteristic path length** is defined as the average of all the shortest path lengths between all possible pair of nodes. If l_i is the average path length between the node i and all the other nodes, the characteristic path length is computed as follows:

$$\frac{1}{q(q-1)} \sum_{i \in V} l_i$$

Here, V is the set of nodes in the graph and $q = |V|$ represents its *order*. This is one of the most commonly used measures of how efficiently information is spread across a network. Networks having shorter characteristic path lengths promote the quick transfer of information and reduce costs. Characteristic path length can be computed through `networkx` using the following function:

```
nx.average_shortest_path_length(G)
```

This should give us the following:

```
2.1904761904761907
```

However, this metric cannot be always defined since it is not possible to compute a path among all the nodes in *disconnected graphs*. For this reason, **network efficiency** is also widely used.

Global and local efficiency

Global efficiency is the average of the inverse shortest path length for all pairs of nodes. Such a metric can be seen as a measure of how efficiently information is exchanged across a network. Consider that l_{ij} is the shortest path between a node i and a node j. The network efficiency is defined as follows:

$$\frac{1}{q(q-1)} \sum_{i \, \in V} \frac{1}{l_{ij}}$$

Efficiency is at a maximum when a graph is fully connected, while it is minimal for completely disconnected graphs. Intuitively, the shorter the path, the lower the measure.

The **local efficiency** of a node can be computed by considering only the neighborhood of the node in the calculation, without the node itself. Global efficiency is computed in `networkx` using the following command:

```
nx.global_efficiency(G)
```

The output should be as follows:

```
0.6111111111111109
```

Average local efficiency is computed in `networkx` using the following command:

```
nx.local_efficiency(G)
```

The output should be as follows:

```
0.6666666666666667
```

In the following screenshot, two examples of graphs are depicted. As observed, a fully connected graph on the left presents a higher level of efficiency compared to a circular graph on the right. In a fully connected graph, each node can be reached from any other node in the graph, and information is exchanged rapidly across the network. However, in a circular graph, several nodes should instead be traversed to reach the target node, making it less efficient:

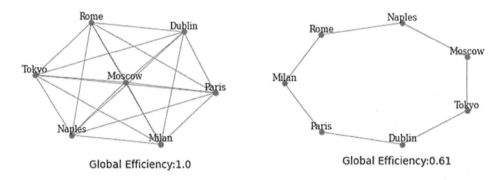

Figure 1.15 – Global efficiency of a fully connected graph (left) and a circular graph (right)

Integration metrics well describe the connection among nodes. However, more information about the presence of groups can be extracted by considering segregation metrics.

Segregation metrics

In this section, some of the most common segregation metrics will be described.

Clustering coefficient

The **clustering coefficient** is a measure of how much nodes cluster together. It is defined as the fraction of **triangles** (complete subgraph of three nodes and three edges) around a node and is equivalent to the fraction of the node's *neighbors* that are neighbors of each other. A global clustering coefficient is computed in `networkx` using the following command:

```
nx.average_clustering(G)
```

This should output the following:

```
0.6666666666666667
```

The local clustering coefficient is computed in `networkx` using the following command:

```
nx.clustering(G)
```

This should output the following:

```
{1: 1.0,
 2: 1.0,
 3: 0.3333333333333333,
 4: 0,
 5: 0.3333333333333333,
 6: 1.0,
 7: 1.0}
```

The output is a Python dictionary containing, for each node (identified by the respective key), the corresponding value. In the graph represented in *Figure 1.16*, two clusters of nodes can be easily identified. By computing the clustering coefficient for each single node, it can be observed that **Rome** has the lowest value. **Tokyo** and **Moscow**, as well as **Paris** and **Dublin**, are instead very well connected within their respective groups (notice the size of each node is drawn proportionally to each node's clustering coefficient). The graph can be seen in the following screenshot:

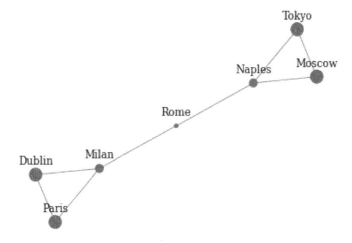

Figure 1.16 – Local clustering coefficient representation

Transitivity

A common variant of the clustering coefficient is known as **transitivity**. This can simply be defined as the ratio between the observed number of **closed triplets** (complete subgraph with three nodes and two edges) and the maximum possible number of closed triplets in the graph. Transitivity can be computed using `networkx`, as follows:

```
nx.transitivity(G)
```

The output should be as follows:

```
0.5454545454545454
```

Modularity

Modularity was designed to quantify the division of a network in aggregated sets of highly interconnected nodes, commonly known as **modules**, **communities**, **groups**, or **clusters**. The main idea is that networks having high modularity will show dense connections within the module and sparse connections between modules.

Consider a social network such as Reddit: members of communities related to video games tend to interact much more with other users in the same community, talking about recent news, favorite consoles, and so on. However, they will probably interact less with users talking about fashion. Differently from many other graph metrics, modularity is often computed by means of optimization algorithms.

Modularity in `networkx` is computed using the `modularity` function of the `networkx.algorithms.community` module, as follows:

```
import networkx.algorithms.community as nx_comm
nx_comm.modularity(G, communities=[{1,2,3}, {4,5,6,7}])
```

Here, the second argument—`communities`—is a list of sets, each representing a partition of the graph. The output should be as follows:

```
0.3671875
```

Segregation metrics help to understand the presence of groups. However, each node in a graph has its own *importance*. To quantify it, we can use centrality metrics.

Centrality metrics

In this section, some of the most common centrality metrics will be described.

Degree centrality

One of the most common and simple centrality metrics is the **degree centrality** metric. This is directly connected with the *degree* of a node, measuring the number of *incident* edges on a certain node i.

Intuitively, the more a node is connected to an other node, the more its degree centrality will assume high values. Note that, if a graph is *directed*, the **in-degree centrality** and **out-degree centrality** will be considered for each node, related to the number of *incoming* and *outcoming* edges, respectively. Degree centrality is computed in networkx by using the following command:

```
nx.degree_centrality(G)
```

The output should be as follows:

```
{1: 0.3333333333333333, 2: 0.3333333333333333, 3: 0.5,
4: 0.3333333333333333, 5: 0.5, 6: 0.3333333333333333, 7:
0.3333333333333333}
```

Closeness centrality

The **closeness centrality** metric attempts to quantify how much a node is close (well connected) to other nodes. More formally, it refers to the average distance of a node i to all other nodes in the network. If l_{ij} is the shortest path between node i and node j, the closeness centrality is defined as follows:

$$\frac{1}{\Sigma_{i \in V, i!=j}\, l_{ij}}$$

Here, V is the set of nodes in the graph. Closeness centrality can be computed in networkx using the following command:

```
nx.closeness_centrality(G)
```

The output should be as follows:

```
{1: 0.4, 2: 0.4, 3: 0.5454545454545454, 4: 0.6, 5:
0.5454545454545454, 6: 0.4, 7: 0.4}
```

Betweenness centrality

The **betweenness centrality** metric evaluates how much a node acts as a **bridge** between other nodes. Even if poorly connected, a node can be strategically connected, helping to keep the whole network connected.

If L_{wj} is the total number of shortest paths between node w and node j and $L_{wj}(i)$ is the total number of shortest paths between w and j passing through node i, then the betweenness centrality is defined as follows:

$$\sum_{w\,!=i\,!=j} \frac{L_{wj}(i)}{L_{wj}}$$

If we observe the formula, we can notice that the higher the number of shortest paths passing through node i, the higher the value of the betweenness centrality. Betweenness centrality is computed in `networkx` by using the following command:

```
nx.betweenness_centrality(G)
```

The output should be as follows:

```
{1: 0.0, 2: 0.0, 3: 0.5333333333333333, 4: 0.6, 5:
0.5333333333333333, 6: 0.0, 7: 0.0}
```

In *Figure 1.17*, we illustrate the difference between *degree centrality*, *closeness centrality*, and *betweenness centrality*. **Milan** and **Naples** have the highest degree centrality. **Rome** has the highest closeness centrality since it is the closest to any other node. It also shows the highest betweenness centrality because of its crucial role in connecting the two visible clusters and keeping the whole network connected.

You can see the differences here:

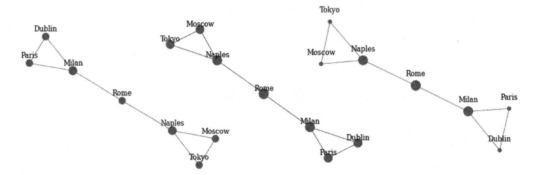

Figure 1.17 – Degree centrality (left), closeness centrality (center), and betweenness centrality (right)

Centrality metrics allow us to measure the importance of a node inside the network. Finally, we will mention resilience metrics, which enable us to measure the vulnerability of a graph.

Resilience metrics

There are several metrics that measure a network's resilience. Assortativity is one of the most used.

Assortativity coefficient

Assortativity is used to quantify the tendency of nodes being connected to similar nodes. There are several ways to measure such correlations. One of the most commonly used methods is the **Pearson correlation coefficient** between the degrees of directly connected nodes (nodes on two opposite ends of a link). The coefficient assumes positive values when there is a correlation between nodes of a similar degree, while it assumes negative values when there is a correlation between nodes of a different degree. Assortativity using the Pearson correlation coefficient is computed in networkx by using the following command:

```
nx.degree_pearson_correlation_coefficient(G)
```

The output should be as follows:

```
-0.6
```

Social networks are mostly assortative. However, the so-called *influencers* (famous singers, football players, fashion bloggers) tend to be *followed* (incoming edges) by several standard users, while tending to be connected with each other and showing a disassortative behavior.

It is important to remark that the previously presented properties are a subset of all the possible metrics used to describe graphs. A wider set of metrics and algorithms can be found at https://networkx.org/documentation/stable/reference/algorithms/.

Benchmarks and repositories

Now that we have understood the basic concepts and notions about graphs and network analysis, it is now time to dive into some practical examples that will help us to start to put into practice the general concepts we have learned so far. In this section, we will present some examples and toy problems that are generally used to study the properties of networks, as well as benchmark performances and effectiveness of networks' algorithms. We will also provide some useful links of repositories where network datasets can be found and downloaded, together with some tips on how to parse and process them.

Examples of simple graphs

We start by looking at some very simple examples of networks. Fortunately, `networkx` already comes with a number of graphs already implemented, ready to be used and played with. Let's start by creating a **fully connected undirected graph**, as follows:

```
complete = nx.complete_graph(n=7)
```

This has $\dfrac{n \cdot (n-1)}{2} = 21$ edges and a clustering coefficient $C=1$. Although fully connected graphs are not very interesting on their own, they represent a fundamental building block that may arise within larger graphs. A fully connected subgraph of n nodes within a larger graph is generally referred to as a **clique** of size n.

> **Definition**
>
> A **clique**, C, in an undirected graph is defined a subset of its vertices, $C \subseteq V$, such that every two distinct vertices in the subset are adjacent. This is equivalent to the condition that the induced subgraph of G induced by C is a fully connected graph.

Cliques represent one of the basic concepts in graph theory and are often also used in mathematical problems where relations need to be encoded. Besides, they also represent the simplest unit when constructing more complex graphs. On the other hand, the task of finding cliques of a given size n in larger graphs (clique problem) is of great interest and it can be shown that it is a **nondeterministic polynomial-time complete (NP-complete)** problem often studied in computer science.

Some simple examples of `networkx` graphs can be seen in the following screenshot:

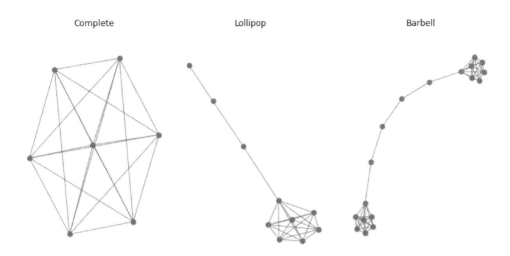

Figure 1.18 – Simple examples of graphs with networkx: (left) fully connected graph; (center) lollipop graph; (right) barbell graph

In *Figure 1.18*, we showed a complete graph along with two other simple examples containing cliques that can be easily generated with networkx, outlined as follows:

- A **lollipop graph** formed by a clique of size *n* and a branch of *m* nodes, as shown in the following code snippet:

```
lollipop = nx.lollipop_graph(m=7, n=3)
```

- A **barbell graph** formed by two cliques of size *m1* and *m2* joined by a branch of nodes, which resembles the sample graph we used previously to characterize some of the global and local properties. The code to generate this is shown in the following snippet:

```
barbell = nx.barbell_graph(m1=7, m2=4)
```

Such simple graphs are basic building blocks that can be used to generate more complex networks by combining them. Merging subgraphs is very easy with networkx and can be done with just a few lines of code, as shown in the following code snippet, where the three graphs are merged together into a single graph and some random edges are placed to connect them:

```
def get_random_node(graph):
    return np.random.choice(graph.nodes)
allGraphs = nx.compose_all([complete, barbell, lollipop])
allGraphs.add_edge(get_random_node(lollipop), get_random_
```

```
node(lollipop))
allGraphs.add_edge(get_random_node(complete), get_random_
node(barbell))
```

Other very simple graphs (that can then be merged and played around with) can be found at `https://networkx.org/documentation/stable/reference/generators.html#module-networkx.generators.classic`.

Generative graph models

Although creating simple subgraphs and merging them is a way to generate new graphs of increasing complexity, networks may also be generated by means of **probabilistic models** and/or **generative models** that let a graph grow by itself. Such graphs usually share interesting properties with real networks and have long been used to create benchmarks and synthetic graphs, especially in times when the amount of data available was not as overwhelming as today. Here, we present some examples of random generated graphs, briefly describing the models that underlie them.

Watts and Strogatz (1998)

This model was used by the authors to study the behavior of **small-world networks**—that is to say, networks that resemble, to some extent, common social networks. The graph is generated by first displacing *n* nodes in a ring and connecting each node with its *k* neighbors. Each edge of such a graph then has a probability *p* of being rewired to a randomly chosen node. By ranging *p*, the Watts and Strogatz model allows a shift from a regular network (*p=0*) to a completely random network (*p=1*). In between, graphs exhibit small-world features; that is, they tend to bring this model closer to social network graphs. These kinds of graphs can be easily created with the following command:

```
graph = nx.watts_strogatz_graph(n=20, k=5, p=0.2)
```

Barabási-Albert (1999)

The model proposed by Albert and Barabási is based on a generative model that allows the creation of random scale-free networks by using a **preferential attachment** schema, where a network is created by progressively adding new nodes and attaching them to already existing nodes, with a preference for nodes that have more neighbors. Mathematically speaking, the underlying idea of this model is that the probability for a new node to be attached to an existing node *i* depends on the degree of the *i*-th node, according to the following formula:

$$p_i = \frac{k_i}{\sum k_j}$$

Thus, nodes with a large number of edges (hubs) tend to develop even more edges, whereas nodes with few links will not develop other links (periphery). Networks generated by this model exhibit a *power-law distribution* for the connectivity (that is, degree) between nodes. Such a behavior is also found in real networks (for example, the **World Wide Web** (**WWW**) network and the actor collaboration network), interestingly showing that it is the popularity of a node (how many edges it already has) rather than its intrinsic node properties that influences the creation of new connections. The initial model has then been extended (and this is the version that is available on `networkx`) to also allow the preferential attachment of new edges or rewiring of existing edges.

The Barabási-Albert model is illustrated in the following screenshot:

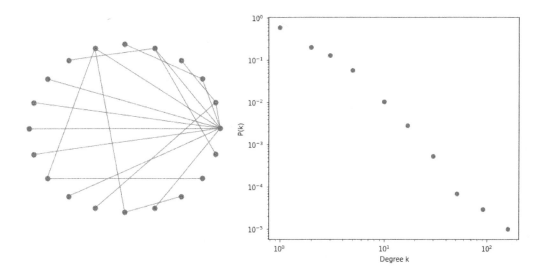

Figure 1.19 – Barabási-Albert model (left) with 20 nodes (right) distribution of connectivity with n=100.000 nodes, showing the scale-free power law distribution

In *Figure 1.19*, we showed an example of the Barabasi-Albert model for a small network, where you can already observe the emergence of hubs (on the left), as well as the probability distribution of the degree of the nodes, which exhibits a scale-free power-law behavior (on the right). The preceding distribution can easily be replicated in `networkx`, as follows:

```
ba_model = nx.extended_barabasi_albert_graph(n,m=1,p=0,q=0)
degree = dict(nx.degree(ba_model)).values()
```

```
bins = np.round(np.logspace(np.log10(min(degree)),
np.log10(max(degree)), 10))
```
```
cnt = Counter(np.digitize(np.array(list(degree)), bins))
```

Benchmarks

Digitalization has profoundly changed our lives, and today, any activity, person, or process generates data, providing a huge amount of information to be drilled, analyzed, and used to promote data-driven decision making. A few decades ago, it was hard to find datasets ready to be used to develop or test new algorithms. On the other hand, there exist today plenty of repositories that provide us with datasets, even of fairly large dimensions, to be downloaded and analyzed. These repositories, where people can share datasets, also provide a benchmark where algorithms can be applied, validated, and compared with each other.

In this section, we will briefly go through some of the main repositories and file formats used in network science, in order to provide you with all the tools needed to import datasets—of different sizes—to analyze and play around with.

In such repositories, you will find network datasets coming from some of the common areas of network science, such as social networks, biochemistry, dynamic networks, documents, co-authoring and citations networks, and networks arising from financial transactions. In *Part 3, Advanced Applications of Graph Machine Learning*, we will discuss some of the most common type of networks (social networks, graphs arising when processing corpus documents, and financial networks) and analyze them more thoroughly by applying the techniques and algorithms described in *Part 2, Machine Learning on Graphs*.

Also, `networkx` already comes with some basic (and very small) networks that are generally used to explain algorithms and basic measures, which can be found at `https://networkx.org/documentation/stable/reference/generators.html#module-networkx.generators.social`. These datasets are, however, generally quite small. For larger datasets, refer to the repositories we present next.

Network Data Repository

The **Network Data Repository** is surely one of the largest repositories of network data (`http://networkrepository.com/`) with several thousand different networks, featuring users and donations from all over the world and top-tier academic institutions. If a network dataset is freely available, chances are that you will find it there. Datasets are classified in about *30 domains*, including biology, economics, citations, social network data, industrial applications (energy, road), and many others. Besides providing the data, the website also provides a tool for interactive visualization, exploration, and comparison of datasets, and we suggest you check it out and explore it.

The data in the Network Data Repository is generally available under the **Matrix Market Exchange Format (MTX)** file format. The MTX file format is basically a file format for specifying dense or sparse matrices, real or complex, via readable text files (**American Standard Code for Information Interchange**, or **ASCII**). For more details, please refer to `http://math.nist.gov/MatrixMarket/formats.html#MMformat`.

A file in MTX format can be easily read in Python using `scipy`. Some of the files we downloaded from the Network Data Repository seemed slightly corrupted and required a minimal fix on a 10.15.2 OSX system. In order to fix them, just make sure the header of the file is compliant with the format specifications; that is, with a double `%` and no spaces at the beginning of the line, as in the following line:

```
%%MatrixMarket matrix coordinate pattern symmetric
```

Matrices should be in coordinate format. In this case, the specification points also to an unweighted, undirected graph (as understood by `pattern` and `symmetric`). Some of the files have some comments after the first header line, which are preceded by a single `%`.

As an example, we consider the **Astro Physics (ASTRO-PH)** collaboration network. The graph is generated using all the scientific papers available from the e-print *arXiv* repository published in the *Astrophysics* category in the period from January 1993 to April 2003. The network is built by connecting (via undirected edges) all the authors that co-authored a publication, thus resulting in a clique that includes all authors of a given paper. The code to generate the graph can be seen here:

```
from scipy.io import mmread
adj_matrix = mmread("ca-AstroPh.mtx")
graph = nx.from_scipy_sparse_matrix(adj_matrix)
```

The dataset has 17,903 nodes, connected by 196,072 edges. Visualizing so many nodes cannot be done easily, and even if we were to do it, it might not be very informative, as understanding the underlying structure would not be very easy with so much information. However, we can get some insights by looking at specific subgraphs, as we will do next.

First, we can start by computing some basic properties we described earlier and put them into a pandas `DataFrame` for our convenience to later use, sort, and analyze. The code to accomplish this is illustrated in the following snippet:

```
stats = pd.DataFrame({
    "centrality": nx.centrality.betweenness_centrality(graph),
    "C_i": nx.clustering(graph),
    "degree": nx.degree(graph)
})
```

We can easily find out that the node with the largest **degree centrality** is the one with ID 6933, which has 503 neighbors (surely a very popular and important scientist in astrophysics!), as illustrated in the following code snippet:

```
neighbors = [n for n in nx.neighbors(graph, 6933)]
```

Of course, also plotting its **ego network** (the node with all its neighbors) would still be a bit messy. One way to produce some subgraphs that can be plotted is by sampling (for example, with a 0.1 ratio) its neighbors in three different ways: random (sorting by index is a sort of random sorting), selecting the most central neighbors, or selecting the neighbors with the largest C_i values. The code to accomplish this is shown in the following code snippet:

```
nTop = round(len(neighbors)*sampling)
idx = {
    "random": stats.loc[neighbors].sort_index().index[:nTop],
    "centrality": stats.loc[neighbors]\
        .sort_values("centrality", ascending=False)\
        .index[:nTop],
    "C_i": stats.loc[neighbors]\
        .sort_values("C_i", ascending=False)\
        .index[:nTop]
}
```

We can then define a simple function for extracting and plotting a subgraph that includes only the nodes related to certain indices, as shown in the following code snippet:

```
def plotSubgraph(graph, indices, center = 6933):
    nx.draw_kamada_kawai(
        nx.subgraph(graph, list(indices) + [center])
    )
```

Using the preceding function, we can plot the different subgraphs, obtained by filtering the ego network using the three different criteria, based on random sampling, centrality, and the clustering coefficient we presented previously. An example is provided here:

```
plotSubgraph(graph, idx["random"])
```

In *Figure 1.20*, we compare these results where the other networks have been obtained by changing the key value to `centrality` and `C_i`. The random representation seems to show some emerging structure with separated communities. The graph with the most central nodes clearly shows an almost fully connected network, possibly made up of all full professors and influential figures in astrophysics science, publishing on multiple topics and collaborating frequently with each other. Finally, the last representation, on the other hand, highlights some specific communities, possibly connected with a specific topic, by selecting the nodes that have a higher clustering coefficient. These nodes might not have a large degree of centrality, but they very well represent specific topics. You can see examples of the ego subgraph here:

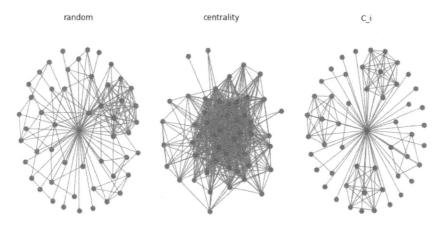

Figure 1.20 – Examples of the ego subgraph for the node that has largest degree in the ASTRO-PH dataset. Neighbors are sampled with a ratio=0.1. (left) random sampling; (center) nodes with largest betweenness centrality; (right) nodes with largest clustering coefficient

Another option to visualize this in `networkx` could also be to use the *Gephi* software that allows for fast filtering and visualizations of graphs. In order to do so, we need to first export the data as **Graph Exchange XML Format** (**GEXF**) (which is a file format that can be imported in Gephi), as follows:

```
nx.write_gext(graph, "ca-AstroPh.gext")
```

Once data is imported in Gephi, with few filters (by centrality or degree) and some computations (modularity), you can easily do plots as nice as the one shown in *Figure 1.21*, where nodes have been colored using modularity in order to highlight clusters. Coloring also allows us to easily spot nodes that connect the different communities and that therefore have large betweenness.

Some of the datasets in the Network Data Repository may also be available in the **EDGE file format** (for instance, the citations networks). The EDGE file format slightly differs from the MTX file format, although it represents the same information. Probably the easiest way to import such files into `networkx` is to convert them by simply rewriting its header. Take, for instance, the **Digital Bibliography and Library** (**DBLP**) citation network.

A sample plot can be seen in the following screenshot:

Figure 1.21 – Example of the visualization ASTRO-PH dataset with Gephi. Nodes are filtered by degree centrality and colored by modularity class; node sizes are proportional to the value of the degree

Here is the code for the header of the file:

```
% asym unweighted
% 49743 12591 12591
```

This can be easily converted to comply with the MTX file format by replacing these lines with the following code:

```
%%MatrixMarket matrix coordinate pattern general
12591 12591 49743
```

Then, you can use the import functions described previously.

Stanford Large Network Dataset Collection

Another valuable source of network datasets is the website of the **Stanford Network Analysis Platform (SNAP)** (https://snap.stanford.edu/index.html), which is a general-purpose network analysis library that was written in order to handle even fairly large graphs, with hundreds of millions of nodes and billions of edges. It is written in C++ to achieve top computational performance, but it also features interfaces with Python in order to be imported and used in native Python applications.

Although `networkx` is currently the main library to study `networkx`, SNAP or other libraries (more on this shortly) can be orders of magnitude faster than `networkx`, and they may be used in place of `networkx` for tasks that require higher performance. In the SNAP website, you will find a specific web page for **Biomedical Network Datasets** (https://snap.stanford.edu/biodata/index.html), besides other more general networks (https://snap.stanford.edu/data/index.html), covering similar domains and datasets as the Network Data Repository described previously.

Data is generally provided in a **text file format** containing a list of edges. Reading such files can be done with `networkx` in one code line, using the following command:

```
g = nx.read_edgelist("amazon0302.txt")
```

Some graphs might have extra information, other than about edges. Extra information is included in the archive of the dataset as a separated file—for example, where some metadata of the nodes is provided and is related to the graph via the *id* node.

Graphs can also be read directly using the SNAP library and its interface via Python. If you have a working version of SNAP on your local machine, you can easily read the data as follows:

```
from snap import LoadEdgeList, PNGraph
graph = LoadEdgeList(PNGraph, "amazon0302.txt", 0, 1, '\t')
```

Keep in mind that at this point, you will have an instance of a `PNGraph` object of the SNAP library, and you can't directly use `networkx` functionalities on this object. If you want to use some `networkx` functions, you first need to convert the `PNGraph` object to a `networkx` object. To make this process simpler, in the supplementary material for this book (available at `https://github.com/PacktPublishing/Graph-Machine-Learning`), we have written some functions that will allow you to seamlessly swap back and forth between `networkx` and SNAP, as illustrated in the following code snippet:

```
networkx_graph = snap2networkx(snap_graph)
snap_graph = networkx2snap(networkx_graph)
```

Open Graph Benchmark

This is the most recent update (dated May 2020) in the graph benchmark landscape, and this repository is expected to gain increasing importance and support in the coming years. The **Open Graph Benchmark (OGB)** has been created to address one specific issue: current benchmarks are actually too small compared to real applications to be useful for **machine learning (ML)** advances. On one hand, some of the models developed on small datasets turn out to not be able to scale to large datasets, proving them unsuitable in real-world applications. On the other hand, large datasets also allow us to increase the capacity (complexity) of the models used in ML tasks and explore new algorithmic solutions (such as neural networks) that can benefit from a large sample size to be efficiently trained, allowing us to achieve very high performance. The datasets belong to diverse domains and they have been ranked on three different dataset sizes (small, medium, and large) where the small-size graphs, despite their name, already have more than 100,000 nodes and/or more than 1 million edges. On the other hand, large graphs feature networks with more than 100 million nodes and more than 1 billion edges, facilitating the development of scalable models.

Beside the datasets, the OGB also provides, in a *Kaggle fashion*, an end-to-end ML pipeline that standardizes the data loading, experimental setup, and model evaluation. OGB creates a platform to compare and evaluate models against each other, publishing a *leaderboard* that allows tracking of the performance evolution and advancements on specific tasks of node, edge, and graph property prediction. For more details on the datasets and on the OGB project, please refer to `https://arxiv.org/pdf/2005.00687.pdf`.

Dealing with large graphs

When approaching a use case or an analysis, it is very important to understand how large the data we focus on is or will be in the future, as the dimension of the datasets may very well impact both the technologies we use and the analysis that we can do. As already mentioned, some of the approaches that have been developed on small datasets hardly scale to real-world applications and larger datasets, making them useless in practice.

When dealing with (possibly) large graphs, it is crucial to understand potential bottlenecks and limitation of the tools, technologies, and/or algorithms we use, assessing which part of our application/analysis may not scale when increasing the number of nodes or edges. Even more importantly, it is crucial to structure a data-driven application, however simple or at early **proof of concept** (**POC**) stages, in a way that would allow its scaling out in the future when data/users would increase, without rewriting the whole application.

Creating a data-driven application that resorts to graphical representation/modeling is a challenging task that requires a design and implementation that is a lot more complicated than simply importing `networkx`. In particular, it is often useful to decouple the component that processes the graph—named **graph processing engine**—from the one that allows querying and traversing the graph—the **graph storage layer**. We will further discuss these concepts in *Chapter 9, Building a Data-Driven Draft-Powered Application*. Nevertheless, given the focus of the book on ML and analytical techniques, it makes sense to focus more on graph processing engines than on graph storage layers. We therefore find it useful to provide you already at this stage with some of the technologies that are used for graph processing engines to deal with large graphs, crucial when scaling out an application.

In this respect, it is important to classify graph processing engines into two categories (that impact the tools/libraries/algorithms to be used), depending whether the graph can fit a *shared memory machine* or requires *distributed architectures* to be processed and analyzed.

Note that there is no absolute definition of large and small graphs, but it also depends on the chosen architecture. Nowadays, thanks to the vertical scaling of infrastructures, you can find servers with **random-access memory** (**RAM**) larger than 1 **terabyte** (**TB**) (usually called *fat nodes*), and with tens of thousands of **central processing units** (**CPUs**) for multithreading in most cloud-provider offerings, although these infrastructures might not be economically viable. Even without scaling out to such extreme architectures, graphs with millions of nodes and tens of millions of edges can nevertheless be easily handled in single servers with ~100 **gigabytes** (**GB**) of RAM and ~50 CPUs.

Although `networkx` is a very popular, user-friendly, and intuitive library, when scaling out to such reasonably large graphs it may not be the best available choice. `networkx`, being natively written in pure Python, which is an interpreted language, can be substantially outperformed by other graph engines fully or partly written in more performant programming languages (such as C++ and Julia) and that make use of multithreading, such as the following:

- **SNAP** (`http://snap.stanford.edu/`), which we have already seen in the previous section, is a graph engine developed at Stanford and is written in C++ with available bindings in Python.

- **igraph** (`https://igraph.org/`) is a C library and features bindings in Python, R, and Mathematica.

- **graph-tool** (`https://graph-tool.skewed.de/`), despite being a Python module, has core algorithms and data-structures written in C++ and uses OpenMP parallelization to scale on multi-core architectures.

- **NetworKit** (`https://networkit.github.io/`) is also written in C++ with OpenMP boost for parallelization for its core functionalities, integrated in a Python module.

- **LightGraphs** (`https://juliagraphs.org/LightGraphs.jl/latest/`) is a library written in Julia that aims to mirroring `networkx` functionalities in a more performant and robust library.

All the preceding libraries are valid alternatives to `networkx` when achieving better performance becomes an issue. Improvements can be very substantial, with speed-ups varying from 30 to 300 times faster, with the best performance generally achieved by LightGraphs.

In the forthcoming chapters, we will mostly focus on `networkx` in order to provide a consistent presentation and provide the user with basic concepts on network analysis. We want you to be aware that other options are available, as this becomes extremely relevant when pushing the edge from a performance standpoint.

Summary

In this chapter, we refreshed concepts such as graphs, nodes, and edges. We reviewed graph *representation* methods and explored how to *visualize* graphs. We also defined *properties* that are used to characterize networks, or parts of them.

We went through a well-known Python library to deal with graphs, `networkx`, and learned how to use it to apply theoretical concepts in practice.

We then ran examples and toy problems that are generally used to study the properties of networks, as well as benchmark performance and effectiveness of network algorithms. We also provided you with some useful links of repositories where network datasets can be found and downloaded, together with some tips on how to parse and process them.

In the next chapter, we will go beyond defining notions of ML on graphs. We will learn how more advanced and latent properties can be automatically found by specific ML algorithms.

2
Graph Machine Learning

Machine learning is a subset of artificial intelligence that aims to provide systems with the ability to *learn* and improve from data. It has achieved impressive results in many different applications, especially where it is difficult or unfeasible to explicitly define rules to solve a specific task. For instance, we can train algorithms to recognize spam emails, translate sentences into other languages, recognize objects in an image, and so on.

In recent years, there has been an increasing interest in applying machine learning to *graph-structured data*. Here, the primary objective is to automatically learn suitable representations to make predictions, discover new patterns, and understand complex dynamics in a better manner with respect to "traditional" machine learning approaches.

This chapter will first review some of the basic machine learning concepts. Then, an introduction to graph machine learning will be provided, with a particular focus on **representation learning**. We will then analyze a practical example to guide you through the comprehension of the theoretical concepts.

The following topics will be covered in this chapter:

- A refresher on machine learning
- What is machine learning on graphs and why is it important?
- A general taxonomy to navigate among graph machine learning algorithms

Technical requirements

We will be using Jupyter notebooks with *Python 3.8* for all of our exercises. The following is a list of the Python libraries that need to be installed for this chapter using `pip`. For example, run `pip install networkx==2.5` on the command line, and so on:

```
Jupyter==1.0.0
networkx==2.5
matplotlib==3.2.2
node2vec==0.3.3
karateclub==1.0.19
scipy==1.6.2
```

All the code files relevant to this chapter are available at `https://github.com/PacktPublishing/Graph-Machine-Learning/tree/main/Chapter02`.

Understanding machine learning on graphs

Of the branches of artificial intelligence, **machine learning** is one that has attracted the most attention in recent years. It refers to a class of computer algorithms that automatically learn and improve their skills through experience *without being explicitly programmed*. Such an approach takes inspiration from nature. Imagine an athlete who faces a novel movement for the first time: they start slowly, carefully imitating the gesture of a coach, trying, making mistakes, and trying again. Eventually, they will improve, becoming more and more confident.

Now, how does this concept translate to machines? It is essentially an optimization problem. The goal is to find a mathematical model that is able to achieve the best possible performance on a particular task. Performance can be measured using a specific performance metric (also known as a **loss function** or **cost function**). In a common learning task, the algorithm is provided with data, possibly lots of it. The algorithm uses this data to iteratively make decisions or predictions for the specific task. At each iteration, decisions are evaluated using the loss function. The resulting *error* is used to update the model parameters in a way that, hopefully, means the model will perform better. This process is commonly called **training**.

More formally, let's consider a particular task, T, and a performance metric, P, which allows us to quantify how good an algorithm is performing on T. According to Mitchell (Mitchell et al., 1997), an algorithm is said to learn from experience, E, if its performance at task T, measured by P, improves with experience E.

Basic principles of machine learning

Machine learning algorithms fall into three main categories, known as *supervised*, *unsupervised*, and *semi-supervised* learning. These learning paradigms depend on the way data is provided to the algorithm and how performance is evaluated.

Supervised learning is the learning paradigm used when we know the answer to the problem. In this scenario, the dataset is composed of samples of pairs of the form *<x,y>*, where *x* is the input (for example, an image or a voice signal) and *y* is the corresponding desired output (for example, what the image represents or what the voice is saying). The input variables are also known as *features*, while the output is usually referred to as *labels*, *targets*, and *annotations*. In supervised settings, performance is often evaluated using a *distance function*. This function measures the differences between the prediction and the expected output. According to the type of labels, supervised learning can be further divided into the following:

- **Classification**: Here, the labels are discrete and refer to the "class" the input belongs to. Examples of classification are determining the object in a photo or predicting whether an email is spam or not.

- **Regression**: The target is continuous. Examples of regression problems are predicting the temperature in a building or predicting the selling price of any particular product.

Unsupervised learning differs from supervised learning since the answer to the problem is not known. In this context, we do not have any labels and only the inputs, *<x>*, are provided. The goal is thus deducing structures and patterns, attempting to find similarities.

Discovering groups of similar examples (clustering) is one of these problems, as well as giving new representations of the data in a high-dimensional space.

In **semi-supervised learning**, the algorithm is trained using a combination of labeled and unlabeled data. Usually, to direct the research of structures present in the unlabeled input data, a limited amount of labeled data is used.

It is also worth mentioning that **reinforcement learning** is used for training machine learning models to make a sequence of decisions. The artificial intelligence algorithm faces a game-like situation, getting *penalties* or *rewards* based on the actions performed. The role of the algorithm is to understand how to act in order to maximize rewards and minimize penalties.

Minimizing the error on the training data is not enough. The keyword in machine learning is *learning*. It means that algorithms must be able to achieve the same level of performance even on unseen data. The most common way of evaluating the generalization capabilities of machine learning algorithms is to divide the dataset into two parts: the **training set** and the **test set**. The model is trained on the training set, where the loss function is computed and used to update the parameters. After training, the model's performance is evaluated on the test set. Moreover, when more data is available, the test set can be further divided into **validation** and **test** sets. The validation set is commonly used for assessing the model's performance during training.

When training a machine learning algorithm, three situations can be observed:

- In the first situation, the model reaches a low level of performance over the training set. This situation is commonly known as **underfitting**, meaning that the model is not powerful enough to address the task.

- In the second situation, the model achieves a high level of performance over the training set but struggles at generalizing over testing data. This situation is known as **overfitting**. In this case, the model is simply memorizing the training data, without actually understanding the true relations among them.

- Finally, the ideal situation is when the model is able to achieve (possibly) the highest level of performance over both training and testing data.

An example of overfitting and underfitting is given by the risk curve shown in *Figure 2.1*. From the figure, it is possible to see how the performances on the training and test sets change according to the complexity of the model (the number of parameters to be fitted):

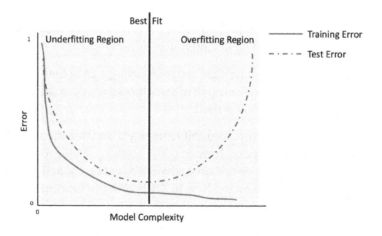

Figure 2.1 – Risk curve describing the prediction error on training and test set error in the function of the model complexity (number of parameters of the model)

Overfitting is one of the main problems that affect machine learning practitioners. It can occur due to several reasons. Some of the reasons can be as follows:

- The dataset can be ill-defined or not sufficiently representative of the task. In this case, adding more data could help to mitigate the problem.

- The mathematical model used for addressing the problem is too powerful for the task. In this case, proper constraints can be added to the loss function in order to reduce the model's "power." Such constraints are called **regularization** terms.

Machine learning has achieved impressive results in many fields, becoming one of the most diffused and effective approaches in computer vision, pattern recognition, and natural language processing, among others.

The benefit of machine learning on graphs

Several machine learning algorithms have been developed, each with its own advantages and limitations. Among those, it is worth mentioning regression algorithms (for example, linear and logistic regression), instance-based algorithms (for example, k-nearest neighbor or support vector machines), decision tree algorithms, Bayesian algorithms (for example, naïve Bayes), clustering algorithms (for example, k-means), and artificial neural networks.

But what is the key to all of this success?

Essentially, one thing: machine learning can automatically address tasks that are easy for humans to do. These tasks can be too complex to describe using traditional computer algorithms and, in some cases, they have shown even better capabilities than human beings. This is especially true when dealing with graphs—they can differ in several more ways than an image or audio signal because of their complex structure. By using graph machine learning, we can create algorithms to automatically detect and interpret recurring latent patterns.

For these reasons, there has been an increasing interest in *learning representations* for graph-structured data and many machine learning algorithms have been developed for handling graphs. For example, we might be interested in determining the role of a protein in a biological interaction graph, predicting the evolution of a collaboration network, recommending new products to a user in a social network, and many more (we will discuss these and more applications in *Chapter 10, The Future of Graphs*).

Due to their nature, graphs can be analyzed at different levels of granularity: at the node, edge, and graph level (the whole graph), as depicted in *Figure 2.2*. For each of those levels, different problems could be faced and, as a consequence, specific algorithms should be used:

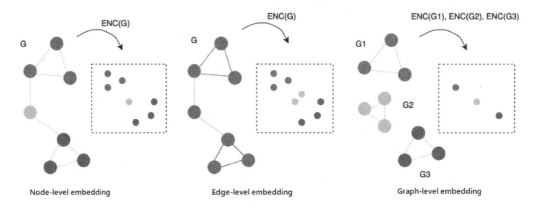

Figure 2.2 – Visual representation of the three different levels of granularity in graphs

In the following bullet points, we will give some examples of machine learning problems that could be faced for each of those levels:

- **Node level**: Given a (possibly large) graph, $G = (V, E)$, the goal is to classify each vertex, $v \in V$, into the right class. In this setting, the dataset includes G and a list of pairs, $< vi, yi >$, where vi is a node of graph G and yi is the class to which the node belongs.

- **Edge level**: Given a (possibly large) graph, $G = (V, E)$, the goal is to classify each edge, $e \in E$, into the right class. In this setting, the dataset includes G and a list of pairs, $< ei, yi >$, where ei is an edge of graph G and yi is the class to which the edge belongs. Another typical task for this level of granularity is **link prediction**, the problem of predicting the existence of a link between two existing nodes in a graph.

- **Graph level**: Given a dataset with m different graphs, the task is to build a machine learning algorithm capable of classifying a graph into the right class. We can then see this problem as a classification problem, where the dataset is defined by a list of pairs, $<Gi, yi>$, where Gi is a graph and yi is the class the graph belongs to.

In this section, we discussed some basic concepts of machine learning. Moreover, we have enriched our description by introducing some of the common machine learning problems when dealing with graphs. Having those theoretical principles as a basis, we will now introduce some more complex concepts relating to graph machine learning.

The generalized graph embedding problem

In classical machine learning applications, a common way to process the input data is to build from a set of features, in a process called **feature engineering**, which is capable of giving a compact and meaningful representation of each instance present in the dataset.

The dataset obtained from the feature engineering step will be then used as input for the machine learning algorithm. If this process usually works well for a large range of problems, it may not be the optimal solution when we are dealing with graphs. Indeed, due to their well-defined structure, finding a suitable representation capable of incorporating all the useful information might not be an easy task.

The first, and most straightforward, way of creating features capable of representing structural information from graphs is the *extraction of certain statistics*. For instance, a graph could be represented by its degree distribution, efficiency, and all the metrics we described in the previous chapter.

A more complex procedure consists of applying specific kernel functions or, in other cases, engineering-specific features that are capable of incorporating the desired properties into the final machine learning model. However, as you can imagine, this process could be really time-consuming and, in certain cases, the features used in the model could represent just a subset of the information that is really needed to get the best performance for the final model.

In the last decade, a lot of work has been done in order to define new approaches for creating meaningful and compact representations of graphs. The general idea behind all these approaches is to create algorithms capable of *learning* a good representation of the original dataset such that geometric relationships in the new space reflect the structure of the original graph. We usually call the process of learning a good representation of a given graph **representation learning** or **network embedding**. We will provide a more formal definition as follows.

Representation learning (network embedding) is the task that aims to learn a mapping function, $f: G \rightarrow \mathbb{R}^n$, from a discrete graph to a continuous domain. Function f will be capable of performing a low-dimensional vector representation such that the properties (local and global) of graph G are preserved.

Once mapping f is learned, it could be applied to the graph and the resulting mapping could be used as a feature set for a machine learning algorithm. A graphical example of this process is visible in *Figure 2.3*:

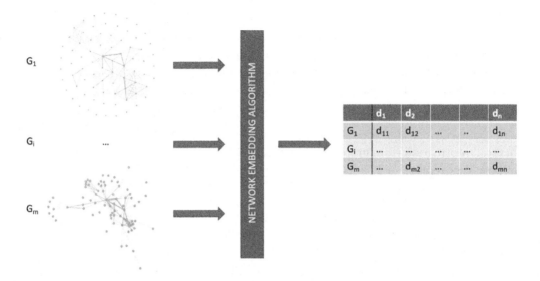

Figure 2.3 – Example of a workflow for a network embedding algorithm

Mapping function f can also be applied in order to learn the vector representation for nodes and edges. As we already mentioned, machine learning problems on graphs could occur at different levels of granularity. As a consequence, different embedding algorithms have been developed in order to learn functions to generate the vectorial representation of nodes ($f: V \rightarrow \mathbb{R}^n$) (also known as **node embedding**) or edges ($f: E \rightarrow \mathbb{R}^n$) (also known as **edge embedding**). Those mapping functions try to build a vector space such that the geometric relationships in the new space reflect the structure of the original graph, node, or edges. As a result, we will see that graphs, nodes, or edges that are similar in the original space will also be similar in the new space.

In other words, in the space generated by the embedding function, similar structures will have *a small Euclidean distance*, while dissimilar structures will have *a large Euclidean distance*. It is important to highlight that while most embedding algorithms generate a mapping in Euclidean vector spaces, there has recently been an interest in non-Euclidean mapping functions.

Let's now see a practical example of what an embedding space looks like, and how similarity can be seen in the new space. In the following code block, we show an example using a particular embedding algorithm known as **Node to Vector** (**Node2Vec**). We will describe how it works in the next chapter. At the moment, we will just say that the algorithm will map each node of graph G in a vector:

```python
import networkx as nx
from node2vec import Node2Vec
import matplotlib.pyplot as plt

G = nx.barbell_graph(m1=7, m2=4)
node2vec = Node2Vec(G, dimensions=2)
model = node2vec.fit(window=10)

fig, ax = plt.subplots()
for x in G.nodes():
    v = model.wv.get_vector(str(x))
    ax.scatter(v[0],v[1], s=1000)
    ax.annotate(str(x), (v[0],v[1]), fontsize=12)
```

In the preceding code, we have done the following:

1. We generated a barbell graph (described in the previous chapter).

2. The Node2Vec embedding algorithm is then used in order to map each node of the graph in a vector of two dimensions.

3. Finally, the two-dimensional vectors generated by the embedding algorithm, representing the nodes of the original graph, are plotted.

The result is shown in *Figure 2.4*:

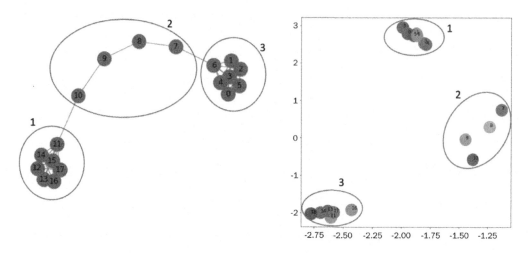

Figure 2.4 – Application of the Node2Vec algorithm to a graph (left) to generate the embedding vector
of its nodes (right)

From *Figure 2.4*, it is easy to see that nodes that have a similar structure are close to each
other and are distant from nodes that have dissimilar structures. It is also interesting
to observe how good Node2Vec is at discriminating group 1 from group 3. Since the
algorithm uses neighboring information of each node to generate the representation, the
clear discrimination of those two groups is possible.

Another example on the same graph can be performed using the **Edge to Vector**
(**Edge2Vec**) algorithm in order to generate a mapping for the edges for the same graph, *G*:

```
from node2vec.edges import HadamardEmbedder
edges_embs = HadamardEmbedder(keyed_vectors=model.wv)
fig, ax = plt.subplots()
for x in G.edges():
    v = edges_embs[(str(x[0]), str(x[1]))]
    ax.scatter(v[0],v[1], s=1000)
    ax.annotate(str(x), (v[0],v[1]), fontsize=12)
```

In the preceding code, we have done the following:

1. We generated a barbell graph (described in the previous chapter).

2. The `HadamardEmbedder` embedding algorithm is applied to the result of the Node2Vec algorithm (`keyed_vectors=model.wv`) used in order to map each edge of the graph in a vector of two dimensions.

3. Finally, the two-dimensional vectors generated by the embedding algorithm, representing the nodes of the original graph, are plotted.

The results are shown in *Figure 2.5*:

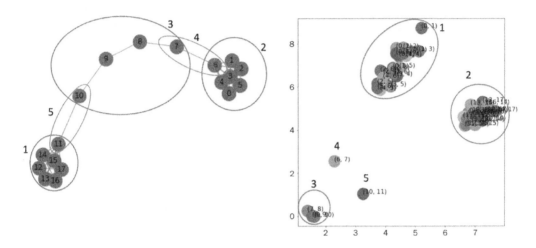

Figure 2.5 – Application of the Hadamard algorithm to a graph (left) to generate the embedding vector of its edges (right)

As for node embedding, in *Figure 2.5*, we reported the results of the edge embedding algorithm. From the figure, it is easy to see that the edge embedding algorithm clearly identifies similar edges. As expected, edges belonging to groups 1, 2, and 3 are clustered in well-defined and well-grouped regions. Moreover, the (6,7) and (10,11) edges, belonging to groups 4 and 5, respectively, are well clustered in specific groups.

Finally, we will provide an example of a **Graph to Vector (Grap2Vec)** embedding algorithm. This algorithm maps a single graph in a vector. As for another example, we will discuss this algorithm in more detail in the next chapter. In the following code block, we provide a Python example showing how to use the Graph2Vec algorithm in order to generate the embedding representation on a set of graphs:

```python
import random
import matplotlib.pyplot as plt
from karateclub import Graph2Vec
n_graphs = 20
def generate_random():
    n = random.randint(5, 20)
    k = random.randint(5, n)
    p = random.uniform(0, 1)
    return nx.watts_strogatz_graph(n,k,p)


Gs = [generate_random() for x in range(n_graphs)]


model = Graph2Vec(dimensions=2)
model.fit(Gs)
embeddings = model.get_embedding()


fig, ax = plt.subplots(figsize=(10,10))
for i,vec in enumerate(embeddings):
    ax.scatter(vec[0],vec[1], s=1000)
    ax.annotate(str(i), (vec[0],vec[1]), fontsize=16)
```

In this example, the following has been done:

1. 20 Watts-Strogatz graphs (described in the previous chapter) have been generated with random parameters.

2. We have then executed the graph embedding algorithm in order to generate a two-dimensional vector representation of each graph.

3. Finally, the generated vectors are plotted in their Euclidean space.

The results of this example are shown in *Figure 2.6*:

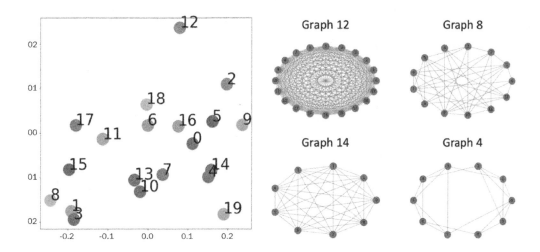

Figure 2.6 – Plot of two embedding vectors generated by the Graph2Vec algorithm applied to 20 randomly generated Watts-Strogatz graphs (left). Extraction of two graphs with a large Euclidean distance (Graph 12 and Graph 8 at the top right) and two graphs with a low Euclidean distance (Graph 14 and Graph 4 at the bottom right) is shown

As we can see from *Figure 2.6*, graphs with a large Euclidean distance, such as graph 12 and graph 8, have a different structure. The former is generated with the nx.watts_ strogatz_graph(20,20,0.2857) parameter and the latter with the nx.watts_ strogatz_graph(13,6,0.8621) parameter. In contrast, a graph with a low Euclidean distance, such as graph 14 and graph 8, has a similar structure. Graph 14 is generated with the nx.watts_strogatz_graph(9,9,0.5091) command, while graph 4 is generated with nx.watts_strogatz_graph(10,5,0.5659).

In the scientific literature, a plethora of embedding methods has been developed. We will describe in detail and use some of them in the next section of this book. These methods are usually classified into two main types: *transductive* and *inductive*, depending on the update procedure of the function when new samples are added. If new nodes are provided, transductive methods update the model (for example, re-train) to infer information about the nodes, while in inductive methods, models are expected to generalize to new nodes, edges, or graphs that were not observed during training.

The taxonomy of graph embedding machine learning algorithms

A wide variety of methods to generate a compact space for graph representation have been developed. In recent years, a trend has been observed of researchers and machine learning practitioners converging toward a unified notation to provide a common definition to describe such algorithms. In this section, we will be introduced to a simplified version of the taxonomy defined in the paper *Machine Learning on Graphs: A Model and Comprehensive Taxonomy* (`https://arxiv.org/abs/2005.03675`).

In this formal representation, every graph, node, or edge embedding method can be described by two fundamental components, named the encoder and the decoder. The **encoder (ENC)** maps the input into the embedding space, while the **decoder (DEC)** decodes structural information about the graph from the learned embedding (*Figure 2.7*).

The framework described in the paper follows an intuitive idea: if we are able to encode a graph such that the decoder is able to retrieve all the necessary information, then the embedding must contain a compressed version of all this information and can be used to downstream machine learning tasks:

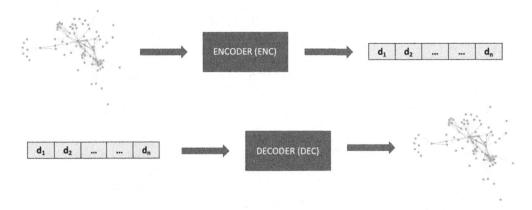

Figure 2.7 – Generalized encoder (ENC) and decoder (DEC) architecture for embedding algorithms

In many graph-based machine learning algorithms for representation learning, the decoder is usually designed to map pairs of node embeddings to a real value, usually representing the proximity (distance) of the nodes in the original graphs. For example, it is possible to implement the decoder such that, given the embedding representation of two nodes, $z_i = ENC(V_i)$ and $z_j = ENC(V_j)$, $DEC(z_i, z_j) = 1$ if in the input graph an edge connecting the two nodes, z_i, z_j, exists. In practice, more effective *proximity functions* can be used to measure the similarity between nodes.

The categorization of embedding algorithms

Inspired by the general framework depicted in *Figure 2.7*, we will now provide a categorization of the various embedding algorithms into four main groups. Moreover, in order to help you to better understand this categorization, we shall provide simple code snapshots in pseudo-code. In our pseudo-code formalism, we denote G as a generic networkx graph, with graphs_list as a list of networkx graphs and model as a generic embedding algorithm:

- **Shallow embedding methods**: These methods are able to learn and return only the embedding values for the learned input data. *Node2Vec*, *Edge2Vec*, and *Graph2Vec*, which we previously discussed, are examples of shallow embedding methods. Indeed, they can only return a vectorial representation of the data they learned during the *fit* procedure. It is not possible to obtain the embedding vector for unseen data. A typical way to use these methods is as follows:

```
model.fit(graphs_list)
embedding = model.get_embedding()[i]
```

  In the code, a generic shallow embedding method is trained on a list of graphs (line 1). Once the model is fitted, we can only get the embedding vector of the *i*th graph belonging to graphs_list (line 2). Unsupervised and supervised shallow embedding methods will be described, respectively, in *Chapter 3*, *Unsupervised Graph Learning*, and *Chapter 4*, *Supervised Graph Learning*.

- **Graph autoencoding methods**: These methods do not simply learn how to map the input graphs in vectors; they learn a more general mapping function, $f(G)$, capable of also generating the embedding vector for unseen instances. A typical way to use them is as follows:

```
model.fit(graphs_list)
embedding = model.get_embedding(G)
```

  The model is trained on graphs_list (line 1). Once the model is fitted on the input training set, it is possible to use it to generate the embedding vector of a new unseen graph, G. Graph autoencoding methods will be described in *Chapter 3*, *Unsupervised Graph Learning*.

- **Neighborhood aggregation methods**: These algorithms can be used to extract embeddings at the graph level, where nodes are labeled with some properties. Moreover, as for the graph autoencoding methods, the algorithms belonging to this class are able to learn a general mapping function, $f(G)$, also capable of generating the embedding vector for unseen instances.

A nice property of those algorithms is the possibility to build an embedding space where not only the internal structure of the graph is taken into account but also some external information, defined as properties of its nodes. For instance, with this method, we can have an embedding space capable of identifying, at the same time, graphs with similar structures and different properties on nodes. Unsupervised and supervised neighborhood aggregation methods will be described in *Chapter 3, Unsupervised Graph Learning*, and *Chapter 4, Supervised Graph Learning*, respectively.

- **Graph regularization methods**: Methods based on graph regularization are slightly different from the ones listed in the preceding points. Here, we do not have a graph as input. Instead, the objective is to learn from a set of features by exploiting their "interaction" to regularize the process. In more detail, a graph can be constructed from the features by considering feature similarities. The main idea is based on the assumption that nearby nodes in a graph are likely to have the same labels. Therefore, the loss function is designed to constrain the labels to be consistent with the graph structure. For example, regularization might constrain neighboring nodes to share similar embeddings, in terms of their distance in the L2 norm. For this reason, the encoder only uses X node features as input.

  The algorithms belonging to this family learn a function, $f(X)$, that maps a specific set of features (X) to an embedding vector. As for the graph autoencoding and neighborhood aggregation methods, this algorithm is also able to apply the learned function to new, unseen features. Graph regularization methods will be described in *Chapter 4, Supervised Graph Learning*.

For algorithms belonging to the group of shallow embedding methods and neighborhood aggregation methods, it is possible to define an *unsupervised* and *supervised* version. The ones belonging to graph autoencoding methods are suitable in unsupervised tasks, while the algorithms belonging to graph regularization methods are used in semi-supervised/supervised settings.

For unsupervised algorithms, the embedding of a specific dataset is performed only using the information contained in the input dataset, such as nodes, edges, or graphs. For the supervised setting, external information is used to guide the embedding process. That information is usually classed as a label, such as a pair, $<Gi,yi>$, that assigns to each graph a specific class. This process is more complex than the unsupervised one since the model tries to find the best vectorial representation in order to find the best assignment of a label to an instance. In order to clarify this concept, we can think, for instance, of the *convolutional neural networks* for image classification. During their training process, neural networks try to classify each image into the right class by performing the fitting of various convolutional filters at the same time. The goal of those convolutional filters is to find a compact representation of the input data in order to maximize the prediction performances. The same concept is also valid for supervised graph embedding, where the algorithm tries to find the best graph representation in order to maximize the performance of a class assignment task.

From a more mathematical perspective, all these models are trained with a proper loss function. This function can be generalized using two terms:

- The first is used in supervised settings to minimize the difference between the prediction and the target.

- The second is used to evaluate the similarity between the input graph and the one reconstructed after the ENC + DEC steps (which is the structure reconstruction error).

Formally, it can be defined as follows:

$$Loss = \alpha L_{sup}(y, \hat{y}) + L_{rec}(G, \hat{G})$$

Here, $\alpha L_{sup}(y, \hat{y})$ is the loss function in the supervised settings. The model is optimized to minimize, for each instance, the error between the right (y) and the predicted class ($\hat{y}$). $L_{rec}(G, \hat{G})$ is the loss function representing the reconstruction error between the input graph (G) and the one obtained after the ENC + DEC process ($\hat{G}$). For unsupervised settings, we have the same loss but $\alpha = 0$, since we do not have a target variable to use.

It is important to highlight the main role that these algorithms play when we try to solve a machine learning problem on a graph. They can be used *passively* in order to transform a graph into a feature vector suitable for a classical machine learning algorithm or for data visualization tasks. But they can also be used *actively* during the learning process, where the machine learning algorithm finds a compact and meaningful solution to a specific problem.

Summary

In this chapter, we refreshed some basic *machine learning* concepts and discovered how they can be applied to graphs. We defined basic *graph machine learning* terminology with a particular focus on *graph representation learning*. A taxonomy of the main graph machine learning algorithms was presented in order to clarify what differentiates the various ranges of solutions developed over the years. Finally, practical examples were provided to begin understanding how the theory can be applied to practical problems.

In the next chapter, we will revise the main graph-based machine learning algorithms. We will analyze their behavior and see how they can be used in practice.

Section 2 – Machine Learning on Graphs

In this section, the reader will become aware of the main existing machine learning models for graph representation learning: their purpose, how they work, and how they can be implemented.

This section comprises the following chapters:

- *Chapter 3, Unsupervised Graph Learning*
- *Chapter 4, Supervised Graph Learning*
- *Chapter 5, Problems with Machine Learning on Graphs*

3
Unsupervised Graph Learning

Unsupervised machine learning refers to the subset of machine learning algorithms that do not exploit any target information during training. Instead, they work on their own to find clusters, discover patterns, detect anomalies, and solve many other problems for which there is no teacher and no correct answer known *a priori*.

As per many other machine learning algorithms, unsupervised models have found large applications in the graph representation learning domain. Indeed, they represent an extremely useful tool for solving various downstream tasks, such as node classification and community detection, among others.

In this chapter, an overview of recent unsupervised graph embedding methods will be provided. Given a graph, the goal of these techniques is to automatically learn a latent representation of it, in which the key structural components are somehow preserved.

The following topics will be covered in this chapter:

- The unsupervised graph embedding roadmap
- Shallow embedding methods
- Autoencoders
- Graph neural networks

Technical requirements

We will be using Jupyter notebooks with Python 3.9 for all of our exercises. The following is a list of the Python libraries that need to be installed for this chapter using `pip`. For example, run `pip install networkx==2.5` on the command line, and so on:

```
Jupyter==1.0.0
networkx==2.5
matplotlib==3.2.2
karateclub==1.0.19
node2vec==0.3.3
tensorflow==2.4.0
scikit-learn==0.24.0
git+https://github.com/palash1992/GEM.git
git+https://github.com/stellargraph/stellargraph.git
```

In the rest of this book, if not clearly stated, we will refer to the Python commands `import networkx as nx`.

All the code files relevant to this chapter are available at `https://github.com/PacktPublishing/Graph-Machine-Learning/tree/main/Chapter03`.

The unsupervised graph embedding roadmap

Graphs are complex mathematical structures defined in a non-Euclidean space. Roughly speaking, this means that it is not always easy to define what is close to what; it might also be hard to say what *close* even means. Imagine a social network graph: two users can be respectively connected and yet share very different features—one might be interested in fashion and clothes, while the other might be interested in sports and videogames. Can we consider them as "close"?

For this reason, unsupervised machine learning algorithms have found large applications in graph analysis. Unsupervised machine learning is the class of machine learning algorithms that can be trained without the need for manually annotated data. Most of those models indeed make use of only information in the adjacency matrix and the node features, without any knowledge of the downstream machine learning task.

How is this possible? One of the most used solutions is to learn embeddings that preserve the graph structure. The learned representation is usually optimized so that it can be used to reconstruct the pair-wise node similarity, for example, the **adjacency matrix**. These techniques bring an important feature: the learned representation can encode latent relationships among nodes or graphs, allowing us to discover hidden and complex novel patterns.

Many algorithms have been developed in relation to unsupervised graph machine learning techniques. However, as previously reported by different scientific papers (`https://arxiv.org/abs/2005.03675`), those algorithms can be grouped into macro-groups: shallow embedding methods, autoencoders, and **Graph Neural Networks** (**GNNs**), as graphically described in the following chart:

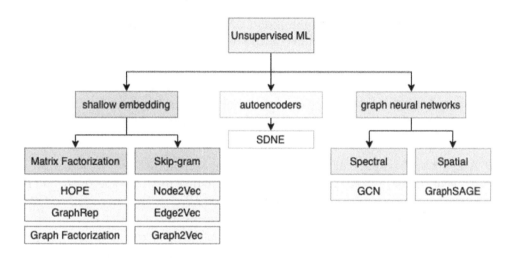

Figure 3.1 – The hierarchical structure of the different unsupervised embedding algorithms described in this book

In the following sections, you will learn the main principles behind each group of algorithms. We will try to provide the idea behind the most well-known algorithms in the field as well as how they can be used for solving real problems.

Shallow embedding methods

As already introduced in *Chapter 2*, *Graph Machine Learning*, with shallow embedding methods, we identify a set of algorithms that are able to learn and return only the embedding values for the learned input data.

In this section, we will explain in detail some of those algorithms. Moreover, we will enrich the descriptions by providing several examples of how to use those algorithms in Python. For all the algorithms described in this section, we will use the implementation provided in the following libraries: **Graph Embedding Methods (GEM)**, **Node to Vector (Node2Vec)**, and Karate Club.

Matrix factorization

Matrix factorization is a general decomposition technique widely used in different domains. A consistent number of graph embedding algorithms use this technique in order to compute the node embedding of a graph.

We will start by providing a general introduction to the matrix factorization problem. After the introduction of the basic principles, we will describe two algorithms, namely **Graph Factorization (GF)** and **Higher-Order Proximity Preserved Embedding (HOPE)**, which use matrix factorization to build the node embedding of a graph.

Let $W \in \mathbb{R}^{m \times n}$ be the input data. Matrix factorization decomposes $W \approx V \times H$ with $V \in \mathbb{R}^{m \times d}$ and $H \in \mathbb{R}^{d \times n}$ called the **source** and **abundance** matrix, respectively, and d is the number of dimensions of the generated embedding space. The matrix factorization algorithm learns the V and H matrices by minimizing a loss function that can change according to the specific problem we want to solve. In its general formulation, the loss function is defined by computing the reconstruction error using the Frobenius norm as $\|W - V \times H\|_F^2$.

Generally speaking, all the unsupervised embedding algorithms based on matrix factorization use the same principle. They all factorize an input graph expressed as a matrix in different components. The main difference between each method lies in the loss function used during the optimization process. Indeed, different loss functions allow creating an embedding space that emphasizes specific properties of the input graph.

Graph factorization

The GF algorithm was one of the first models to reach good computational performance in order to perform the node embedding of a given graph. By following the principle of matrix factorization that we previously described, the GF algorithm factorizes the adjacency matrix of a given graph.

Formally, let $G = (V, E)$ be the graph we want to compute the node embedding with and let $A \in \mathbb{R}^{|V| \times |V|}$ be its adjacency matrix. The loss function (L) used in this matrix factorization problem is as follows:

$$L = \frac{1}{2} \sum_{(i,j) \in E} (A_{i,j} - Y_{i,:} Y_{j,:}^T)^2 + \frac{\lambda}{2} \sum_i \|Y_{i,:}\|^2$$

In the preceding equation, $(i, j) \in E$ represents one of the edges in G while $Y \in \mathbb{R}^{|V| \times d}$ is the matrix containing the d-dimensional embedding. Each row of the matrix represents the embedding of a given node. Moreover, a regularization term (λ) of the embedding matrix is used to ensure that the problem remains well-posed even in the absence of sufficient data.

The loss function used in this method was mainly designed to improve GF performances and scalability. Indeed, the solution generated by this method could be noisy. Moreover, it should be noted, by looking at its matrix factorization formulation, that GF performs a strong symmetric factorization. This property is particularly suitable for undirected graphs, where the adjacency matrix is symmetric, but could be a potential limitation for undirected graphs.

In the following code, we will show how to perform the node embedding of a given `networkx` graph using Python and the GEM library:

```python
import networkx as nx
from gem.embedding.gf import GraphFactorization
G = nx.barbell_graph(m1=10, m2=4)
gf = GraphFactorization(d=2, data_set=None, max_iter=10000,
eta=1*10**-4, regu=1.0)
gf.learn_embedding(G)
embeddings = gf.get_embedding()
```

In the preceding example, the following have been done:

1. `networkx` is used to generate a **barbell graph** (G) used as input for the GF factorization algorithm.

2. The `GraphFactorization` class is used to generate a d=2-dimensional embedding space.

3. The computation of the node embeddings of the input graph is performed using `gf.learn_embedding(G)`.

4. The computed embeddings are extracted by calling the `gf.get_embedding()` method.

The results of the previous code are shown in the following graph:

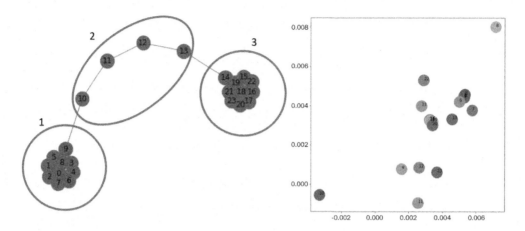

Figure 3.2 – Application of the GF algorithm to a graph (left) to generate the embedding vector of its nodes (right)

From *Figure 3.2*, it is possible to see how nodes belonging to groups 1 and 3 are mapped together in the same region of space. Those points are separated by the nodes belonging to group 2. This mapping allows us to well separate groups 1 and 3 from group 2. Unfortunately, there is no clear separation between groups 1 and 3.

Higher-order proximity preserved embedding

HOPE is another graph embedding technique based on the matrix factorization principle. This method allows preserving higher-order proximity and does not force its embeddings to have any symmetric properties. Before starting to describe the method, let's understand what first-order proximity and high-order proximity mean:

- **First-order proximity**: Given a graph, $G = (V, E)$, where the edges have a weight, W_{ij}, for each vertex pair (v_i, v_j), we say they have a first-order proximity equal to W_{ij} if the edge $(v_i, v_j) \in E$. Otherwise, the first-order proximity between the two nodes is 0.

- **Second- and high-order proximity**: With the second-order proximity, we can capture the two-step relations between each pair of vertices. For each vertex pair (v_i, v_j), we can see the second-order proximity as a two-step transition from v_i to v_j. High-order proximity generalizes this concept and allows us to capture a more global structure. As a consequence, high-order proximity can be viewed as a k-step $(k \geq 3)$ transition from v_i to v_j.

Given the definition of proximity, we can now describe the HOPE method. Formally, let $G = (V, E)$ be the graph we want to compute the embedding for and let $A \in \mathbb{R}^{|V| \times |V|}$ be its adjacency matrix. The loss function (L) used by this problem is as follows:

$$L = \|S - Y_s \times Y_t^T\|_F^2$$

In the preceding equation, $S \in \mathbb{R}^{|V| \times |V|}$ is a similarity matrix generated from graph G and $Y_s \in \mathbb{R}^{|V| \times d}$ and $Y_t \in \mathbb{R}^{|V| \times d}$ are two embedding matrices representing a d-dimensional embedding space. In more detail, Y_s represents the source embedding and Y_t represents the target embedding.

HOPE uses those two matrices in order to capture asymmetric proximity in directed networks where the direction from a source node and a target node is present. The final embedding matrix, Y, is obtained by simply concatenating, column-wise, the Y_s and Y_t matrices. Due to this operation, the final embedding space generated by HOPE will have $2 * d$ dimensions.

As we already stated, the S matrix is a similarity matrix obtained from the original graph, G. The goal of S is to obtain high-order proximity information. Formally, it is computed as $S = M_g \cdot M_l$, where M_g and M_l are both polynomials of matrices.

In its original formulation, the authors of HOPE suggested different ways to compute M_g and M_l. Here we report a common and easy method to compute those matrices, **Adamic-Adar (AA)**. In this formulation, $M_g = I$ (the identity matrix) while $M_l = A \cdot D \cdot A$,

where D is a diagonal matrix computed as $D_{ij} = 1/ (\sum (A_{ij} + A_{ji}))$. Other formulations to compute M_g and M_l are the **Katz Index**, **Rooted PageRank (RPR)**, and **Common Neighbors (CN)**.

In the following code, we will show how to perform the node embedding of a given `networkx` graph using Python and the GEM library:

```python
import networkx as nx
from gem.embedding.hope import HOPE
G = nx.barbell_graph(m1=10, m2=4)
gf = HOPE(d=4, beta=0.01)
gf.learn_embedding(G)
embeddings = gf.get_embedding()
```

The preceding code is similar to the one used for GF. The only difference is in the class initialization since here we use HOPE. According to the implementation provided by GEM, the d parameter, representing the dimension of the embedding space, will define the number of columns of the final embedding matrix, Y, obtained after the column-wise concatenation of Y_s and Y_t.

As a consequence, the number of columns of Y_s and Y_t is defined by the floor division (the // operator in Python) of the value assigned to d. The results of the code are shown in the following graph:

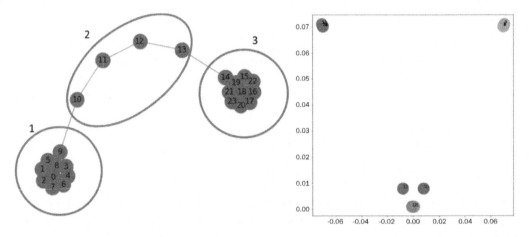

Figure 3.3 – Application of the HOPE algorithm to a graph (left) to generate the embedding vector of its nodes (right)

In this case, the graph is undirected and thus there is no difference between the source and target nodes. *Figure 3.3* shows the first two dimensions of the embeddings matrix representing Y_s. It is possible to see how the embedding space generated by HOPE provides, in this case, a better separation of the different nodes.

Graph representation with global structure information

Graph representation with global structure information (GraphRep), such as HOPE, allows us to preserve higher-order proximity without forcing its embeddings to have symmetric properties. Formally, let $G = (V, E)$ be the graph we want to compute the node embeddings for and let $A \in \mathbb{R}^{|V| \times |V|}$ be its adjacency matrix. The loss function (L) used by this problem is as follows:

$$L_k = \| X^k - Y_s^k \times Y_t^{k^T} \|_F^2 \ 1 \leq k \leq K$$

In the preceding equation, $X^k \in \mathbb{R}^{|V| \times |V|}$ is a matrix generated from graph G in order to get the kth order of proximity between nodes.

$Y_s^k \in \mathbb{R}^{|V| \times d}$ and $Y_t^k \in \mathbb{R}^{|V| \times d}$ are two embedding matrices representing a d-dimensional embedding space of the kth order of proximity for the source and target nodes, respectively.

The X^k matrix is computed according to the following equation:
$$X^k = \prod_k (D^{-1}A)$$
Here, D is a diagonal matrix known as the **degree matrix** computed using the following equation:

$$D_{ij} = \{ \begin{array}{ll} \sum_p A_{ip}, & i = j \\ 0, & i \neq j \end{array}$$

$X^1 = D^{-1}A$ represents the (one-step) probability transition matrix, where X_{ij}^1 is the probability of a transition from v_i to vertex v_j within one step. In general, for a generic value of k, X_{ij}^k represents the probability of a transition from v_i to vertex v_j within k steps.

For each order of proximity, k, an independent optimization problem is fitted. All the k embedding matrices generated are then column-wise concatenated to get the final source embedding matrices.

In the following code, we will show how to perform the node embedding of a given networkx graph using Python and the karateclub library:

```
import networkx as nx
from karateclub.node_embedding.neighbourhood.grarep import
GraRep
G = nx.barbell_graph(m1=10, m2=4)
gr = GraRep(dimensions=2, order=3)
gr.fit(G)
embeddings = gr.get_embedding()
```

We initialize the GraRep class from the karateclub library. In this implementation, the dimension parameter represents the dimension of the embedding space, while the order parameter defines the maximum number of orders of proximity between nodes. The number of columns of the final embedding matrix (stored, in the example, in the embeddings variable) is dimension*order, since, as we said, for each proximity order an embedding is computed and concatenated in the final embedding matrix.

To specify, since two dimensions are computed in the example, `embeddings[:,:2]` represents the embedding obtained for $k=1$, `embeddings[:,2:4]` for $k=2$, and `embeddings[:,4:]` for $k=3$. The results of the code are shown in the following graph:

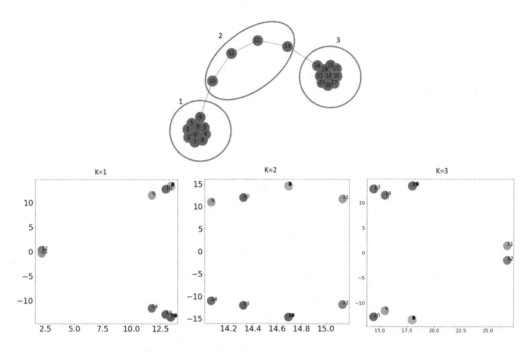

Figure 3.4 – Application of the GraphRep algorithm to a graph (top) to generate the embedding vector of its nodes (bottom) for different values of k

From the preceding graph, it is easy to see how different orders of proximity allow us to get different embeddings. Since the input graph is quite simple, in this case, already with $k=1$, a well-separated embedding space is obtained. To specify, the nodes belonging to groups 1 and 3 in all the proximity orders have the same embedding values (they are overlapping in the scatter plot).

In this section, we described some matrix factorization methods for unsupervised graph embedding. In the next section, we will introduce a different way to perform unsupervised graph embedding using skip-gram models.

Skip-gram

In this section, we will provide a quick description of the skip-gram model. Since it is widely used by different embedding algorithms, a high-level description is needed to better understand the different methods. Before going deep into a detailed description, we will first give a brief overview.

The skip-gram model is a simple neural network with one hidden layer trained in order to predict the probability of a given word being present when an input word is present. The neural network is trained by building the training data using a text corpus as a reference. This process is described in the following chart:

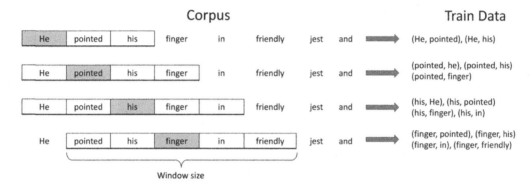

Figure 3.5 – Example of the generation of training data from a given corpus. In the filled boxes, the target word. In the dash boxes, the context words identified by a window size of length 2

The example described in *Figure 3.5* shows how the algorithm to generate the training data works. A *target* word is selected and a rolling window of fixed size *w* is built around that word. The words inside the rolling windows are known as *context* words. Multiple pairs of *(target word, context word)* are then built according to the words inside the rolling window.

Once the training data is generated from the whole corpus, the skip-gram model is trained to predict the probability of a word being a context word for the given target. During its training, the neural network learns a compact representation of the input words. This is why the skip-gram model is also known as **Word to Vector (Word2Vec)**.

The structure of the neural network representing the skip-gram model is described in the following chart:

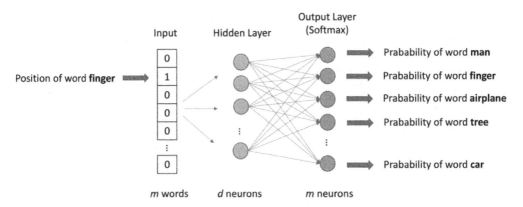

Figure 3.6 – Structure of the neural network of the skip-gram model. The number of d neurons in the hidden layer represents the final size of the embedding space

The input of the neural network is a binary vector of size m. Each element of the vector represents a word in the dictionary of the language we want to embed the words in. When, during the training process, a *(target word, context word)* pair is given, the input array will have 0 in all its entries with the exception of the entry representing the "target" word, which will be equal to 1. The hidden layer has d neurons. The hidden layer will learn the embedding representation of each word, creating a d-dimensional embedding space.

Finally, the output layer of the neural network is a dense layer of m neurons (the same size as the input vector) with a *softmax* activation function. Each neuron represents a word of the dictionary. The value assigned by the neuron corresponds to the probability of that word being "related" to the input word. Since softmax can be hard to compute when the size of m increases, a *hierarchical softmax* approach is always used.

The final goal of the skip-gram model is not to actually learn the task we previously described but to build a compact d-dimensional representation of the input words. Thanks to this representation, it is possible to easily extract an embedding space for the words using the weight of the hidden layer. Another common approach to creating a skip-gram model, which will be not described here, is *context-based*: **Continuous Bag-of-Words (CBOW)**.

Since the basic concepts behind the skip-gram model have been introduced, we can start to describe a series of unsupervised graph embedding algorithms built upon this model. Generally speaking, all the unsupervised embedding algorithms based on the skip-gram model use the same principle.

Starting from an input graph, they extract from it a set of walks. Those walks can be seen as a text corpus where each node represents a word. Two words (representing nodes) are near each other in the text if they are connected by an edge in a walk. The main difference between each method lies in the way those walks are computed. Indeed, as we will see, different walk generation algorithms can emphasize particular local or global structures of the graph.

DeepWalk

The DeepWalk algorithm generates the node embedding of a given graph using the skip-gram model. In order to provide a better explanation of this model, we need to introduce the concept of **random walks**.

Formally, let G be a graph and let v_i be a vertex selected as the starting point. We select a neighbor of v_i at random and we move toward it. From this point, we randomly select another point to move. This process is repeated t times. The random sequence of t vertices selected in this way is a random walk of length t. It is worth mentioning that the algorithm used to generate the random walks does not impose any constraint on how they are built. As a consequence, there is no guarantee that the local neighborhood of the node is well preserved.

Using the notion of random walk, the DeepWalk algorithm generates a random walk of a size of at most t for each node. Those random walks will be given as input to the skip-gram model. The embedding generated using skip-gram will be used as the final node embedding. In the following figure (*Figure 3.7*), we can see a step-by-step graphical representation of the algorithm:

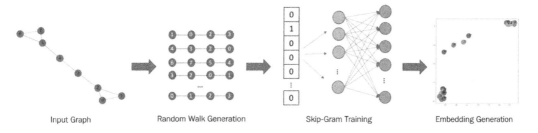

Input Graph   Random Walk Generation   Skip-Gram Training   Embedding Generation

Figure 3.7 – All the steps used by the DeepWalk algorithm to generate the node embedding of a given graph

Here is a step-by-step explanation of the algorithm graphically described in the preceding chart:

1. **Random Walk Generation**: For each node of input graph G, a set of γ random walks with a fixed maximum length (t) is computed. It should be noted that the length t is an upper bound. There are no constraints forcing all the paths to have the same length.

2. **Skip-Gram Training**: Using all the random walks generated in the previous step, a skip-gram model is trained. As we described earlier, the skip-gram model works on words and sentences. When a graph is given as input to the skip-gram model, as visible in *Figure 3.7*, a graph can be seen as an input text corpus, while a single node of the graph can be seen as a word of the corpus.

   A random walk can be seen as a sequence of words (a sentence). The skip-gram is then trained using the "fake" sentences generated by the nodes in the random walk. The parameters for the skip-gram model previously described (window size, w, and embed size, d) are used in this step.

3. **Embedding Generation**: The information contained in the hidden layers of the trained skip-gram model is used in order to extract the embedding of each node.

In the following code, we will show how to perform the node embedding of a given `networkx` graph using Python and the `karateclub` library:

```
import networkx as nx
from karateclub.node_embedding.neighbourhood.deepwalk import
DeepWalk
G = nx.barbell_graph(m1=10, m2=4)
dw = DeepWalk(dimensions=2)
dw.fit(G)
embeddings = dw.get_embedding()
```

The code is quite simple. We initialize the `DeepWalk` class from the `karateclub` library. In this implementation, the `dimensions` parameter represents the dimension of the embedding space. Other parameters worth mentioning that the `DeepWalk` class accepts are as follows:

- `walk_number`: The number of random walks to generate for each node
- `walk_length`: The length of the generated random walks
- `window_size`: The window size parameter of the skip-gram model

Finally, the model is fitted on graph G using `dw.fit(G)` and the embeddings are extracted using `dw.get_embedding()`.

The results of the code are shown in the following figure:

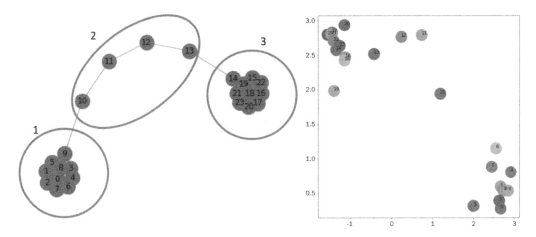

Figure 3.8 – Application of the DeepWalk algorithm to a graph (left) to generate the embedding vector of its nodes (right)

From the previous graph, we can see how DeepWalk is able to separate region 1 from region 3. Those two groups are contaminated by the nodes belonging to region 2. Indeed, for those nodes, a clear distinction is not visible in the embedding space.

Node2Vec

The **Node2Vec** algorithm can be seen as an extension of DeepWalk. Indeed, as with DeepWalk, Node2Vec also generates a set of random walks used as input to a skip-gram model. Once trained, the hidden layers of the skip-gram model are used to generate the embedding of the node in the graph. The main difference between the two algorithms lies in the way the random walks are generated.

Indeed, if DeepWalk generates random walks without using any bias, in Node2Vec a new technique to generate biased random walks on the graph is introduced. The algorithm to generate the random walks combines graph exploration by merging **Breadth-First Search (BFS)** and **Depth-First Search (DFS)**. The way those two algorithms are combined in the random walk's generation is regularized by two parameters, p and q. p defines the probability of a random walk getting back to the previous node, while q defines the probability that a random walk can pass through a previously unseen part of the graph.

Due to this combination, Node2Vec can preserve high-order proximities by preserving local structures in the graph as well as global community structures. This new method of random walk generation allows solving the limitation of DeepWalk preserving the local neighborhood properties of the node.

In the following code, we will show how to perform the node embedding of a given networkx graph using Python and the node2vec library:

```
import networkx as nx
from node2vec import Node2Vec
G = nx.barbell_graph(m1=10, m2=4)
draw_graph(G)
node2vec = Node2Vec(G, dimensions=2)
model = node2vec.fit(window=10)
embeddings = model.wv
```

Also, for Node2Vec, the code is straightforward. We initialize the Node2Vec class from the node2vec library. In this implementation, the dimensions parameter represents the dimension of the embedding space. The model is then fitted using node2vec.fit(window=10). Finally, the embeddings are obtained using model.wv.

It should be noted that model.wv is an object of the Word2VecKeyedVectors class. In order to get the embedding vector of a specific node with nodeid as the ID, we can use the trained model, as follows: model.wv[str(nodeId)]. Other parameters worth mentioning that the Node2Vec class accepts are as follows:

- num_walks: The number of random walks to generate for each node
- walk_length: The length of the generated random walks
- p, q: The p and q parameters of the random walk's generation algorithm

The results of the code are shown in *Figure 3.9*:

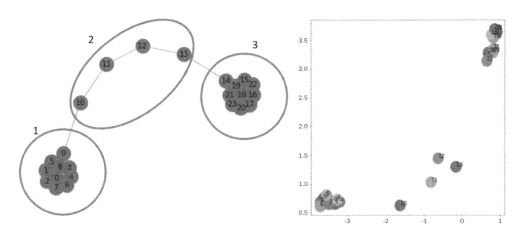

Figure 3.9 – Application of the Node2Vec algorithm to a graph (left) to generate the embedding vector of its nodes (right)

As is visible from *Figure 3.9*, Node2Vec allows us to obtain a better separation between nodes in the embedding space compared to DeepWalk. To specify, regions 1 and 3 are well clustered in two regions of space. Region 2 instead is well placed in the middle of the two groups without any overlap.

Edge2Vec

Contrary to the other embedding function, the **Edge to Vector (Edge2Vec)** algorithm generates the embedding space on edges, instead of nodes. This algorithm is a simple side effect of the embedding generated by using Node2Vec. The main idea is to use the node embedding of two adjacent nodes to perform some basic mathematical operations in order to extract the embedding of the edge connecting them.

Formally, let v_i and v_j be two adjacent nodes and let $f(v_i)$ and $f(v_j)$ be their embeddings computed with Node2Vec. The operators described in *Table 3.1* can be used in order to compute the embedding of their edge:

Operator	Equation	Class Name
Average	$\dfrac{f(v_i) + f(v_j)}{2}$	AverageEmbedder
Hadamard	$f(v_i) * f(v_j)$	HadamardEmbedder
Weighted-L1	$\lvert f(v_i) - f(v_j) \rvert$	WeightedL1Embedder
Weighted-L2	$\lvert f(v_i) - f(v_j) \rvert^2$	WeightedL2Embedder

Table 3.1 – Edge embedding operators with their equation and class name in the Node2Vec library

In the following code, we will show how to perform the node embedding of a given `networkx` graph using Python and the Node2Vec library:

```
from node2vec.edges import HadamardEmbedder
embedding = HadamardEmbedder(keyed_vectors=model.wv)
```

The code is quite simple. The `HadamardEmbedder` class is instantiated with only the `keyed_vectors` parameter. The value of this parameter is the embedding model generated by Node2Vec. In order to use other techniques to generate the edge embedding, we just need to change the class and select one from the ones listed in *Table 3.1*. An example of the application of this algorithm is shown in the following figure:

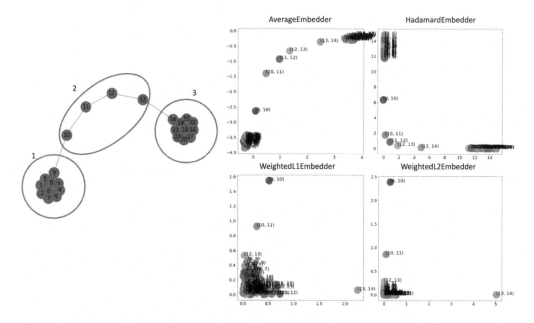

Figure 3.11 – Application of the Edge2Vec algorithm to a graph (top) to generate the embedding vector of its nodes (bottom) using different methods

From *Figure 3.11*, we can see how different embedding methods generate completely different embedding spaces. `AverageEmbedder` and `HadamardEmbedder`, in this example, generate well-separated embeddings for regions 1, 2, and 3.

For `WeightedL1Embedder` and `WeightedL2Embedder`, however, the embedding space is not well separated since the edge embeddings are concentrated in a single region without showing clear clusters.

Graph2Vec

The methods we previously described generated the embedding space for each node or edge on a given graph. **Graph to Vector (Graph2Vec)** generalizes this concept and generates embeddings for the whole graph.

To specify, given a set of graphs, the Graph2Vec algorithms generate an embedding space where each point represents a graph. This algorithm generates its embedding using an evolution of the Word2Vec skip-gram model known as **Document to Vector (Doc2Vec)**. We can graphically see a simplification of this model in *Figure 3.12*:

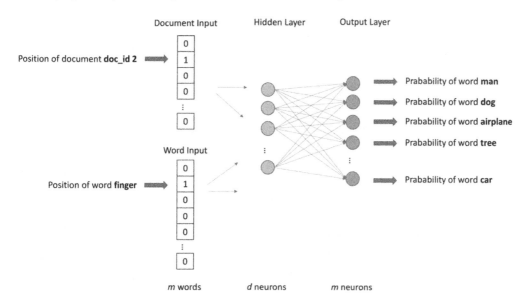

Figure 3.12 – Simplified graphical representation of the Doc2Vec skip-gram model. The number of d neurons in the hidden layer represents the final size of the embedding space

Compared to the simple Word2Vec, Doc2Vec also accepts another binary array representing the document containing the input word. Given a "target" document and a "target" word, the model then tries to predict the most probable "context" word with respect to the input "target" word and document.

With the introduction of the Doc2Vec model, we can now describe the Graph2Vec algorithm. The main idea behind this method is to view an entire graph as a document and each of its subgraphs, generated as an ego graph (see *Chapter 1, Getting Started with Graphs*) of each node, as words that comprise the document.

In other words, a graph is composed of subgraphs as a document is composed of sentences. According to this description, the algorithm can be summarized into the following steps:

1. **Subgraph generation**: A set of rooted subgraphs is generated around every node.

2. **Doc2Vec training**: The Doc2Vec skip-gram is trained using the subgraphs generated by the previous step.

3. **Embedding generation**: The information contained in the hidden layers of the trained Doc2Vec model is used in order to extract the embedding of each node.

In the following code, as we already did in *Chapter 2, Graph Machine Learning*, we will show how to perform the node embedding of a set of `networkx` graphs using Python and the `karateclub` library:

```python
import matplotlib.pyplot as plt
from karateclub import Graph2Vec
n_graphs = 20
def generate_random():
    n = random.randint(5, 20)
    k = random.randint(5, n)
    p = random.uniform(0, 1)
    return nx.watts_strogatz_graph(n,k,p)

Gs = [generate_random() for x in range(n_graphs)]

model = Graph2Vec(dimensions=2)
model.fit(Gs)
embeddings = model.get_embedding()
```

In this example, the following have been done:

1. 20 Watts-Strogatz graphs have been generated with random parameters.

2. We then initialize the Graph2Vec class from the `karateclub` library with two dimensions. In this implementation, the `dimensions` parameter represents the dimension of the embedding space.

3. The model is then fitted on the input data using `model.fit(Gs)`.

4. The vector containing the embeddings is extracted using `model.get_embedding()`.

The results of the code are shown in the following figure:

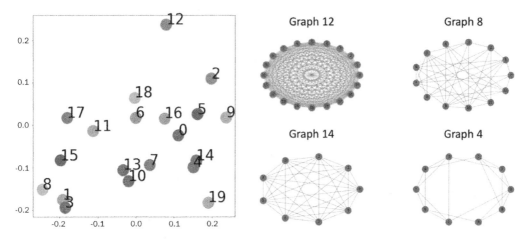

Figure 3.13 – Application of the Graph2Vec algorithm to a graph (left) to generate the embedding vector of its nodes (right) using different methods

From *Figure 3.13*, it is possible to see the embedding space generated for the different graphs.

In this section, we described different shallow embedding methods based on matrix factorization and the skip-gram model. However, in the scientific literature, a lot of unsupervised embedding algorithms exist, such as Laplacian methods. We refer those of you who are interested in exploring those methods to look at the paper *Machine Learning on Graphs: A Model and Comprehensive Taxonomy* available at `https://arxiv.org/pdf/2005.03675.pdf`.

We will continue our description of the unsupervised graph embedding method in the next sections. We will describe more complex graph embedding algorithms based on autoencoders.

Autoencoders

Autoencoders are an extremely powerful tool that can effectively help data scientists to deal with high-dimensional datasets. Although first presented around 30 years ago, in recent years, autoencoders have become more and more widespread in conjunction with the general rise of neural network-based algorithms. Besides allowing us to compact sparse representations, they can also be at the base of generative models, representing the first inception of the famous **Generative Adversarial Network (GAN)**, which is, using the words of Geoffrey Hinton:

"The most interesting idea in the last 10 years in machine learning"

An autoencoder is a neural network where the inputs and outputs are basically the same, but that is characterized by a small number of units in the hidden layer. Loosely speaking, it is a neural network that is trained to reconstruct its inputs using a significantly lower number of variables and/or degree of freedom.

Since an autoencoder does not need a labeled dataset, it can be seen as an example of unsupervised learning and a dimensionality-reduction technique. However, different from other techniques such as **Principal Component Analysis (PCA)** and matrix factorization, autoencoders can learn non-linear transformation thanks to the non-linear activation functions of their neurons:

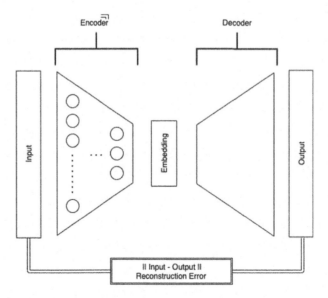

Figure 3.14 – Diagram of the autoencoder structure. The colors in the input and output layers represent the fact that the values should be as similar as possible. In fact, the training of the network is done in order to match these values and minimize the reconstruction error

Figure 3.14 shows a simple example of an autoencoder. You can see how the autoencoder can generally be seen as composed of two parts:

- An encoder network that processes the input through one or more units and maps it into an encoded representation that reduces the dimension of the inputs (under-complete autoencoders) and/or constrains its sparsity (over-complete regularized autoencoders)

- A decoder network that reconstructs the input signal from the encoded representation of the middle layer

The encoder-decoder structure is then trained to minimize the ability of the full network to reconstruct the input. In order to completely specify an autoencoder, we need a loss function. The error between the inputs and the outputs can be computed using different metrics and indeed the choice of the correct form for the "reconstruction" error is a critical point when building an autoencoder.

Some common choices for the loss functions that measure the reconstruction error are **mean square error**, **mean absolute error**, **cross-entropy**, and **KL divergence**.

In the following sections, we will show you how to build an autoencoder starting with some basic concepts and then applying those concepts to graph structures. But before diving in, we feel compelled to give you a very brief introduction to the frameworks that will allow us to do this: TensorFlow and Keras.

TensorFlow and Keras – a powerful combination

Released as open source by Google in 2017, TensorFlow is now the standard, de facto framework that allows symbolic computations and differential programming. It basically allows you to build a symbolic structure that describes how inputs are combined in order to produce the outputs, defining what is generally called a **computational graph** or a **stateful dataflow graph**. In this graph, nodes are the variable (scalar, arrays, tensors) and edges represent operations connecting the inputs (edge source) to the output (edge target) of a single operation.

In TensorFlow, such a graph is static (this is indeed one of the main differences with respect to another very popular framework in this context: `torch`) and can be executed by feeding data into it, as inputs, clearing the "dataflow" attribute mentioned previously.

By abstracting the computation, TensorFlow is a very general tool that can run on multiple backends: on machines powered by CPUs, GPUs, or even ad hoc, specifically designed processing units such as TPUs. Besides, TensorFlow-powered applications can also be deployed on different devices, ranging from single and distributed servers to mobile devices.

Besides abstracting computation, TensorFlow also allows you to symbolically differentiate your computational graph with respect to any of its variables, resulting in a new computational graph that can also be differentiated to produce higher-order derivatives. This approach is generally referred to as symbol-to-symbol derivative and it is indeed extremely powerful, especially in the context of the optimization of the generic loss function, which requires gradient estimations (such as gradient descent techniques).

As you might know, the problem of optimizing a loss function with respect to many parameters is central in the training of any neural network via backpropagation. This is surely the main reason why TensorFlow has become very popular in the past few years and why it was designed and produced in the first place by Google.

Diving in depth into the usage of TensorFlow is beyond the scope of this book and indeed you can find out more through the description given in dedicated books. In the following sections, we will use some of its main functionalities and provide you with the basic tools for building neural networks.

Since its last major release, 2.x, the standard way of building a model with TensorFlow is using the Keras API. Keras was natively a side external project with respect to TensorFlow, aimed at providing a common and simple API to use several differential programming frameworks, such as TensorFlow, Teano, and CNTK, for implementing a neural network model. It generally abstracts the low-level implementation of the computation graph and provides you with the most common layers used when building neural networks (although custom layers can also be easily implemented), such as the following:

- Convolutional layers
- Recurrent layers
- Regularization layers
- Loss functions

Keras also exposes APIs that are very similar to scikit-learn, the most popular library for machine learning in the Python ecosystem, making it very easy for data scientists to build, train, and integrate neural network-based models in their applications.

In the next section, we will show you how to build and train an autoencoder using Keras. We'll start applying these techniques to images in order to progressively apply the key concepts to graph structures.

Our first autoencoder

We'll start by implementing an autoencoder in its simplest form, that is, a simple feed-forward network trained to reconstruct its input. We'll apply this to the Fashion-MNIST dataset, which is a dataset similar to the famous MNIST dataset that features hand-written numbers on a black and white image.

MNIST has 10 categories and consists of 60k + 10k (train dataset + test dataset) 28x28 pixel grayscale images that represent a piece of clothing (`T-shirt`, `Trouser`, `Pullover`, `Dress`, `Coat`, `Sandal`, `Shirt`, `Sneaker`, `Bag`, and `Ankle boot`). The Fashion-MNIST dataset is a harder task than the original MNIST dataset and it is generally used for benchmarking algorithms.

The dataset is already integrated in the Keras library and can be easily imported using the following code:

```
from tensorflow.keras.datasets import fashion_mnist
(x_train, y_train), (x_test, y_test) = fashion_mnist.load_
data()
```

It is usually good practice to rescale the inputs with an order of magnitude of around 1 (for which activation functions are most efficient) and make sure that the numerical data is in single-precision (32 bits) instead of double-precision (64 bits). This is due to the fact that it is generally desirable to promote speed rather than precision when training a neural network, which is a computationally expensive process. In certain cases, the precision could even be lowered to half-precision (16 bits). We transform the input with the following:

```
x_train = x_train.astype('float32') / 255.
x_test = x_test.astype('float32') / 255.
```

We can grasp the type of inputs we are dealing with by plotting some of the samples from the training set using the following code:

```
n = 10
plt.figure(figsize=(20, 4))
for i in range(n):
    ax = plt.subplot(1, n, i + 1)
    plt.imshow(x_train[i])
    plt.title(classes[y_train[i]])
    plt.gray()
    ax.get_xaxis().set_visible(False)
```

```
        ax.get_yaxis().set_visible(False)
plt.show()
```

In the preceding code, `classes` represents the mapping between integers and class names, for example, `T-shirt`, `Trouser`, `Pullover`, `Dress`, `Coat`, `Sandal`, `Shirt`, `Sneaker`, `Bag`, and `Ankle boot`:

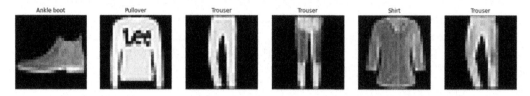

Figure 3.15 – Some samples taken from the training set of the Fashion-MNIST dataset

Now that we have imported the inputs, we can build our autoencoder network by creating the encoder and the decoder. We will be doing this using the Keras functional API, which provides more generality and flexibility compared to the so-called Sequential API. We start by defining the encoder network:

```
from tensorflow.keras.layers import Conv2D, Dropout,
MaxPooling2D, UpSampling2D, Input
input_img = Input(shape=(28, 28, 1))
x = Conv2D(16, (3, 3), activation='relu', padding='same')
(input_img)
x = MaxPooling2D((2, 2), padding='same')(x)
x = Conv2D(8, (3, 3), activation='relu', padding='same')(x)
x = MaxPooling2D((2, 2), padding='same')(x)
x = Conv2D(8, (3, 3), activation='relu', padding='same')(x)
encoded = MaxPooling2D((2, 2), padding='same')(x)
```

Our network is composed of a stack of three levels of the same pattern composed of the same two-layer building block:

- `Conv2D`, a two-dimensional convolutional kernel that is applied to the input and effectively corresponds to having weights shared across all the input neurons. After applying the convolutional kernel, the output is transformed using the ReLU activation function. This structure is replicated for n hidden planes, with n being 16 in the first stacked layer and 8 in the second and third stacked layers.

- `MaxPooling2D`, which down-samples the inputs by taking the maximum value over the specified window (2x2 in this case).

Using the Keras API, we can also have an overview of how the layers transformed the inputs using the `Model` class, which converts the tensors into a user-friendly model ready to be used and explored:

```
Model(input_img, encoded).summary()
```

This provides a summary of the encoder network visible in *Figure 3.16*:

```
Model: "model_4"
_____
Layer (type)                 Output Shape              Param #
=================================================================
input_2 (InputLayer)         [(None, 28, 28, 1)]       0

gaussian_noise (GaussianNois (None, 28, 28, 1)         0

conv2d_7 (Conv2D)            (None, 28, 28, 16)        160

max_pooling2d_3 (MaxPooling2 (None, 14, 14, 16)        0

conv2d_8 (Conv2D)            (None, 14, 14, 8)         1160

max_pooling2d_4 (MaxPooling2 (None, 7, 7, 8)           0

conv2d_9 (Conv2D)            (None, 7, 7, 8)           584

max_pooling2d_5 (MaxPooling2 (None, 4, 4, 8)           0
=================================================================
Total params: 1,904
Trainable params: 1,904
Non-trainable params: 0
_____
```

Figure 3.16 – Overview of the encoder network

As can be seen, at the end of the encoding phase, we have a (4, 4, 8) tensor, which is more than six times smaller than our original initial inputs (28x28). We can now build the decoder network. Note that the encoder and decoder do not need to have the same structure and/or shared weights:

```
x = Conv2D(8, (3, 3), activation='relu', padding='same')
(encoded)
x = UpSampling2D((2, 2))(x)
x = Conv2D(8, (3, 3), activation='relu', padding='same')(x)
x = UpSampling2D((2, 2))(x)
x = Conv2D(16, (3, 3), activation='relu')(x)
x = UpSampling2D((2, 2))(x)
```

```
decoded = Conv2D(1, (3, 3), activation='sigmoid',
padding='same')(x)
```

In this case, the decoder network resembles the encoder structure where the down-sampling of the input achieved using the `MaxPooling2D` layer has been replaced by the `UpSampling2D` layer, which basically repeats the input over a specified window (2x2 in this case, effectively doubling the tensor in each direction).

We have now fully defined the network structure with the encoder and decoder layers. In order to completely specify our autoencoder, we also need to specify a loss function. Moreover, to build the computational graph, Keras also needs to know which algorithms should be used in order to optimize the network weights. Both bits of information, the loss function and optimizer to be used, are generally provided to Keras when *compiling* the model:

```
autoencoder = Model(input_img, decoded)
autoencoder.compile(optimizer='adam', loss='binary_
crossentropy')
```

We can now finally train our autoencoder. Keras `Model` classes provide APIs that are similar to scikit-learn, with a `fit` method to be used to train the neural network. Note that, owing to the nature of the autoencoder, we are using the same information as the input and output of our network:

```
autoencoder.fit(x_train, x_train,
                epochs=50,
                batch_size=128,
                shuffle=True,
                validation_data=(x_test, x_test))
```

Once the training is finished, we can examine the ability of the network to reconstruct the inputs by comparing input images with their reconstructed version, which can be easily computed using the `predict` method of the Keras `Model` class as follows:

```
decoded_imgs = autoencoder.predict(x_test)
```

In *Figure 3.17*, we show the reconstructed images. As you can see, the network is quite good at reconstructing unseen images, especially when considering the large-scale features. Details might have been lost in the compression (see, for instance, the logo on the t-shirts) but the overall relevant information has indeed been captured by our network:

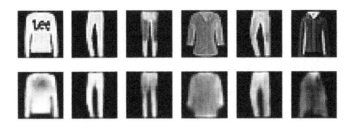

Figure 3.17 – Examples of the reconstruction done on the test set by the trained autoencoder

It can also be very interesting to represent the encoded version of the images in a two-dimensional plane using T-SNE:

```
from tensorflow.keras.layers import Flatten
embed_layer = Flatten()(encoded)
embeddings = Model(input_img, embed_layer).predict(x_test)
tsne = TSNE(n_components=2)
emb2d = tsne.fit_transform(embeddings)
x, y = np.squeeze(emb2d[:, 0]), np.squeeze(emb2d[:, 1])
```

The coordinates provided by T-SNE are shown in *Figure 3.18*, colored by the class the sample belongs to. The clustering of the different clothing can clearly be seen, particularly for some classes that are very well separated from the rest:

Figure 3.18 – T-SNE transformation of the embeddings extracted from the test set, colored by the class that the sample belongs to

Autoencoders are, however, rather prone to overfitting, as they tend to re-create exactly the images of the training and not generalize well. In the following subsection, we will see how overfitting can be prevented in order to build more robust and reliable dense representations.

Denoising autoencoders

Besides allowing us to compress a sparse representation into a denser vector, autoencoders are also widely used to process a signal in order to filter out noise and extract only a relevant (characteristic) signal. This can be very useful in many applications, especially when identifying anomalies and outliers.

Denoising autoencoders are a small variation of what has been implemented. As described in the previous section, basic autoencoders are trained using the same image as input and output. Denoising autoencoders corrupt the input using some noise of various intensity, while keeping the same noise-free target. This could be achieved by simply adding some Gaussian noise to the inputs:

```
noise_factor = 0.1
x_train_noisy = x_train + noise_factor * np.random.
normal(loc=0.0, scale=1.0, size=x_train.shape)
x_test_noisy = x_test + noise_factor * np.random.
normal(loc=0.0, scale=1.0, size=x_test.shape)

x_train_noisy = np.clip(x_train_noisy, 0., 1.)
x_test_noisy = np.clip(x_test_noisy, 0., 1.)
```

The network can then be trained using the corrupted input, while for the output the noise-free image is used:

```
noisy_autoencoder.fit(x_train_noisy, x_train,
                epochs=50,
                batch_size=128,
                shuffle=True,
                validation_data=(x_test_noisy, x_test))
```

Such an approach is generally valid when datasets are large and when the risk of overfitting the noise is rather limited. When datasets are smaller, an alternative to avoid the network "learning" the noise as well (thus learning the mapping between a static noisy image to its noise-free version) is to add training stochastic noise using a `GaussianNoise` layer.

Note that in this way, the noise may change between epochs and prevent the network from learning a static corruption superimposed to our training set. In order to do so, we change the first layers of our network in the following way:

```
input_img = Input(shape=(28, 28, 1))
noisy_input = GaussianNoise(0.1)(input_img)
x = Conv2D(16, (3, 3), activation='relu', padding='same')
(noisy_input)
```

The difference is that instead of having statically corrupted samples (that do not change in time), the noisy inputs now keep changing between epochs, thus avoiding the network learning the noise as well.

The `GaussianNoise` layer is an example of a regularization layer, that is, a layer that helps reduce overfitting of a neural network by inserting a random part in the network. `GaussianNoise` layers make models more robust and able to generalize better, avoiding autoencoders learning the identity function.

Another common example of a regularization layer is the dropout layers that effectively set to 0 some of the inputs (at random with a probability, p_0) and rescale the other inputs by a $1/1 - p_0$ factor in order to (statistically) keep the sum over all the units constant, with and without dropout.

Dropout corresponds to randomly killing some of the connections between layers in order to reduce output dependence to specific neurons. You need to keep in mind that regularization layers are only active at training, while at test time they simply correspond to identity layers.

In *Figure 3.19*, we compare the network reconstruction of a noisy input (input) for the previous unregularized trained network and the network with a `GaussianNoise` layer. As can be seen (compare, for instance, the images of trousers), the model with regularization tends to develop stronger robustness and reconstructs the noise-free outputs:

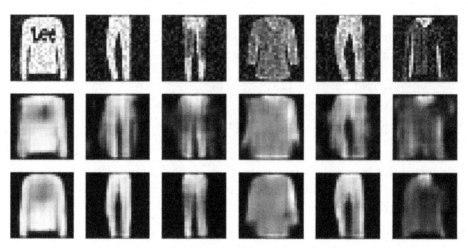

Figure 3.19 – Comparison with reconstruction for noisy samples. Top row: noisy input; middle row: reconstructed output using a vanilla autoencoder; bottom row: reconstructed output using a denoising autoencoder

Regularization layers are often used when dealing with deep neural networks that tend to overfit and are able to learn identity functions for autoencoders. Often, dropout or `GaussianNoise` layers are introduced, repeating a similar pattern composed of regularization and learnable layers that we usually refer to as **stacked denoising layers**.

Graph autoencoders

Once the basic concepts of autoencoders are understood, we can now turn to apply this framework to graph structures. If on one hand the network structure, decomposed into an encoder-decoder structure with a low-dimensional representation in between, still applies, the definition of the loss function to be optimized needs a bit of caution when dealing with networks. First, we need to adapt the reconstruction error to a meaningful formulation that can adapt to the peculiarities of graph structures. But to do so, let's first introduce the concepts of first- and higher-order proximity.

When applying autoencoders to graph structures, the input and output of the network should be a graph representation, as, for instance, the adjacency matrix. The reconstruction loss could then be defined as the Frobenius norm of the difference between the input and output matrices. However, when applying autoencoders to such graph structures and adjacency matrices, two critical issues arise:

- Whereas the presence of links indicates a relation or similarity between two vertices, their absence does not generally indicate a dissimilarity between vertices.

- The adjacency matrix is extremely sparse and therefore the model will naturally tend to predict a 0 rather than a positive value.

To address such peculiarities of graph structures, when defining the reconstruction loss, we need to penalize more errors done for the non-zero elements rather than that for zero elements. This can be done using the following loss function:

$$\mathcal{L}_{2nd} = \sum_{i=1}^{n} \left\| (\tilde{X}_\iota - X_i) \odot b_i \right\|$$

Here, $\odot$ is the Hadamard element-wise product, where $b_{ij} = \beta > 1$ if there is an edge between nodes i and j, and 0 otherwise. The preceding loss guarantees that vertices that share a neighborhood (that is, their adjacency vectors are similar) will also be close in the embedding space. Thus, the preceding formulation will naturally preserve second-order proximity for the reconstructed graph.

On the other hand, you can also promote first-order proximity in the reconstructed graph, thus enforcing connected nodes to be close in the embedding space. This condition can be enforced by using the following loss:

$$\mathcal{L}_{1th} = \sum_{i,j=1}^{n} s_{ij} \left\| y_j - y_i \right\|_2^2$$

Here, y_i and y_j are the two representation of nodes i and j in the embedding space. This loss function forces neighboring nodes to be close in the embedding space. In fact, if two nodes are tightly connected, s_{ij} will be large. As a consequence, their difference in the embedding space, $\left\| y_j - y_i \right\|_2^2$, should be limited (indicating the two nodes are close in the embedding space) to keep the loss function small. The two losses can also be combined into a single loss function, where, in order to prevent overfitting, a regularization loss can be added that is proportional to the norm of the weight coefficients:

$$\mathcal{L}_{tot} = \mathcal{L}_{2nd} + \alpha \cdot \mathcal{L}_{tot} + v \cdot \mathcal{L}_{reg} = \mathcal{L}_{2nd} + \alpha \cdot \mathcal{L}_{tot} + v \cdot \left\| W \right\|_F^2$$

In the preceding equation, *W* represents all the weights used across the network. The preceding formulation was proposed in 2016 by Wang et al., and it is now known as **Structural Deep Network Embedding (SDNE)**.

Although the preceding loss could also be directly implemented with TensorFlow and Keras, you can already find this network integrated in the GEM package we referred to previously. As before, extracting the node embedding can be done similarly in a few lines of code, as follows:

```
G=nx.karate_club_graph()
sdne=SDNE(d=2, beta=5, alpha=1e-5, nu1=1e-6, nu2=1e-6,
          K=3,n_units=[50, 15,], rho=0.3, n_iter=10,
          xeta=0.01,n_batch=100,
          modelfile=['enc_model.json','dec_model.json'],
          weightfile=['enc_weights.hdf5','dec_weights.hdf5'])
sdne.learn_embedding(G)
embeddings = m1.get_embedding()
```

Although very powerful, these graph autoencoders encounter some issues when dealing with large graphs. For these cases, the input of our autoencoder is one row of the adjacency matrix that has as many elements as the nodes in the network. In large networks, this size can easily be of the order of millions or tens of millions.

In the next section, we describe a different strategy for encoding the network information that in some cases may iteratively aggregate embeddings only over local neighborhoods, making it scalable to large graphs.

Graph neural networks

GNNs are deep learning methods that work on graph-structured data. This family of methods is also known as **geometric deep learning** and is gaining increasing interest in a variety of applications, including social network analysis and computer graphics.

According to the taxonomy defined in *Chapter 2, Graph Machine Learning*, the encoder part takes as input both the graph structure and the node features. Those algorithms can be trained either with or without supervision. In this chapter, we will focus on unsupervised training, while the supervised setting will be explored in *Chapter 4, Supervised Graph Learning*.

If you are familiar with the concept of a **Convolutional Neural Network (CNN)**, you might already know that they are able to achieve impressive results when dealing with regular Euclidean spaces, such as text (one-dimensional), images (two-dimensional), and videos (three-dimensional). A classic CNN consists of a sequence of layers and each layer extracts multi-scale localized spatial features. Those features are exploited by deeper layers to construct more complex and highly expressive representations.

In recent years, it has been observed that concepts such as multi-layer and locality are also useful for processing graph-structured data. However, graphs are defined over a *non-Euclidean space*, and finding a generalization of a CNN for graphs is not straightforward, as described in *Figure 3.20*:

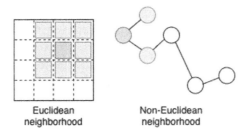

Euclidean
neighborhood

Non-Euclidean
neighborhood

Figure 3.20 – Visual difference between Euclidean and non-Euclidean neighborhoods

The original formulation of GNN was proposed by Scarselli et al. back in 2009. It relies on the fact that each node can be described by its features and its neighborhood. Information coming from the neighborhood (which represents the concept of locality in the graph domain) can be aggregated and used to compute more complex and high-level features. Let's understand in more detail how it can be done.

At the beginning, each node, v_i, is associated with a state. Let's start with a random embedding, h_i^t (ignoring node attributes for simplicity). At each iteration of the algorithm, nodes accumulate input from their neighbors using a simple neural network layer:

$$h_i^t = \sum_{v_j \in N(v_i)} \sigma\left(W h_j^{t-1} + b\right)$$

Here, $W \in \mathbb{R}^{d \times d}$ and $b \in \mathbb{R}^d$ are trainable parameters (where d is the dimension of the embedding), σ is a non-linear function, and t represents the tth iteration of the algorithm. The equation is applied recursively until a particular objective is reached. Notice that, at each iteration, the *previous state* (the state computed at the previous iteration) is exploited in order to compute that the new state has happened with *recurrent neural networks*.

Variants of GNNs

Starting from this first idea, several attempts have been made in recent years to re-address the problem of learning from graph data. In particular, variants of the previously described GNN have been proposed, with the aim of improving its representation learning capability. Some of them are specifically designed to process specific types of graphs (direct, indirect, weighted, unweighted, static, dynamic, and so on).

Also, several modifications have been proposed for the propagation step (convolution, gate mechanisms, attention mechanisms, and skip connections, among others), with the aim of improving representation at different levels. Also, different training methods have been proposed to improve learning.

When dealing with unsupervised representation learning, one of the most common approaches is to use an encoder to embed the graph (the encoder is formulated as one of the GNN variants) and then use a simple decoder to reconstruct the adjacency matrix. The loss function is usually formulated as the similarity between the original adjacency matrix and the reconstructed one. Formally, it can be defined as follows:

$$Z = GNN(X, A)$$
$$\hat{A} = ZZ^T$$

Here, $A \in \mathbb{R}^{N \times N}$ is the adjacency matrix representation and $X \in \mathbb{R}^{N \times d}$ is the matrix of node attributes. Another common variant of this approach, especially used when dealing with graph classification/representation learning, is to train against a *target distance*. The idea is to embed two pairs of graphs simultaneously obtaining a combined representation. The model is then trained such that this representation matches the distance. A similar strategy can be also adopted when dealing with node classification/representation learning by using a node similarity function.

Graph Convolutional Neural Network (GCN)-based encoders are one of the most diffused variants of GNN for unsupervised learning. GCNs are GNN models inspired by many of the basic ideas behind CNN. Filter parameters are typically shared over all locations in the graph and several layers are concatenated to form a deep network.

There are essentially two types of convolutional operations for graph data, namely **spectral approaches** and **non-spectral (spatial)** approaches. The first, as the name suggests, defines convolution in the spectral domain (that is, decomposing graphs in a combination of simpler elements). Spatial convolution formulates the convolution as aggregating feature information from neighbors.

Spectral graph convolution

Spectral approaches are related to spectral graph theory, the study of the characteristics of a graph in relation to the characteristic polynomial, eigenvalues, and eigenvectors of the matrices associated with the graph. The convolution operation is defined as the multiplication of a signal (node features) by a kernel. In more detail, it is defined in the Fourier domain by determining the *eigendecomposition of the graph Laplacian* (think about the graph Laplacian as an adjacency matrix normalized in a special way).

While this definition of spectral convolution has a strong mathematical foundation, the operation is computationally expensive. For this reason, several works have been done to approximate it in an efficient way. ChebNet by Defferrard et al., for instance, is one of the first seminal works on spectral graph convolution. Here, the operation is approximated by using the concept of the Chebyshev polynomial of order K (a special kind of polynomial used to efficiently approximate functions).

Here, K is a very useful parameter because it determines the locality of the filter. Intuitively, for $K=1$, only the node features are fed into the network. With $K=2$, we average over two-hop neighbors (neighbors of neighbors) and so on.

Let $X \in \mathbb{R}^{N \times d}$ be the matrix of node features. In classical neural network processing, this signal would be composed of layers of the following form:

$$H^l = \sigma(XW)$$

Here, $W \in \mathbb{R}^{N \times N}$ is the layer weights and σ represents some non-linear activation function. The drawback of this operation is that it processes each node signal independently without taking into account connections between nodes. To overcome this limitation, a simple (yet effective) modification can be done, as follows:

$$H^l = \sigma(AXW)$$

By introducing the adjacency matrix, $A \in \mathbb{R}^{N \times N}$, a new linear combination between each node and its corresponding neighbors is added. This way, the information depends only on the neighborhood and parameters are applied on all the nodes, simultaneously.

It is worth noting that this operation can be repeated in sequence several times, thus creating a deep network. At each layer, the node descriptors, X, will be replaced with the output of the previous layer, H^{l-1}.

The preceding presented equation, however, has some limitations and cannot be applied as it stands. The first limitation is that by multiplying by A, we consider all the neighbors of the node but not the node itself. This problem can be easily overcome by adding self-loops in the graph, that is, adding the $\hat{A} = A + I$ identity matrix.

The second limitation is related to the adjacency matrix itself. Since it is typically not normalized, we will observe large values in the feature representation of high-degree nodes and small values in the feature representation of low-degree nodes. This will lead to several problems during training since optimization algorithms are often sensitive to feature scale. Several methods have been proposed for normalizing A.

In Kipf and Welling, 2017 (one of the well-known GCN models), for example, the normalization is performed by multiplying A by the *diagonal node degree matrix D*, such that all the rows sum to 1: $D^{-1}A$. More specifically, they used symmetric normalization ($D^{-1/2}AD^{-1/2}$), such that the proposed propagation rule becomes as follows:

$$H^l = \sigma\left(\hat{D}^{-\frac{1}{2}}\hat{A}\hat{D}^{-\frac{1}{2}}XW\right)$$

Here, $\hat{D}$ is the diagonal node degree matrix of $\hat{A}$.

In the following example, we will create a GCN as defined in Kipf and Welling and we will apply this propagation rule for embedding a well-known network: a Zachary's karate club graph:

1. To begin, it is necessary to import all the Python modules. We will use `networkx` to load the *barbell graph*:

```python
import networkx as nx
import numpy as np
G = nx.barbell_graph(m1=10,m2=4)
```

2. To implement the GC propagation rule, we need an adjacency matrix representing G. Since this network does not have node features, we will use the $I \in \mathbb{R}^{N \times N}$ identity matrix as the node descriptor:

```python
A = nx.to_numpy_matrix(G)
I = np.eye(G.number_of_nodes())
```

3. We now add the self-loop and prepare the diagonal node degree matrix:

```python
from scipy.linalg import sqrtm

A_hat = A + I
D_hat = np.array(np.sum(A_hat, axis=0))[0]
D_hat = np.array(np.diag(D_hat))
D_hat = np.linalg.inv(sqrtm(D_hat))
A_norm = D_hat @ A_hat @ D_hat
```

4. Our GCN will be composed of two layers. Let's define the layers' weights and the propagation rule. Layer weights, *W*, will be initialized using *Glorot uniform initialization* (even if other initialization methods can be also used, for example, by sampling from a Gaussian or uniform distribution):

```python
def glorot_init(nin, nout):
    sd = np.sqrt(6.0 / (nin + nout))
    return np.random.uniform(-sd, sd, size=(nin, nout))
class GCNLayer():
  def __init__(self, n_inputs, n_outputs):
      self.n_inputs = n_inputs
      self.n_outputs = n_outputs
      self.W = glorot_init(self.n_outputs, self.n_inputs)
      self.activation = np.tanh
  def forward(self, A, X):
      self._X = (A @ X).T
      H = self.W @ self._X
      H = self.activation(H)
      return H.T # (n_outputs, N)
```

5. Finally, let's create our network and compute the forward pass, that is, propagate the signal through the network:

```python
gcn1 = GCNLayer(G.number_of_nodes(), 8)
gcn2 = GCNLayer(8, 4)
gcn3 = GCNLayer(4, 2)
H1 = gcn1.forward(A_norm, I)
H2 = gcn2.forward(A_norm, H1)

H3 = gcn3.forward(A_norm, H2)
```

H3 now contains the embedding computed using the GCN propagation rule. Notice that we chose 2 as the number of outputs, meaning that the embedding is bi-dimensional and can be easily visualized. In *Figure 3.21*, you can see the output:

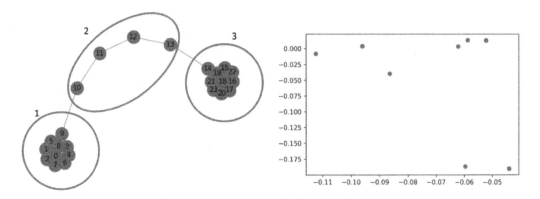

Figure 3.21 – Application of the graph convolutional layer to a graph (left) to generate the embedding vector of its nodes (right)

You can observe the presence of two quite well-separated communities. This is a nice result, considering that we have not trained the network yet!

Spectral graph convolution methods have achieved noteworthy results in many domains. However, they present some drawbacks. Consider, for example, a very big graph with billions of nodes: a spectral approach requires the graph to be processed simultaneously, which can be impractical from a computational point of view.

Furthermore, spectral convolution often assumes a fixed graph, leading to poor generalization capabilities on new, different graphs. To overcome these issues, spatial graph convolution represents an interesting alternative.

Spatial graph convolution

Spatial graph convolutional networks perform the operations directly on the graph by aggregating information from spatially close neighbors. Spatial convolution has many advantages: weights can be easily shared across a different location of the graph, leading to a good generalization capability on different graphs. Furthermore, the computation can be done by considering subsets of nodes instead of the entire graph, potentially improving computational efficiency.

GraphSAGE is one of the algorithms that implement spatial convolution. One of the main characteristics is its ability to scale over various types of networks. We can think of GraphSAGE as composed of three steps:

1. **Neighborhood sampling**: For each node in a graph, the first step is to find its k-neighborhood, where *k* is defined by the user for determining how many hops to consider (neighbors of neighbors).

2. **Aggregation**: The second step is to aggregate, for each node, the node features describing the respective neighborhood. Various types of aggregation can be performed, including average, pooling (for example, taking the best feature according to certain criteria), or an even more complicated operation, such as using recurrent units (such as LSTM).

3. **Prediction**: Each node is equipped with a simple neural network that learns how to perform predictions based on the aggregated features from the neighbors.

GraphSAGE is often used in supervised settings, as we will see in *Chapter 4*, *Supervised Graph Learning*. However, by adopting strategies such as using a similarity function as the target distance, it can also be effective for learning embedding without explicitly supervising the task.

Graph convolution in practice

In practice, GNNs have been implemented in many machine learning and deep learning frameworks, including TensorFlow, Keras, and PyTorch. For the next example, we will be using StellarGraph, the Python library for machine learning on graphs.

In the following example, we will learn about embedding vectors in an unsupervised manner, without a target variable. The method is inspired by Bai et al. 2019 and is based on the simultaneous embedding of pairs of graphs. This embedding should match a ground-truth distance between graphs:

1. First, let's load the required Python modules:

```
import numpy as np
import stellargraph as sg
from stellargraph.mapper import FullBatchNodeGenerator
from stellargraph.layer import GCN

import tensorflow as tf
from tensorflow.keras import layers, optimizers, losses, metrics, Model
```

2. We will be using the PROTEINS dataset for this example, which is available in StellarGraph and consists of 1,114 graphs with 39 nodes and 73 edges on average for each graph. Each node is described by four attributes and belongs to one of two classes:

```
dataset = sg.datasets.PROTEINS()
graphs, graph_labels = dataset.load()
```

3. The next step is to create the model. It will be composed of two GC layers with 64 and 32 output dimensions followed by ReLU activation, respectively. The output will be computed as the Euclidean distance of the two embeddings:

```
generator = sg.mapper.PaddedGraphGenerator(graphs)


# define a GCN model containing 2 layers of size 64 and
32, respectively.
# ReLU activation function is used to add non-linearity
between layers
gc_model = sg.layer.GCNSupervisedGraphClassification(
 [64, 32], ["relu", "relu"], generator, pool_all_
layers=True)
# retrieve the input and the output tensor of the GC
layer such that they can be connected to the next layer

inp1, out1 = gc_model.in_out_tensors()
inp2, out2 = gc_model.in_out_tensors()
vec_distance = tf.norm(out1 - out2, axis=1)


# create the model. It is also useful to create a
specular model in order to easily retrieve the embeddings
pair_model = Model(inp1 + inp2, vec_distance)
 embedding_model = Model(inp1, out1)
```

4. It is now time to prepare the dataset for training. To each pair of input graphs, we will assign a similarity score. Notice that any notion of graph similarity can be used in this case, including graph edit distances. For simplicity, we will be using the distance between the spectrum of the Laplacian of the graphs:

```
def graph_distance(graph1, graph2):
    spec1 = nx.laplacian_spectrum(graph1.to_
```

```
networkx(feature_attr=None))
    spec2 = nx.laplacian_spectrum(graph2.to_
networkx(feature_attr=None))
    k = min(len(spec1), len(spec2))
    return np.linalg.norm(spec1[:k] - spec2[:k])
```

```
graph_idx = np.random.RandomState(0).randint(len(graphs),
size=(100, 2))
targets = [graph_distance(graphs[left], graphs[right])
for left, right in graph_idx]
train_gen = generator.flow(graph_idx, batch_size=10,
targets=targets)
```

5. Finally, let's compile and train the model. We will be using an adaptive moment estimation optimizer (Adam) with the learning rate parameter set to 1e-2. The loss function we will be using is defined as the minimum squared error between the prediction and the ground-truth distance computed as previously. The model will be trained for 500 epochs:

```
pair_model.compile(optimizers.Adam(1e-2), loss="mse")
pair_model.fit(train_gen, epochs=500, verbose=0)
```

6. After training, we are now ready to inspect and visualize the learned representation. Since the output is 32-dimensional, we need a way to qualitatively evaluate the embeddings, for example, by plotting them in a bi-dimensional space. We will use T-SNE for this purpose:

```
# retrieve the embeddings
embeddings = embedding_model.predict(generator.
flow(graphs))
# TSNE is used for dimensionality reduction
from sklearn.manifold import TSNE
tsne = TSNE(2)
  two_d = tsne.fit_transform(embeddings)
```

Let's plot the embeddings. In the plot, each point (embedded graph) is colored according to the corresponding label (blue=0, red=1). The results are visible in *Figure 3.22*:

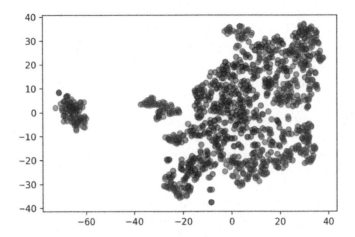

Figure 3.22 – The PROTEINS dataset embedding using GCNs

This is just one of the possible methods for learning embeddings for graphs. More advanced solutions can be experimented with to better fit the problem of interest.

Summary

In this chapter, we have learned how unsupervised machine learning can be effectively applied to graphs to solve real problems, such as node and graph representation learning.

In particular, we first analyzed shallow embedding methods, a set of algorithms that are able to learn and return only the embedding values for the learned input data.

We then learned how autoencoder algorithms can be used to encode the input by preserving important information in a lower-dimensional space. We have also seen how this idea can be adapted to graphs, by learning about embeddings that allow us to reconstruct the pair-wise node/graph similarity.

Finally, we introduced the main concepts behind GNNs. We have seen how well-known concepts, such as convolution, can be applied to graphs.

In the next chapter, we will revise these concepts in a supervised setting. There, a target label is provided and the objective is to learn a mapping between the input and the output.

4
Supervised Graph Learning

Supervised learning (**SL**) most probably represents the majority of practical **machine learning** (**ML**) tasks. Thanks to more and more active and effective data collection activities, it is very common nowadays to deal with labeled datasets.

This is also true for graph data, where labels can be assigned to nodes, communities, or even to an entire structure. The task, then, is to learn a mapping function between the input and the label (also known as a target or an annotation).

For example, given a graph representing a social network, we might be asked to guess which user (node) will close their account. We can learn this predictive function by training graph ML on **retrospective data**, where each user is labeled as "faithful" or "quitter" based on whether they closed their account after a few months.

In this chapter, we will explore the concept of SL and how it can be applied on graphs. Therefore, we will also be providing an overview of the main supervised graph embedding methods. The following topics will be covered:

- The supervised graph embedding roadmap
- Feature-based methods
- Shallow embedding methods

- Graph regularization methods
- Graph **convolutional neural networks (CNNs)**

Technical requirements

We will be using *Jupyter* Notebooks with *Python* 3.8 for all of our exercises. In the following code block, you can see a list of the Python libraries that will be installed for this chapter using `pip` (for example, run `pip install networkx==2.5` on the command line):

```
Jupyter==1.0.0
networkx==2.5
matplotlib==3.2.2
node2vec==0.3.3
karateclub==1.0.19
scikit-learn==0.24.0
pandas==1.1.3
numpy==1.19.2
tensorflow==2.4.1
neural-structured-learning==1.3.1
stellargraph==1.2.1
```

In the rest of this book, if not clearly stated, we will refer to nx as the result of the `import networkx as nx` Python command.

All code files relevant to this chapter are available at `https://github.com/PacktPublishing/Graph-Machine-Learning/tree/main/Chapter04`.

The supervised graph embedding roadmap

In SL, a training set consists of a sequence of ordered pairs (x, y), where x is a set of input features (often signals defined on graphs) and y is the output label assigned to it. The goal of the ML models, then, is to learn the function mapping each x value to each y value. Common supervised tasks include predicting user properties in a large social network or predicting molecules' attributes, where each molecule is a graph.

Sometimes, however, not all instances can be provided with a label. In this scenario, a typical dataset consists of a small set of labeled instances and a larger set of unlabeled instances. For such situations, **semi-SL (SSL)** is proposed, whereby algorithms aim to exploit label dependency information reflected by available label information in order to learn the predicting function for the unlabeled samples.

With regard to supervised graph ML techniques, many algorithms have been developed. However as previously reported by different scientific papers (`https://arxiv.org/abs/2005.03675`), they can be grouped into macro-groups such as **feature-based methods**, **shallow embedding methods**, **regularization methods**, and **graph neural networks (GNNs)**, as graphically depicted in the following diagram:

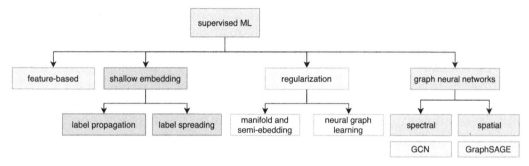

Figure 4.1 – Hierarchical structure of the different supervised embedding algorithms described in this book

In the following sections, you will learn the main principles behind each group of algorithms. We will try to provide insight into the most well-known algorithms in the field as well, as these can be used to solve real-world problems.

Feature-based methods

One very simple (yet powerful) method for applying ML on graphs is to consider the encoding function as a simple embedding lookup. When dealing with supervised tasks, one simple way of doing this is to exploit graph properties. In *Chapter 1, Getting Started with Graphs*, we have learned how graphs (or nodes in a graph) can be described by means of structural properties, each "encoding" important information from the graph itself.

Let's forget graph ML for a moment: in classical supervised ML, the task is to find a function that maps a set of (descriptive) features of an instance to a particular output. Such features should be carefully engineered so that they are sufficiently representative to learn that concept. Therefore, as the number of petals and the sepal length might be good descriptors for a flower, when describing a graph we might rely on its average degree, its global efficiency, and its characteristic path length.

This shallow approach acts in two steps, outlined as follows:

1. Select a set of *good* descriptive graph properties.

2. Use such properties as input for a traditional ML algorithm.

Unfortunately, there is no general definition of *good* descriptive properties, and their choice strictly depends on the specific problem to solve. However, you can still compute a wide variety of graph properties and then perform *feature selection* to select the most informative ones. **Feature selection** is a widely studied topic in ML, but providing details about the various methods is outside the scope of this book. However, we refer you to the book *Machine Learning Algorithms – Second Edition* (`https://subscription.packtpub.com/book/big_data_and_business_intelligence/9781789347999`), published by Packt Publishing, for further reading on this subject.

Let's now see a practical example of how such a basic method can be applied. We will be performing a supervised graph classification task by using a `PROTEINS` dataset. The `PROTEINS` dataset contains several graphs representing protein structures. Each graph is labeled, defining whether the protein is an enzyme or not. We will follow these next steps:

1. First, let's load the dataset through the `stellargraph` Python library, as follows:

```
from stellargraph import datasets
from IPython.display import display, HTML
dataset = datasets.PROTEINS()
graphs, graph_labels = dataset.load()
```

2. For computing graph properties, we will be using `networkx`, as described in *Chapter 1, Getting Started with Graphs*. To that end, we need to convert graphs from the `stellargraph` format to the `networkx` format. This can be done in two steps: first, convert the graphs from the `stellargraph` representation to `numpy` adjacency matrices. Then, use the adjacency matrices to retrieve the `networkx` representation. In addition, we also transform the labels (which are stored as a `pandas` Series) to a `numpy` array, which can be better exploited by the evaluation functions, as we will see in the next steps. The code is illustrated in the following snippet:

```
# convert from StellarGraph format to numpy adj matrices
adjs = [graph.to_adjacency_matrix().A for graph in
graphs]
# convert labels from Pandas.Series to numpy array
labels = graph_labels.to_numpy(dtype=int)
```

3. Then, for each graph, we compute global metrics to describe it. For this example, we have chosen the number of edges, the average cluster coefficient, and the global efficiency. However, we suggest you compute several other properties you may find worth exploring. We can extract the graph metrics using `networkx`, as follows:

```
import numpy as np
import networkx as nx
metrics = []
for adj in adjs:
    G = nx.from_numpy_matrix(adj)
    # basic properties
    num_edges = G.number_of_edges()
    # clustering measures
    cc = nx.average_clustering(G)
    # measure of efficiency
    eff = nx.global_efficiency(G)
    metrics.append([num_edges, cc, eff])
```

4. We can now exploit `scikit-learn` utilities to create train and test sets. In our experiments, we will be using 70% of the dataset as the training set and the remainder as the test set. We can do that by using the `train_test_split` function provided by `scikit-learn`, as follows:

```
from sklearn.model_selection import train_test_split
X_train, X_test, y_train, y_test = train_test_
split(metrics, labels, test_size=0.3, random_state=42)
```

5. It's now time for training a proper ML algorithm. We chose a **support vector machine (SVM)** for this task. More precisely, the SVM is trained to minimize the difference between the predicted labels and the actual labels (the ground truth). We can do this by using the `SVC` module of `scikit-learn`, as follows:

```
from sklearn import svm
from sklearn.metrics import accuracy_score, precision_
score, recall_score, f1_score
clf = svm.SVC()
clf.fit(X_train, y_train)
 y_pred = clf.predict(X_test)
print('Accuracy', accuracy_score(y_test,y_pred))
 print('Precision', precision_score(y_test,y_pred))
 print('Recall', recall_score(y_test,y_pred))
 print('F1-score', f1_score(y_test,y_pred))
```

This should be the output of the previous snippet of code:

```
Accuracy 0.7455
Precision 0.7709
Recall 0.8413
F1-score 0.8045
```

We used `Accuracy`, `Precision`, `Recall`, and `F1-score` to evaluate how well the algorithm is performing on the test set. We achieved about 80% for the F1 score, which is already quite good for such a naïve task.

Shallow embedding methods

As we already described in *Chapter 3, Unsupervised Graph Learning*, shallow embedding methods are a subset of graph embedding methods that learn node, edge, or graph representation for only a finite set of input data. They cannot be applied to other instances different from the ones used to train the model. Before starting our discussion, it is important to define how supervised and unsupervised shallow embedding algorithms differ.

The main difference between unsupervised and supervised embedding methods essentially lies in the task they attempt to solve. Indeed, if unsupervised shallow embedding algorithms try to learn a good graph, node, or edge representation in order to build well-defined clusters, the supervised algorithms try to find the best solution for a prediction task such as node, label, or graph classification.

In this section, we will explain in detail some of those supervised shallow embedding algorithms. Moreover, we will enrich our description by providing several examples of how to use those algorithms in Python. For all the algorithms described in this section, we will present a custom implementation using the base classes available in the `scikit-learn` library.

Label propagation algorithm

The label propagation algorithm is a well-known semi-supervised algorithm widely applied in data science and used to solve the node classification task. More precisely, the algorithm *propagates* the label of a given node to its neighbors or to nodes having a high probability of being reached from that node.

The general idea behind this approach is quite simple: given a graph with a set of labeled and unlabeled nodes, the labeled nodes propagate their label to the nodes having the highest probability of being reached. In the following diagram, we can see an example of a graph having labeled and unlabeled nodes:

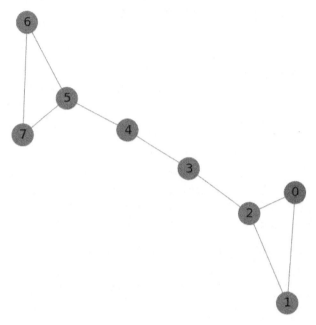

Figure 4.2 – Example of a graph with two labeled nodes (class 0 in red and class 1 in green) and six unlabeled nodes

According to *Figure 4.2*, using the information of the labeled nodes (node **0** and **6**), the algorithm will calculate the probability of moving to another unlabeled node. The nodes having the highest probability from a labeled node will get the label of that node.

Formally, let $G = (V, E)$ be a graph and let $Y = \{y_1, \dots, y_p\}$ be a set of labels. Since the algorithm is semi-supervised, just a subset of nodes will have an assigned label. Moreover, let $A \in \mathbb{R}^{|V| \times |V|}$ be the adjacency matrix of the input graph G and $D \in \mathbb{R}^{|V| \times |V|}$ be the diagonal degree matrix where each element $d_{ij} \in D$ is defined as follows:

$$d_{ij} = \{ \begin{matrix} 0 \; if \; i \neq j \\ \deg(v_i) \; if \; i = j \end{matrix}$$

In other words, the only nonzero elements of the degree matrix are the diagonal elements whose values are given by the degree of the node represented by the row. In the following figure, we can see the diagonal degree matrix of the graph represented in *Figure 4.2*:

$$D = \begin{bmatrix} 2 & 0 & 0 & 0 & 0 & 0 & 0 & 0 \\ 0 & 2 & 0 & 0 & 0 & 0 & 0 & 0 \\ 0 & 0 & 3 & 0 & 0 & 0 & 0 & 0 \\ 0 & 0 & 0 & 2 & 0 & 0 & 0 & 0 \\ 0 & 0 & 0 & 0 & 2 & 0 & 0 & 0 \\ 0 & 0 & 0 & 0 & 0 & 3 & 0 & 0 \\ 0 & 0 & 0 & 0 & 0 & 0 & 2 & 0 \\ 0 & 0 & 0 & 0 & 0 & 0 & 0 & 2 \end{bmatrix}$$

Figure 4.3 – Diagonal degree matrix for the graph in Figure 4.2

From *Figure 4.3*, it is possible to see how only the diagonal elements of the matrix contain nonzero values, and those values represent the degree of the specific node. We also need to introduce the transition matrix $L = D^{-1}A$. This matrix defines the probability of a node being reached from another node. More precisely, $l_{ij} \in L$ is the probability of reaching node v_j from node v_i. The following figure shows the transition matrix L for the graph depicted in *Figure 4.2*:

$$L = \begin{bmatrix} 0 & 0.5 & 0.5 & 0 & 0 & 0 & 0 & 0 \\ 0.5 & 0 & 0.5 & 0 & 0 & 0 & 0 & 0 \\ 0.33 & 0.33 & 0 & 0.33 & 0 & 0 & 0 & 0 \\ 0 & 0 & 0.5 & 0 & 0.5 & 0 & 0 & 0 \\ 0 & 0 & 0 & 0.5 & 0 & 0.5 & 0 & 0 \\ 0 & 0 & 0 & 0 & 0.33 & 0 & 0.33 & 0.33 \\ 0 & 0 & 0 & 0 & 0 & 0.5 & 0 & 0.5 \\ 0 & 0 & 0 & 0 & 0 & 0.5 & 0.5 & 0 \end{bmatrix}$$

Figure 4.4 – Transition matrix for the graph in Figure 4.2

In *Figure 4.4*, the matrix shows the probability of reaching an end node given a start node. For instance, from the first row of the matrix, we can see how from node 0 it is possible to reach, with equal probability of 0.5, only nodes 1 and 2. If we defined with Y^0 the initial label assignment, the probability of label assignment for each node obtained using the L matrix can be computed as $Y^1 = LY^0$. The Y^1 matrix computed for the graph in *Figure 4.2* is shown in the following figure:

$$Y^1 = \begin{bmatrix} 0 & 0.5 & 0.5 & 0 & 0 & 0 & 0 & 0 \\ 0.5 & 0 & 0.5 & 0 & 0 & 0 & 0 & 0 \\ 0.33 & 0.33 & 0 & 0.33 & 0 & 0 & 0 & 0 \\ 0 & 0 & 0.5 & 0 & 0.5 & 0 & 0 & 0 \\ 0 & 0 & 0 & 0.5 & 0 & 0.5 & 0 & 0 \\ 0 & 0 & 0 & 0 & 0.33 & 0 & 0.33 & 0.33 \\ 0 & 0 & 0 & 0 & 0 & 0.5 & 0 & 0.5 \\ 0 & 0 & 0 & 0 & 0 & 0.5 & 0.5 & 0 \end{bmatrix} * \begin{bmatrix} 1 & 0 \\ 0 & 0 \\ 0 & 0 \\ 0 & 0 \\ 0 & 0 \\ 0 & 0 \\ 0 & 1 \\ 0 & 0 \end{bmatrix} = \begin{bmatrix} 0 & 0 \\ 0.5 & 0 \\ 0.33 & 0 \\ 0 & 0 \\ 0 & 0 \\ 0 & 0.33 \\ 0 & 0 \\ 0 & 0.5 \end{bmatrix}$$

Figure 4.5 – Solution obtained using the matrix for the graph in Figure 4.2

From *Figure 4.5*, we can see that using the transition matrix, node 1 and node 2 have a probability of being assigned to the [1   0] label of 0.5 and 0.33 respectively, while node 5 and node 6 have a probability of being assigned to the [0   1] label of 0.33 and 0.5, respectively.

Moreover, if we better analyze *Figure 4.5*, we can see two main problems, as follows:

- With this solution, it is possible to assign only to nodes [1 2] and [5 7] a probability associated with a label.

- The initial labels of nodes 0 and 6 are different from the one defined in Y^0.

In order to solve the first point, the algorithm will perform n different iterations; at each iteration t, the algorithm will compute the solution for that iteration, as follows:

$$Y^t = LY^{t-1}$$

The algorithm stops its iteration when a certain condition is met. The second problem is solved by the label propagation algorithm by imposing, in the solution of a given iteration t, the labeled nodes to have the initial class values. For example, after computing the result visible in *Figure 4.5*, the algorithm will force the first line of the result matrix to be [1   0] and the seventh line of the matrix to be [0   1].

Here, we propose a modified version of the LabelPropagation class available in the scikit-learn library. The main reason behind this choice is given by the fact that the LabelPropagation class takes as input a matrix representing a dataset. Each row of the matrix represents a sample, and each column represents a feature.

Before performing a fit operation, the LabelPropagation class internally executes the _build_graph function. This function will build, using a parametric kernel (**k-nearest neighbors (kNN)** and radial basis functions are available for use inside the _get_kernel function), a graph describing the input dataset. As a result, the original dataset is transformed into a graph (in its adjacency matrix representation) where each node is a sample (a row of the input dataset) and each edge is an *interaction* between the samples.

In our specific case, the input dataset is already a graph, so we need to define a new class capable of dealing with a `networkx` graph and performing the computation operation on the original graph. The goal is achieved by creating a new class—namely, `GraphLabelPropagation`—by extending the `ClassifierMixin`, `BaseEstimator`, and `ABCMeta` base classes. The algorithm proposed here is mainly used in order to help you understand the concept behind the algorithm. The whole algorithm is provided in the `04_supervised_graph_machine_learning/02_Shallow_embeddings.ipynb` notebook available in the GitHub repository of this book. In order to describe the algorithm, we will use only the `fit(X,y)` function as a reference. The code is illustrated in the following snippet:

```python
class GraphLabelPropagation(ClassifierMixin, BaseEstimator,
metaclass=ABCMeta):

    def fit(self, X, y):
        X, y = self._validate_data(X, y)
        self.X_ = X
        check_classification_targets(y)
        D = [X.degree(n) for n in X.nodes()]
        D = np.diag(D)

        # label construction
        # construct a categorical distribution for
classification only
        unlabeled_index = np.where(y==-1)[0]
        labeled_index = np.where(y!=-1)[0]
        unique_classes = np.unique(y[labeled_index])

        self.classes_ = unique_classes
        Y0 = np.array([self.build_label(y[x], len(unique_
classes)) if x in labeled_index else np.zeros(len(unique_
classes)) for x in range(len(y))])

        A = inv(D)*nx.to_numpy_matrix(G)
        Y_prev = Y0
        it = 0
        c_tool = 10
```

```
        while it < self.max_iter & c_tool > self.tol:
            Y = A*Y_prev
            #force labeled nodes
            Y[labeled_index] = Y0[labeled_index]
            it +=1
            c_tol = np.sum(np.abs(Y-Y_prev))
            Y_prev = Y

        self.label_distributions_ = Y
        return self
```

The fit(X,y) function takes as input a networkx graph *X* and an array *y* representing the labels assigned to each node. Nodes without labels should have a representative value of -1. The while loop performs the real computation. More precisely, it computes the Y^t value at each iteration and forces the labeled nodes in the solution to be equal to their original input value. The algorithm performs the computation until the two stop conditions are satisfied. In this implementation, the following two criteria have been used:

- **Number of iterations**: The algorithm runs the computation until a given number of iterations has been performed.

- **Solution tolerance error**: The algorithm runs the computation until the absolute difference of the solution obtained in two consecutive iterations, y^{t-1} and y^t, is lower than a given threshold value.

The algorithm can be applied to the example graph depicted in *Figure 4.2* using the following code:

```
glp = GraphLabelPropagation()
y = np.array([-1 for x in range(len(G.nodes()))])
y[0] = 0
y[6] = 1
glp.fit(G,y)
glp.predict_proba(G)
```

The result obtained by the algorithm is shown in the following diagram:

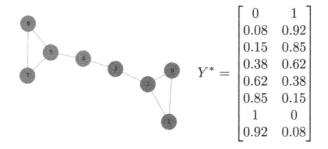

$$Y^* = \begin{bmatrix} 0 & 1 \\ 0.08 & 0.92 \\ 0.15 & 0.85 \\ 0.38 & 0.62 \\ 0.62 & 0.38 \\ 0.85 & 0.15 \\ 1 & 0 \\ 0.92 & 0.08 \end{bmatrix}$$

Figure 4.6 – Result of the label propagation algorithm on the graph of Figure 4.2: on the left, the final labeled graph; on the right, the final probability assignment matrix

In *Figure 4.6*, we can see the results of the algorithm applied to the example shown in *Figure 4.2*. From the final probability assignment matrix, it is possible to see how the probability of the initial labeled nodes is 1 due to the constraints of the algorithm and how nodes that are "near" to labeled nodes get their label.

Label spreading algorithm

The label spreading algorithm is another semi-supervised shallow embedding algorithm. It was built in order to overcome one big limitation of the label propagation method: the **initial labeling**. Indeed, according to the label propagation algorithm, the initial labels cannot be modified in the training process and, in each iteration, they are forced to be equal to their original value. This constraint could generate incorrect results when the initial labeling is affected by errors or noise. As a consequence, the error will be propagated in all nodes of the input graph.

In order to solve this limitation, the label spreading algorithm tries to relax the constraint of the original labeled data, allowing the labeled input nodes to change their label during the training process.

Formally, let $G = (V, E)$ be a graph and let $Y = \{y_1, ..., y_p\}$ be a set of labels (since the algorithm is semi-supervised, just a subset of nodes will have an assigned label), and let $A \in \mathbb{R}^{|V| \times |V|}$ and $D \in \mathbb{R}^{|V| \times |V|}$ be the adjacency matrix diagonal degree matrix of graph G, respectively. Instead of computing the probability transition matrix, the label spreading algorithm uses the normalized graph **Laplacian matrix**, defined as follows:

$$\mathcal{L} = D^{-1/2} A D^{-1/2}$$

As with label propagation, this matrix can be seen as a sort of compact low-dimensional representation of the connections defined in the whole graph. This matrix can be easily computed using `networkx` with the following code:

```
from scipy.linalg import fractional_matrix_power
D_inv = fractional_matrix_power(D, -0.5)
L = D_inv*nx.to_numpy_matrix(G)*D_inv
```

As a result, we get the following:

$$\mathcal{L} = \begin{bmatrix} 0 & 0.5 & 0.40824829 & 0 & 0 & 0 & 0 & 0 \\ 0.5 & 0 & 0.40824829 & 0 & 0 & 0 & 0 & 0 \\ 0.40824829 & 0.40824829 & 0 & 0.40824829 & 0 & 0 & 0 & 0 \\ 0 & 0 & 0.40824829 & 0 & 0.5 & 0 & 0 & 0 \\ 0 & 0 & 0 & 0.5 & 0 & 0.40824829 & 0 & 0 \\ 0 & 0 & 0 & 0 & 0.40824829 & 0 & 0.40824829 & 0.40824829 \\ 0 & 0 & 0 & 0 & 0 & 0.40824829 & 0 & 0.5 \\ 0 & 0 & 0 & 0 & 0 & 0.40824829 & 0.5 & 0 \end{bmatrix}$$

Figure 4.7 – The normalized graph Laplacian matrix

The most important difference between the label spreading and label propagation algorithms is related to the function used to extract the labels. If we defined with Y^0 the initial label assignment, the probability of a label assignment for each node obtained using the $\mathcal{L}$ matrix can be computed as follows:

$$Y^1 = \alpha\mathcal{L}Y^0 + (1 - \alpha)Y^0$$

As with label propagation, label spreading has an iterative process to compute the final solution. The algorithm will perform n different iterations; in each iteration t, the algorithm will compute the solution for that iteration, as follows:

$$Y^t = \alpha\mathcal{L}Y^{t-1} + (1 - \alpha)Y^0$$

The algorithm stops its iteration when a certain condition is met. It is important to underline the term $(1 - \alpha)Y^0$ of the equation. Indeed, as we said, label spreading does not force the labeled element of the solution to be equal to its original value. Instead, the algorithm uses a regularization parameter $\alpha \epsilon [0,1)$ to weight the influence of the original solution at each iteration. This allows us to explicitly impose the "quality" of the original solution and its influence in the final solution.

As with the label propagation algorithm, in the following code snippet, we propose a modified version of the `LabelSpreading` class available in the `scikit-learn` library due to the motivations we already mentioned in the previous section. We propose the `GraphLabelSpreading` class by extending our `GraphLabelPropagation` class, since the only difference will be in the `fit()` method of the class. The whole algorithm is provided in the `04_supervised_graph_machine_learning/02_Shallow_embeddings.ipynb` notebook available in the GitHub repository of this book:

```python
class GraphLabelSpreading(GraphLabelPropagation):

    def fit(self, X, y):
        X, y = self._validate_data(X, y)
        self.X_ = X
        check_classification_targets(y)
        D = [X.degree(n) for n in X.nodes()]
        D = np.diag(D)
        D_inv = np.matrix(fractional_matrix_power(D,-0.5))
        L = D_inv*nx.to_numpy_matrix(G)*D_inv

        # label construction
        # construct a categorical distribution for
classification only
        labeled_index = np.where(y!=-1)[0]
        unique_classes = np.unique(y[labeled_index])
        self.classes_ = unique_classes

        Y0 = np.array([self.build_label(y[x], len(unique_
classes)) if x in labeled_index else np.zeros(len(unique_
classes)) for x in range(len(y))])

        Y_prev = Y0
        it = 0
        c_tool = 10
        while it < self.max_iter & c_tool > self.tol:
            Y = (self.alpha*(L*Y_prev))+((1-self.alpha)*Y0)
            it +=1
            c_tol = np.sum(np.abs(Y-Y_prev))
            Y_prev = Y
```

```
            self.label_distributions_ = Y
            return self
```

Also in this class, the `fit ()` function is the focal point. The function takes as input a `networkx` graph X and an array y representing the labels assigned to each node. Nodes without labels should have a representative value of -1. The `while` loop computes the Y^t value at each iteration, weighting the influence of the initial labeling via the parameter α. Also, for this algorithm, the number of iterations and the difference between two consecutive solutions are used as stop criteria.

The algorithm can be applied to the example graph depicted in *Figure 4.2* using the following code:

```
gls = GraphLabelSpreading()
y = np.array([-1 for x in range(len(G.nodes()))])
y[0] = 0
y[6] = 1
gls.fit(G,y)
  gls.predict_proba(G)
```

In the following diagram, the result obtained by the algorithm is shown:

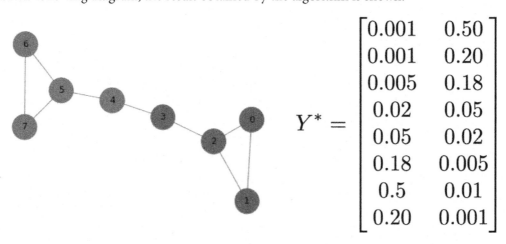

$$Y^* = \begin{bmatrix} 0.001 & 0.50 \\ 0.001 & 0.20 \\ 0.005 & 0.18 \\ 0.02 & 0.05 \\ 0.05 & 0.02 \\ 0.18 & 0.005 \\ 0.5 & 0.01 \\ 0.20 & 0.001 \end{bmatrix}$$

Figure 4.8 – Result of the label propagation algorithm on graph in Figure 4.2: on the left, the final labeled graph; on the right, the final probability assignment matrix

The result visible in the diagram shown in *Figure 4.8* looks similar to the one obtained using the label propagation algorithm. The main difference is related to the probability of label assignment. Indeed, in this case, it is possible to see how nodes 0 and 6 (the ones having an initial labeling) have a probability of 0.5, which is significantly lower compared to the probability of 1 obtained using the label propagation algorithm. This behavior is expected since the influence of the initial label assignment is weighted by the regularization parameter α.

In the next section, we will continue our description of supervised graph embedding methods. We will describe how network-based information helps regularize the training and create more robust models.

Graph regularization methods

Shallow embedding methods described in the previous section show how topological information and relations between data points can be encoded and leveraged in order to build more robust classifiers and address semi-supervised tasks. In general terms, network information can be extremely useful in constraining models and enforcing the output to be smooth within neighboring nodes. As we have already seen in previous sections, this idea can be efficiently used in semi-supervised tasks, when propagating the information on neighbor unlabeled nodes.

On the other hand, this can also be used to regularize the learning phase in order to create more robust models that tend to better generalize to unseen examples. Both the label propagation and the label spreading algorithms we have seen previously can be implemented as a cost function to be minimized when we add an additional regularization term. Generally, in supervised tasks, we can write the cost function to be minimized in the following form:

$$\mathcal{L}(x) = \sum_{i \in L} \mathcal{L}_s(y_i, f(x_i)) + \sum_{i,j \in L,U} \mathcal{L}_g(f(x_i), f(x_j), G)$$

Here, L and U represent the labeled and unlabeled samples, and the second term acts as a regularization term that depends on the topological information of the graph G.

In this section, we will further describe such an idea and see how this can be very powerful, especially when regularizing the training of neural networks, which—as you might know—naturally tend to overfit and/or need large amounts of data to be trained efficiently.

Manifold regularization and semi-supervised embedding

Manifold regularization (Belkin et al., 2006) extends the label propagation framework by parametrizing the model function in the **reproducing kernel Hilbert space (RKHS)** and using as a supervised loss function (first term in the previous equation) the **mean square error (MSE)** or the hinge loss. In other words, when training an SVM or a least squares fit, they apply a graph regularization term based on the Laplacian matrix L, as follows:

$$\sum_{i,j \in L,U} W_{ij} \|f(x_i) - f(x_j)\|_2^2 = \overline{f} L \overline{f}$$

For this reason, these methods are generally labeled as **Laplacian regularization,** and such a formulation leads to **Laplacian regularized least squares (LapRLS)** and **LapSVM** classifications. Label propagation and label spreading can be seen as a special case of manifold regularization. Besides, these algorithms can also be used in the case of no-labeled data (first term in the equation disappearing) reducing to **Laplacian eigenmaps**.

On the other hand, they can also be used in the case of a fully labeled dataset, in which case the preceding terms constrain the training phase to regularize the training and achieve more robust models. Moreover, being the classifier parametrized in the RKHS, the model can be used on unobserved samples and does not require test samples to belong to the input graph. In this sense, it is therefore an *inductive* model.

Manifold learning still represents a form of shallow learning, whereby the parametrized function does not leverage on any form of intermediate embeddings. **Semi-supervised embedding** (Weston et al., 2012) extends the concepts of graph regularization to deeper architectures by imposing the constraint and the smoothness of the function on intermediate layers of a neural network. Let's define g_{h_k} as the intermediate output of the kth hidden layer. The regularization term proposed in the semi-supervised embedding framework reads as follows:

$$\mathcal{L}_G^{h_k} = \sum_{i,j \in L,U} \mathcal{L}(W_{ij}, g_{h_k}(x_i), g_{h_k}(x_i))$$

Depending on where the regularization is imposed, three different configurations (shown in *Figure 4.9*) can be achieved, as follows:

- Regularization is applied to the final output of the network. This corresponds to a generalization of the manifold learning technique to multilayer neural networks.

- Regularization is applied to an intermediate layer of the network, thus regularizing the embedding representation.

- Regularization is applied to an auxiliary network that shares the first k-1 layers. This basically corresponds to training an unsupervised embedding network while simultaneously training a supervised network. This technique basically imposes a derived regularization on the first k-1 layers that are constrained by the unsupervised network as well and simultaneously promotes an embedding of the network nodes.

The following diagram shows an illustration of the three different configurations—with their similarities and differences—that can be achieved using a semi-supervised embedding framework:

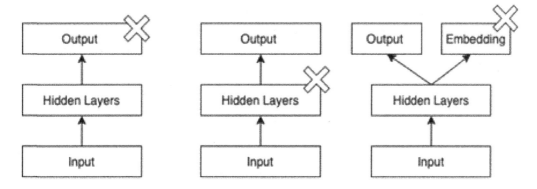

Figure 4.9 – Semi-supervised embedding regularization configurations: graph regularization, indicated by the cross, can be applied to the output (left), to an intermediate layer (center), or to an auxiliary network (right)

In its original formulation, the loss function used for the embeddings is the one derived from the Siamese network formulation, shown as follows:

$$
L\left(W_{ij}, g_{h_k}^{(i)}, g_{h_k}^{(j)}\right) = \{
\begin{array}{l}
\left\| g_{h_k}^{(i)} - g_{h_k}^{(j)} \right\|^2 \ if \ W_{ij} = 1 \\
\max\left(0, m - \left\| g_{h_k}^{(i)} - g_{h_k}^{(j)} \right\|^2\right) if \ W_{ij} = 0
\end{array}
$$

As can be seen by this equation, the loss function ensures the embeddings of neighboring nodes stay close. On the other hand, non-neighbors are instead pulled apart to a distance (at least) specified by the threshold m. As compared to the regularization based on the Laplacian $\bar{f}L\bar{f}$ (although for neighboring points, the penalization factor is effectively recovered), the one shown here is generally easier to be optimized by gradient descent.

The best choice among the three configurations presented in *Figure 4.9* is largely influenced by the data at your disposal as well as on your specific use case—that is, whether you need a regularized model output or to learn a high-level data representation. However, you should always keep in mind that when using softmax layers (usually done at the output layer), the regularization based on the hinge loss may not be very appropriate or suited for log probabilities. In such cases, regularized embeddings and relative loss should instead be introduced at intermediate layers. However, be aware that embeddings lying in deeper layers are generally harder to be trained and require a careful tuning of learning rate and margins to be used.

Neural Graph Learning

Neural graph learning (**NGL**) basically generalizes the previous formulations and, as we will see, makes it possible to seamlessly apply graph regularization to any form of a neural network, including CNNs and **recurrent neural networks** (**RNNs**). In particular, there exists an extremely powerful framework named **Neural Structured Learning** (**NSL**) that allows us to extend in a very few lines of code a neural network implemented in TensorFlow with graph regularization. The networks can be of any kind: natural or synthetic.

When synthetic, graphs can be generated in different ways, using—for instance—embeddings learned in an unsupervised manner and/or by using a similarity/distance metric between samples using their features. You can also generate synthetic graphs using adversarial examples. Adversarial examples are artificially generated samples obtained by perturbing actual (real) examples in such a way that we confound the network, trying to force a prediction error. These very carefully designed samples (obtained by perturbing a given sample in the gradient-descent direction in order to maximize errors) can be connected to their related samples, thus generating a graph. These connections can then be used to train a graph-regularized version of the network, allowing us to obtain models that are more robust against adversarially generated examples.

NGL extends the regularization by augmenting the tuning parameters for graph regularization in neural networks, decomposing the contribution of labeled-labeled, labeled-unlabeled, and unlabeled-unlabeled relations using three parameters, α_1, α_2, and α_3, respectively, as follows:

$$\mathcal{L} = \mathcal{L}_s + \alpha_1 \sum_{i,j \in LL} W_{ij} d\left(g_{h_k}^{(i)}, g_{h_k}^{(j)}\right) + \alpha_2 \sum_{i,j \in LU} W_{ij} d\left(g_{h_k}^{(i)}, g_{h_k}^{(j)}\right) + \alpha_3 \sum_{i,j \in UU} W_{ij} d\left(g_{h_k}^{(i)}, g_{h_k}^{(j)}\right)$$

The function d represents a generic distance between two vectors—for instance, the L2 norm $\|\cdot\|_2$. By varying the coefficients and the definition of g_{h_k}, we can arrive at the different algorithms seen previously as limiting behavior, as follows:

- When $\alpha_i = 0$ $\forall i$ we retrieve the non-regularized version of a neural network.

- When only $\alpha_1 \neq 0$, we recover a fully supervised formulation where relationships between nodes act to regularize the training.

- When we substitute g_{h_k} (which are parametrized by a set of alpha coefficients) with a set of values y_i^* (to be learned) that map each sample to its instance class, we recover the label propagation formulation.

Loosely speaking, the NGL formulations can be seen as a non-linear version of the label propagation and label spreading algorithms, or as a form of a graph-regularized neural network for which the manifold learning or semi-supervising embedding can be obtained.

We will now apply NGL to a practical example, where you will learn how to use graph regularization in neural networks. To do so, we will use the NLS framework (`https://github.com/tensorflow/neural-structured-learning`), which is a library built on top of TensorFlow that makes it possible to implement graph regularization with only a few lines of codes on top of standard neural networks.

For our example, we will be using the `Cora` dataset, which is a labeled dataset that consists of 2,708 scientific papers in computer science that have been classified into seven classes. Each paper represents a node that is connected to other nodes based on citations. In total, there are 5,429 links in the network.

Moreover, each node is further described by a 1,433-long vector of binary values (0 or 1) that represent a dichotomic **bag-of-words** (**BOW**) representation of the paper: a one-hot encoding algorithm indicating the presence/absence of a word in a given vocabulary made up of 1,433 terms. The `Cora` dataset can be downloaded directly from the `stellargraph` library with a few lines of code, as follows:

```
from stellargraph import datasets
dataset = datasets.Cora()
```

```
dataset.download()
G, labels = dataset.load()
```

This returns two outputs, outlined as follows:

- G, which is the citation network containing the network nodes, edges, and the features describing the BOW representation.

- labels, which is a pandas Series that provides the mapping between the paper ID and one of the classes, as follows:

```
['Neural_Networks', 'Rule_Learning', 'Reinforcement_
Learning',
'Probabilistic_Methods', 'Theory', 'Genetic_Algorithms',
'Case_Based']
```

Starting from this information, we create a training set and a validation set. In the training samples, we will include information relating to neighbors (which may or may not belong to the training set and therefore have a label), and this will be used to regularize the training.

Validation samples, on the other hand, will not have neighbor information and the predicted label will only depend on the node features—namely, the BOW representation. Therefore, we will leverage both labeled and unlabeled samples (semi-supervised task) in order to produce an inductive model that can also be used against unobserved samples.

To start with, we conveniently structure the node features as a DataFrame, whereas we store the graph as an adjacency matrix, as follows:

```
adjMatrix = pd.DataFrame.sparse.from_spmatrix(
        G.to_adjacency_matrix(),
        index=G.nodes(), columns=G.nodes()
)
features = pd.DataFrame(G.node_features(), index=G.nodes())
```

Using adjMatrix, we implement a helper function that is able to retrieve the closest topn neighbors of a node, returning the node ID and the edge weight, as illustrated in the following code snippet:

```
def getNeighbors(idx, adjMatrix, topn=5):
    weights = adjMatrix.loc[idx]
    neighbors = weights[weights>0]\
        .sort_values(ascending=False)\
```

```
        .head(topn)
    return [(k, v) for k, v in neighbors.iteritems()]
```

Using the preceding information together with the helper function, we can merge the information into a single DataFrame, as follows:

```
dataset = {
    index: {
        "id": index,
        "words": [float(x)
                    for x in features.loc[index].values],
        "label": label_index[label],
        "neighbors": getNeighbors(index, adjMatrix, topn)
    }
    for index, label in labels.items()
}
df = pd.DataFrame.from_dict(dataset, orient="index")
```

This DataFrame represents the node-centric feature space. This would suffice if we were to use a regular classifier that does not exploit the information of the relationships between nodes. However, in order to allow the computation of the graph-regularization term, we need to join the preceding DataFrame with information relating to the neighborhood of each node. We then define a function able to retrieve and join the neighborhood information, as follows:

```
def getFeatureOrDefault(ith, row):
    try:
        nodeId, value = row["neighbors"][ith]
        return {
            f"{GRAPH_PREFIX}_{ith}_weight": value,
            f"{GRAPH_PREFIX}_{ith}_words": df.loc[nodeId]
["words"]
        }
    except:
        return {
            f"{GRAPH_PREFIX}_{ith}_weight": 0.0,
            f"{GRAPH_PREFIX}_{ith}_words": [float(x) for x in
np.zeros(1433)]
        }
```

```
def neighborsFeatures(row):
    featureList = [getFeatureOrDefault(ith, row) for ith in
range(topn)]
    return pd.Series(
        {k: v
          for feat in featureList for k, v in feat.items()}
    )
```

As shown in the preceding code snippet, when the neighbors are less than `topn`, we set the weight and the one-hot encoding of the words to 0. The `GRAPH_PREFIX` constant is a prefix that is to be prepended to all features that will later be used by the `nsl` library to regularize the training. Although it can be changed, in the following code snippet we will keep its value equal to the default value: `"NL_nbr"`.

This function can be applied to the DataFrame in order to compute the full feature space, as follows:

```
neighbors = df.apply(neighborsFeatures, axis=1)
allFeatures = pd.concat([df, neighbors], axis=1)
```

We now have in `allFeatures` all the ingredients we need to implement our graph-regularized model.

We start by splitting our dataset into a training set and a validation set, as follows:

```
n = int(np.round(len(labels)*ratio))
labelled, unlabelled = model_selection.train_test_split(
    allFeatures, train_size=n, test_size=None, stratify=labels
)
```

By changing the ratio, we can change the amount of labeled versus unlabeled data points. As the ratio decreases, we expect the performance of standard non-regularized classifiers to reduce. However, such a reduction can be compensated by leveraging network information provided by unlabeled data. We thus expect graph-regularized neural networks to provide better performance thanks to the augmented information they leverage. For the following code snippet, we will assume a `ratio` value equal to `0.2`.

Before feeding this data into our neural network, we convert the DataFrame into a TensorFlow tensor and dataset, which is a convenient representation that will allow the model to refer to feature names in its input layers.

Since the input features have different data types, it is best to handle the dataset creation separately for `weights`, `words`, and `labels` values, as follows:

```
train_base = {
    "words": tf.constant([
        tuple(x) for x in labelled["words"].values
    ]),
    "label": tf.constant([
        x for x in labelled["label"].values
    ])
}
train_neighbor_words = {
    k: tf.constant([tuple(x) for x in labelled[k].values])
    for k in neighbors if "words" in k
}
train_neighbor_weights = {
    k: tf.constant([tuple([x]) for x in labelled[k].values])
    for k in neighbors if "weight" in k
}
```

Now that we have the tensor, we can merge all this information into a TensorFlow dataset, as follows:

```
trainSet = tf.data.Dataset.from_tensor_slices({
    k: v
    for feature in [train_base, train_neighbor_words,
                    train_neighbor_weights]
    for k, v in feature.items()
})
```

We can similarly create a validation set. As mentioned previously, since we want to design an inductive algorithm, the validation dataset does not need any neighborhood information. The code is illustrated in the following snippet:

```
validSet = tf.data.Dataset.from_tensor_slices({
    "words": tf.constant([
```

```
        tuple(x) for x in unlabelled["words"].values
    ]),
    "label": tf.constant([
        x for x in unlabelled["label"].values
    ])
  })
```

Before feeding the dataset into the model, we split the features from the labels, as follows:

```
def split(features):
    labels=features.pop("label")
    return features, labels
trainSet = trainSet.map(f)
 validSet = validSet.map(f)
```

That's it! We have generated the inputs to our model. We could also inspect one sample batch of our dataset by printing the values of features and labels, as shown in the following code block:

```
for features, labels in trainSet.batch(2).take(1):
    print(features)
    print(labels)
```

It is now time to create our first model. To do this, we start from a simple architecture that takes as input the one-hot representation and has two hidden layers, composed of a Dense layer plus a Dropout layer with 50 units each, as follows:

```
inputs = tf.keras.Input(
    shape=(vocabularySize,), dtype='float32', name='words'
)
cur_layer = inputs
for num_units in [50, 50]:
    cur_layer = tf.keras.layers.Dense(
        num_units, activation='relu'
    )(cur_layer)
    cur_layer = tf.keras.layers.Dropout(0.8)(cur_layer)
outputs = tf.keras.layers.Dense(
    len(label_index), activation='softmax',
    name="label"
```

```
)(cur_layer)
model = tf.keras.Model(inputs, outputs=outputs)
```

Indeed, we could also train this model without graph regularization by simply compiling the model to create a computational graph, as follows:

```
model.compile(
    optimizer='adam',
    loss='sparse_categorical_crossentropy',
    metrics=['accuracy']
)
```

And then, we could run it as usual, also allowing the history file to be written to disk in order to be monitored using TensorBoard, as illustrated in the following code snippet:

```
from tensorflow.keras.callbacks import TensorBoard
model.fit(
    trainSet.batch(128), epochs=200, verbose=1,
    validation_data=validSet.batch(128),
    callbacks=[TensorBoard(log_dir='/tmp/base)]
)
```

At the end of the process, we should have something similar to the following output:

```
Epoch 200/200
loss: 0.7798 - accuracy: 06795 - val_loss: 1.5948 - val_
accuracy: 0.5873
```

With a top performance around 0.6 in accuracy, we now need to create a graph-regularized version of the preceding model. First of all, we need to recreate our model from scratch. This is important when comparing the results. If we were to use layers already initialized and used in the previous model, the layer weights would not be random but would be used with the ones already optimized in the preceding run. Once a new model has been created, adding a graph regularization technique to be used at training time can be done in just a few lines of code, as follows:

```
import neural_structured_learning as nsl
graph_reg_config = nsl.configs.make_graph_reg_config(
    max_neighbors=2,
    multiplier=0.1,
    distance_type=nsl.configs.DistanceType.L2,
```

```
        sum_over_axis=-1)
graph_reg= nsl.keras.GraphRegularization(
        model, graph_reg_config)
```

Let's analyze the different hyperparameters of the regularization, as follows:

- `max_neighbors` tunes the number of neighbors that ought to be used for computing the regularization loss for each node.

- `multiplier` corresponds to the coefficients that tune the importance of the regularization loss. Since we only consider labeled-labeled and labeled-unlabeled, this effectively corresponds to α_1 and α_2.

- `distance_type` represents the pairwise distance d to be used.

- `sum_over_axis` sets whether the weighted average sum should be calculated with respect to features (when set to `None`) or to samples (when set to -1).

The graph-regularized model can be compiled and run in the same way as before with the following commands:

```
graph_reg.compile(
        optimizer='adam',
        loss='sparse_categorical_crossentropy',
metrics=['accuracy']
)
model.fit(
        trainSet.batch(128), epochs=200, verbose=1,
        validation_data=validSet.batch(128),
        callbacks=[TensorBoard(log_dir='/tmp/nsl)]
)
```

Note that the loss function now also accounts for the graph-regularization term, as defined previously. Therefore, we now also introduce information coming from neighboring nodes that regularizes the training of our neural network. The preceding code, after about 200 iterations, provides the following output:

```
Epoch 200/200
loss: 0.9136 - accuracy: 06405 - scaled_graph_loss: 0.0328 -
val_loss: 1.2526 - val_accuracy: 0.6320
```

As you can see, graph regularization, when compared to the vanilla version, has allowed us to boost the performance in terms of accuracy by about 5%. Not bad at all!

You can perform several experiments, changing the ratio of labeled/unlabeled samples, the number of neighbors to be used, the regularization coefficient, the distance, and more. We encourage you to play around with the notebook that is provided with this book to explore the effect of different parameters yourself.

In the right panel of the following screenshot, we show the dependence of the performance measured by the accuracy as the supervised ratio increases. As expected, performance increases as the ratio increases. On the left panel, we show the accuracy increments on the validation set for various configuration of neighbors and supervised ratio, defined by

$$\Delta a = accuracy_{reg.} - accuracy_{no\ reg}$$

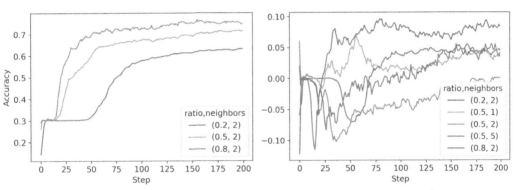

Figure 4.10 – (Left) Accuracy on the validation set for the graph-regularized neural networks with neighbors = 2 and various supervised ratios; (Right) accuracy increments on the validation set for the graph-regularized neural networks compared to the vanilla version

As can be seen in *Figure 4.10*, almost all graph-regularized versions outperform the vanilla models. The only exceptions are configuration neighbors = 2 and ratio = 0.5, for which the two models perform very similarly. However, the curve has a clear positive trend and we reasonably expect the graph-regularized version to outperform the vanilla model for a larger number of epochs.

Note that in the notebook, we also use another interesting feature of TensorFlow for creating the datasets. Instead of using a `pandas` DataFrame, as we did previously, we will create a dataset using the TensorFlow `Example`, `Features`, and `Feature` classes, which, besides providing a high-level description of samples, also allow us to serialize the input data (using `protobuf`) to make them compatible across platforms and programming languages.

If you are interested in further using `TensorFlow` both for prototyping models and deploying them into production via data-driven applications (maybe written in other languages), we strongly advise you to dig further into these concepts.

Planetoid

The methods discussed so far provide graph regularization that is based on the Laplacian matrix. As we have seen in previous chapters, enforcing constraints based on W_{ij} ensures that first-order proximity is preserved. Yang et al. (2016) proposed a method to extend graph regularization in order to also account for higher-order proximities. Their approach, which they named **Planetoid** (short for **Predicting Labels And Neighbors with Embeddings Transductively Or Inductively from Data**), extends skip-gram methods used for computing node embeddings to incorporate node-label information.

As we have seen in the previous chapter, skip-gram methods are based on generating random walks through a graph and then using the generated sequences to learn embeddings via a skip-gram model. The following diagram shows how the unsupervised version is modified to account for the supervised loss:

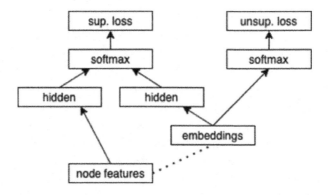

Figure 4.11 – Sketch of the Planetoid architecture: the dashed line represents a parametrized function that allows the method to extend from transductive to inductive

As shown in *Figure 4.11*, embeddings are fed to both of the following:

- A softmax layer to predict the graph context of the sampled random-walk sequences

- A set of hidden layers that combine together with the hidden layers derived from the node features in order to predict the class labels

The cost function to be minimized to train the combined network is composed of a supervised and an unsupervised loss—$\mathcal{L}_s$ and $\mathcal{L}_u$, respectively. The unsupervised loss is analogous to the one used with skip-gram with negative sampling, whereas the supervised loss minimizes the conditional probability and can be written as follows:

$$\mathcal{L}_s = -\sum_{i \in L} \log p(y_i|x_i, e_i)$$

The preceding formulation is *transductive* as it requires samples to belong to the graph in order to be applied. In a semi-supervised task, this method can be efficiently used to predict labels for unlabeled examples. However, it cannot be used for unobserved samples. As shown by the dashed line in *Figure 4.11*, an inductive version of the Planetoid algorithm can be obtained by parametrizing the embeddings as a function of the node features, via dedicated connected layers.

Graph CNNs

In *Chapter 3, Unsupervised Graph Learning*, we have learned the main concepts behind GNNs and **graph convolutional networks** (**GCNs**). We have also learned the difference between spectral graph convolution and spatial graph convolution. More precisely, we have further seen that GCN layers can be used to encode graphs or nodes under unsupervised settings by learning how to preserve graph properties such as node similarity.

In this chapter, we will explore such methods under supervised settings. This time, our goal is to learn graphs or node representations that can accurately *predict node or graph labels*. It is indeed worth noting that the encoding function remains the same. What will change is the objective!

Graph classification using GCNs

Let's consider again our `PROTEINS` dataset. Let's load the dataset as follows:

```
import pandas as pd
from stellargraph import datasets
dataset = datasets.PROTEINS()
graphs, graph_labels = dataset.load()
# necessary for converting default string labels to int
labels = pd.get_dummies(graph_labels, drop_first=True)
```

In the following example, we are going to use (and compare) one of the most widely used GCN algorithms for graph classification: *GCN* by Kipf and Welling:

1. stellargraph, which we are using for building the model, uses tf.Keras as the backend. According to its specific criteria, we need a data generator to feed the model. More precisely, since we are addressing a supervised graph classification problem, we can use an instance of the PaddedGraphGenerator class of stellargraph, which automatically resolves differences in the number of nodes by using padding. Here is the code required for this step:

```
from stellargraph.mapper import PaddedGraphGenerator
generator = PaddedGraphGenerator(graphs=graphs)
```

2. We are now ready to actually create our first model. We will create and stack together four GCN layers through the utility function of stellargraph, as follows:

```
from stellargraph.layer import DeepGraphCNN
from tensorflow.keras import Model
from tensorflow.keras.optimizers import Adam
from tensorflow.keras.layers import Dense, Conv1D,
MaxPool1D, Dropout, Flatten
from tensorflow.keras.losses import binary_crossentropy
import tensorflow as tf
nrows = 35  # the number of rows for the output tensor
layer_dims = [32, 32, 32, 1]
# backbone part of the model (Encoder)
  dgcnn_model = DeepGraphCNN(
    layer_sizes=layer_dims,
    activations=["tanh", "tanh", "tanh", "tanh"],
    k=nrows,
    bias=False,
    generator=generator,
)
```

3. This *backbone* will be concatenated to **one-dimensional (1D)** convolutional layers and fully connected layers using tf.Keras, as follows:

```
# necessary for connecting the backbone to the head
gnn_inp, gnn_out = dgcnn_model.in_out_tensors()
```

```
# head part of the model (classification)
 x_out = Conv1D(filters=16, kernel_size=sum(layer_dims),
strides=sum(layer_dims))(gnn_out)
x_out = MaxPool1D(pool_size=2)(x_out)
 x_out = Conv1D(filters=32, kernel_size=5, strides=1)(x_
out)
x_out = Flatten()(x_out)
 x_out = Dense(units=128, activation="relu")(x_out)
 x_out = Dropout(rate=0.5)(x_out)
predictions = Dense(units=1, activation="sigmoid")(x_out)
```

4. Let's create and compile a model using `tf.Keras` utilities. We will train the model with a `binary_crossentropy` loss function (to measure the difference between predicted labels and ground truth) with the `Adam` optimizer and a *learning rate* of 0.0001. We will also monitor the accuracy metric while training. The code is illustrated in the following snippet:

```
model = Model(inputs=gnn_inp, outputs=predictions)
model.compile(optimizer=Adam(lr=0.0001), loss=binary_
crossentropy, metrics=["acc"])
```

5. We can now exploit `scikit-learn` utilities to create train and test sets. In our experiments, we will be using 70% of the dataset as a training set and the remainder as a test set. In addition, we need to use the `flow` method of the generator to supply them to the model. The code to achieve this is shown in the following snippet:

```
from sklearn.model_selection import train_test_split
train_graphs, test_graphs = train_test_split(
graph_labels, test_size=.3, stratify=labels,)
gen = PaddedGraphGenerator(graphs=graphs)
train_gen = gen.flow(
    list(train_graphs.index - 1),
    targets=train_graphs.values,
    symmetric_normalization=False,
    batch_size=50,
)
test_gen = gen.flow(
    list(test_graphs.index - 1),
```

```
            targets=test_graphs.values,
            symmetric_normalization=False,
            batch_size=1,
    )
```

6. It's now time for training. We train the model for 100 epochs. However, feel free to play with the hyperparameters to gain better performance. Here is the code for this:

```
epochs = 100
history = model.fit(train_gen, epochs=epochs, verbose=1,
    validation_data=test_gen, shuffle=True,)
```

After 100 epochs, this should be the output:

```
Epoch 100/100
loss: 0.5121 - acc: 0.7636 - val_loss: 0.5636 - val_acc:
0.7305
```

Here, we are achieving about 76% accuracy on the training set and about 73% accuracy on the test set.

Node classification using GraphSAGE

In the next example, we will train GraphSAGE to classify nodes of the Cora dataset.

Let's first load the dataset using stellargraph utilities, as follows:

```
dataset = datasets.Cora()
G, nodes = dataset.load()
```

Follow this list of steps to train GraphSAGE to classify nodes of the Cora dataset:

1. As in the previous example, the first step is to split the dataset. We will be using 90% of the dataset as a training set and the remainder for testing. Here is the code for this step:

```
train_nodes, test_nodes = train_test_split(nodes, train_
size=0.1,test_size=None, stratify=nodes)
```

2. This time, we will convert labels using **one-hot representation**. This representation is often used for classification tasks and usually leads to better performance. Specifically, let c be the number of possible targets (seven, in the case of the Cora dataset), and each label will be converted in a vector of size c, where all the elements are 0 except for the one corresponding to the target class. The code is illustrated in the following snippet:

```
from sklearn import preprocessing
label_encoding = preprocessing.LabelBinarizer()
train_labels = label_encoding.fit_transform(train_nodes)
test_labels = label_encoding.transform(test_nodes)
```

3. Let's create a generator to feed the data into the model. We will be using an instance of the GraphSAGENodeGenerator class of stellargraph. We will use the flow method to feed the model with the train and test sets, as follows:

```
from stellargraph.mapper import GraphSAGENodeGenerator
batchsize = 50
n_samples = [10, 5, 7]
generator = GraphSAGENodeGenerator(G, batchsize, n_
samples)
train_gen = generator.flow(train_nodes.index, train_
labels, shuffle=True)
test_gen = generator.flow(test_labels.index, test_
labels)
```

4. Finally, let's create the model and compile it. For this exercise, we will be using a GraphSAGE encoder with three layers of 32, 32, and 16 dimensions, respectively. The encoder will then be connected to a dense layer with *softmax* activation to perform the classification. We will use an Adam optimizer with a *learning rate* of 0.03 and categorical_crossentropy as the loss function. The code is illustrated in the following snippet:

```
from stellargraph.layer import GraphSAGE
from tensorflow.keras.losses import categorical_
crossentropy
graphsage_model = GraphSAGE(layer_sizes=[32, 32, 16],
generator=generator, bias=True, dropout=0.6,)
gnn_inp, gnn_out = graphsage_model.in_out_tensors()
outputs = Dense(units=train_labels.shape[1],
```

```
activation="softmax")(gnn_out)
# create the model and compile
model = Model(inputs=gnn_inp, outputs=outputs)
model.compile(optimizer=Adam(lr=0.003), loss=categorical_
crossentropy, metrics=["acc"],)
```

5. It's now time to train the model. We will train the model for 20 epochs, as follows:

```
model.fit(train_gen, epochs=20, validation_data=test_gen,
verbose=2, shuffle=False)
```

6. This should be the output:

```
Epoch 20/20
loss: 0.8252 - acc: 0.8889 - val_loss: 0.9070 - val_acc:
0.8011
```

We achieved about 89% accuracy over the training set and about 80% accuracy over the test set.

Summary

In this chapter, we have learned how supervised ML can be effectively applied on graphs to solve real problems such as node and graph classification.

In particular, we first analyzed how graph and node properties can be directly used as features to train classic ML algorithms. We have seen shallow methods and simple approaches to learning node, edge, or graph representations for only a finite set of input data.

We have than learned how regularization techniques can be used during the learning phase in order to create more robust models that tend to generalize better.

Finally, we have seen how GNNs can be applied to solve supervised ML problems on graphs.

But what can those algorithms be useful for? In the next chapter, we will explore common problems on graphs that need to be solved through ML techniques.

5
Problems with Machine Learning on Graphs

Graph **machine learning (ML)** approaches can be useful for a wide range of tasks, with applications ranging from drug design to recommender systems in social networks. Furthermore, given the fact that such methods are *general by design* (meaning that they are not tailored to a specific problem), the same algorithm can be used to solve different problems.

There are common problems that can be solved using graph-based learning techniques. In this chapter, we will mention some of the most well studied of these by providing details about how a specific algorithm, among the ones we have already learned about in *Chapter 3, Unsupervised Graph Learning*, and *Chapter 4, Supervised Graph Learning*, can be used to solve a task. After reading this chapter, you will be aware of the formal definition of many common problems you may encounter when dealing with graphs. In addition, you will learn useful ML pipelines that you can reuse on future real-world problems you will deal with.

More precisely, the following topics will be covered in this chapter:

- Predicting missing links in a graph
- Detecting meaningful structures such as communities
- Detecting graph similarities and graph matching

Technical requirements

We will be using *Jupyter* Notebooks with Python 3.8 for all of our exercises. In the following code block, you can see a list of the Python libraries that will be installed for this chapter using `pip` (for example, run `pip install networkx==2.5` on the command line):

```
Jupyter==1.0.0
networkx==2.5
karateclub==1.0.19
scikit-learn==0.24.0
pandas==1.1.3
node2vec==0.3.3
numpy==1.19.2
tensorflow==2.4.1
stellargraph==1.2.1
communities==2.2.0
git+https://github.com/palash1992/GEM.git
```

All code files relevant to this chapter are available at `https://github.com/PacktPublishing/Graph-Machine-Learning/tree/main/Chapter05`.

Predicting missing links in a graph

Link prediction, also known as **graph completion**, is a common problem when dealing with graphs. More precisely, from a partially observed graph—a graph where for a certain pair of nodes it is not possible to exactly know if there is (or there is not) an edge between them—we want to predict whether or not edges exist for the unknown status node pairs, as seen in *Figure 5.1*. Formally, let $G = (V, E)$ be a graph where V is its set of nodes and $E = E_o \cup E_u$ is its set of edges. The set of edges E_o are known as *observed links*, while the set of edges E_u are known as *unknown links*. The goal of the link prediction problem is to exploit the information of V and E_o to estimate E_u. This problem is also common when dealing with temporal graph data. In this setting, let G_t be a graph observed at a given timepoint t, where we want to predict the edges of this graph at a given timepoint $t + 1$. The partially observed graph can be seen here:

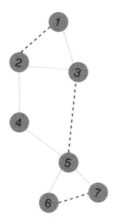

$$E_o = \{\{1, 3\}, \{2, 3\}, \{2, 4\}, \{4, 5\}, \{5, 6\}, \{5, 7\}\}$$

$$E_u = \{\{1, 2\}, \{3, 5\}, \{6, 7\}\}$$

Figure 5.1 – Partially observed graph with observed link $\boldsymbol{E_o}$ (solid lines) and unknown link $\boldsymbol{E_u}$ (dashed lines)

The link prediction problem is widely used in different domains, such as a recommender system in order to propose friendships in social networks or items to purchase on e-commerce websites. It is also used in criminal network investigations in order to find hidden connections between criminal clusters, as well as in bioinformatics for the analysis of protein-protein interactions. In the next sections, we will discuss two families of approaches to solve the link prediction problem—namely, **similarity-based** and **embedding-based** methods.

Similarity-based methods

In this subsection, we show several simple algorithms to solve the label prediction problem. The main shared idea behind all these algorithms is to estimate a similarity function between each couple of nodes in a graph. If, according to the function, the nodes *look similar*, they will have a high probability of being connected by an edge. We will divide these algorithms into two sub-families: **index-based** and **community-based** methods. The former contains all the methods through a simple calculation of an index based on the neighbors of a given couple of nodes. The latter contains more sophisticated algorithms, whereby the index is computed using information about the community to which a given couple of nodes belong. In order to give a practical example of these algorithms, we will use the standard implementation available in the `networkx` library in the `networkx.algorithms.link_prediction` package.

Index-based methods

In this section, we will show some algorithms available in `networkx` to compute the probability of an edge between two disconnected nodes. These algorithms are based on the calculation of a simple index through information obtained by analyzing the neighbors of the two disconnected nodes.

Resource allocation index

The resource allocation index method estimates the probability that two nodes v and u are connected by estimating the *resource allocation index* for all node pairs according to the following formula:

$$Resource\ Allocation\ Index(u, v) = \sum_{w \in N(u) \cap N(v)} \frac{1}{|N(w)|}$$

In the given formula, the $N(v)$ function computes the neighbors of the v nodes and, as visible in the formula, w is a node who is a neighbor of both u and v. This index can be computed in `networkx` using the following code:

```
import networkx as nx
edges = [[1,3],[2,3],[2,4],[4,5],[5,6],[5,7]]
G = nx.from_edgelist(edges)
preds = nx.resource_allocation_index(G,[(1,2),(2,5),(3,4)])
```

The first parameter for the `resource_allocation_index` function is an input graph, while the second parameter is a list of possible edges. We want to compute the probability of a connection. As a result, we get the following output:

```
[(1, 2, 0.5), (2, 5, 0.5), (3, 4, 0.5)]
```

The output is a list containing couples of nodes such as (1,2), (2,5), and (3,4), which form the resource allocation index. According to this output, the probability of having an edge between those couples of nodes is 0.5.

Jaccard coefficient

The algorithm computes the probability of a connection between two nodes u and v, according to the *Jaccard coefficient*, computed as follows:

$$Jaccard\ Coefficient(u, v) = \frac{|N(u) \cap N(v)|}{|N(u) \cup N(v)|}$$

Here, $N(v)$ is used to compute the neighbors of the v node. The function can be used in networkx using the following code:

```
import networkx as nx
edges = [[1,3],[2,3],[2,4],[4,5],[5,6],[5,7]]
G = nx.from_edgelist(edges)
preds = nx.resource_allocation_index(G,[(1,2),(2,5),(3,4)])
```

The resource_allocation_index function has the same parameters as the previous function. The result of the code is shown here:

```
[(1, 2, 0.5), (2, 5, 0.25), (3, 4, 0.3333333333333333)]
```

According to this output, the probability of having an edge between nodes (1,2) is 0.5, while between nodes (2,5) this is 0.25, and between nodes (3,4) this is 0.333.

In networkx, other methods to compute the probability of a connection between two nodes based on their similarity score are nx.adamic_adar_index and nx.preferential_attachment, based on *Adamic/Adar index* and *preferential attachment index* calculations respectively. Those functions have the same parameters as the others, and accept a graph and a list of a couple of nodes where we want to compute the score. In the next section, we will show another family of algorithms based on community detection.

Community-based methods

As with index-based methods, the algorithms belonging to this family also compute an index representing the probability of the disconnected nodes being connected. The main difference between index-based and community-based methods is related to the logic behind them. Indeed, community-based methods, before generating the index, need to compute information about the community belonging to those nodes. In this subsection, we will show—also providing several examples—some common community-based methods.

Community common neighbor

In order to estimate the probability of two nodes being connected, this algorithm computes the number of common neighbors and adds to this value the number of common neighbors belonging to the same community. Formally, for two nodes v and u, the community common neighbor value is computed as follows:

$$Community\ Common\ Neighbor(u,v) = |N(v) \cup N(u)| + \sum_{w \in N(v) \cap N(u)} f(w)$$

In this formula, $N(v)$ is used to compute the neighbors of node v, while $f(w) = 1$ if w belongs to the same community of u and v; otherwise, this is 0. The function can be computed in networkx using the following code:

```
import networkx as nx
edges = [[1,3],[2,3],[2,4],[4,5],[5,6],[5,7]]
 G = nx.from_edgelist(edges)

G.nodes[1]["community"] = 0
G.nodes[2]["community"] = 0
G.nodes[3]["community"] = 0

G.nodes[4]["community"] = 1
G.nodes[5]["community"] = 1
G.nodes[6]["community"] = 1
G.nodes[7]["community"] = 1

preds = nx.cn_soundarajan_hopcroft(G, [(1,2),(2,5),(3,4)])
```

From the preceding code snippet, it is possible to see how we need to assign the `community` property to each node of the graph. This property is used to identify nodes belonging to the same community when computing the function $f(v)$ defined in the previous equation. The community value, as we will see in the next section, can also be automatically computed using specific algorithms. As we already saw, the `cn_soundarajan_hopcroft` function takes the input graph and a couple of nodes for which we want to compute the score. As a result, we get the following output:

```
[(1, 2, 2), (2, 5, 1), (3, 4, 1)]
```

The main difference from the previous function is in the index value. Indeed, we can easily see that the output is not in the range `(0,1)`.

Community resource allocation

As with the previous method, the community resource allocation algorithm merges information obtained from the neighbors of the nodes with the community, as shown in the following formula:

$$Community\ Resource\ Allocation(u, v) = \sum_{w \in N(v) \cap N(u)} \frac{f(w)}{|N(w)|}$$

Here, $N(v)$ is used to compute the neighbors of node v, while $f(w) = 1$ if w belongs to the same community of u and v; otherwise, this is 0. The function can be computed in `networkx` using the following code:

```python
import networkx as nx
edges = [[1,3],[2,3],[2,4],[4,5],[5,6],[5,7]]
  G = nx.from_edgelist(edges)

G.nodes[1]["community"] = 0
G.nodes[2]["community"] = 0
G.nodes[3]["community"] = 0

G.nodes[4]["community"] = 1
G.nodes[5]["community"] = 1
G.nodes[6]["community"] = 1
G.nodes[7]["community"] = 1

preds = nx. ra_index_soundarajan_
hopcroft(G, [(1,2),(2,5),(3,4)])
```

From the preceding code snippet, it is possible to see how we need to assign the `community` property to each node of the graph. This property is used to identify nodes belonging to the same community when computing the function $f(v)$ defined in the previous equation. The community value, as we will see in the next section, can also be automatically computed using specific algorithms. As we already saw, the `ra_index_soundarajan_hopcroft` function takes the input graph and a couple of nodes for which we want to compute the score. As a result, we get the following output:

```
[(1, 2, 0.5), (2, 5, 0), (3, 4, 0)]
```

From the preceding output, it is possible to see the influence of the community in the computation of the index. Since nodes 1 and 2 belong to the same community, they have a higher value in the index. On the contrary, edges (2,5) and (3,4) have a value of 0 since they belong to a different community from each other.

In `networkx`, two other methods to compute the probability of a connection between two nodes based on their similarity score merged with community information are `nx.a within_inter_cluster` and `nx.common_neighbor_centrality`.

In the next section, we will describe a more complex technique based on ML plus edge embedding to perform prediction of unknown edges.

Embedding-based methods

In this section, we describe a more advanced way to perform link prediction. The idea behind this approach is to solve the link prediction problem as a supervised classification task. More precisely, for a given graph, each couple of nodes is represented with a feature vector (x), and a class label (y) is assigned to each of those node couples. Formally, let $G = (V, E)$ be a graph, and for each couple of nodes i, j, we build the following formula:

$$x = [f_{0,0}, \dots, f_{i,j}, \dots, f_{n,n}] \quad y = [y_{0,0}, \dots, y_{i,j}, \dots, y_{n,n}]$$

Here, $f_{ij} \in x$ is the *feature vector* representing the couple of nodes i, j, and $y_{i,j} \in y$ is their *label*. The value for $y_{i,j}$ is defined as follows: $y_{i,j} = 1$ if, in the graph G, the edge connecting node i, j exists; otherwise, $y_{i,j} = 0$. Using the feature vector and the labels, we can then train an ML algorithm in order to predict if a given couple of nodes constitute a plausible edge for the given graph.

If it is easy to build the label vector for each couple of nodes, it is not so straightforward to build the feature space. In order to generate the feature vector for each couple of nodes, we will use some embedding techniques, such as node2vec and edge2vec, already discussed in *Chapter 3, Unsupervised Graph Learning*. Using those embedding algorithms, the generation of the feature space will be greatly simplified. Indeed, the whole process can be summarized in two main steps, outlined as follows:

1. For each node of the graph G, its embedding vector is computed using a node2vec algorithm.

2. For all the possible couple of nodes in the graph, the embedding is computed using an edge2vec algorithm.

We can apply now a generic ML algorithm to the generated feature vector in order to solve the classification problem.

In order to give you a practical explanation of this procedure, we will provide an example in the following code snippet. More precisely, we will describe the whole pipeline (from graph to link prediction) using the networkx, stellargraph, and node2vec libraries. We will split the whole process into different steps in order to simplify our understanding of the different parts. The link prediction problem was applied to the citation network dataset described in *Chapter 1, Getting Started with Graphs in Python*, available at the following link: https://linqs-data.soe.ucsc.edu/public/lbc/cora.tgz.

As a first step, we will build a networkx graph using the citation dataset, as follows:

```
import networkx as nx
import pandas as pd

edgelist = pd.read_csv("cora.cites", sep='\t', header=None,
names=["target", "source"])
G = nx.from_pandas_edgelist(edgelist)
```

Since the dataset is represented as an edge list (see *Chapter 1, Getting Started with Graphs in Python*), we used the from_pandas_edgelist function to build the graph.

As a second step, we need to create, from the graph G, training and test sets. More precisely, our training and test sets should contain not only a subset of real edges of the graph G but also couples of nodes that do not represent a real edge in G. The couples representing real edges will be *positive instances* (class label 1), while the couples that do not represent real edges will be *negative instances* (class label 0). This process can be easily performed as follows:

```
from stellargraph.data import EdgeSplitter


edgeSplitter = EdgeSplitter(G)
 graph_test, samples_test, labels_test = edgeSplitter.train_
test_split(p=0.1, method="global")
```

We used the EdgeSplitter class available in stellargraph. The main constructor parameter of the EdgeSplitter class is the graph (G) we want to use to perform our split. The real splitting is performed using the train_test_split function that will generate the following outputs:

- graph_test is a subset of the original graph *G* containing all the nodes but just a selected subset of edges.

- samples_test is a vector containing in each position a couple of nodes. This vector will contain couples of nodes representing real edges (positive instance) but also couples of nodes that do not represent real edges (negative instance).

- labels_test is a vector having the same length as samples_test. It contains only 0 or 1. The value of 0 is present in the position representing a negative instance in the samples_test vector, while the value of 1 is present in the position representing a positive instance in samples_test.

By following the same procedure used to generate the test set, it is possible to generate the training set, as illustrated in the following code snippet:

```
edgeSplitter = EdgeSplitter(graph_test, G)
 graph_train, samples_train, labels_train = edgeSplitter.train_
test_split(p=0.1, method="global")
```

The main difference in this part of code is related to the initialization of EdgeSplitter. In this case, we also provide graph_test in order to not repeat positive and negative instances generated for the test set.

At this point, we have our training and testing datasets with negative and positive instances. For each of those instances, we now need to generate their feature vector. In this example, we used the `node2vec` library to generate the node embedding. In general, every node embedding algorithm can be used to perform this task. For the training set, we can thus generate the feature vector with the following code:

```
from node2vec import Node2Vec
from node2vec.edges import HadamardEmbedder

node2vec = Node2Vec(graph_train)
 model = node2vec.fit()
edges_embs = HadamardEmbedder(keyed_vectors=model.wv)
 train_embeddings = [edges_embs[str(x[0]),str(x[1])] for x in
samples_train]
```

From the previous code snippet, it is possible to see the following:

- We generate the embedding for each node in the training graph using the `node2vec` library.

- We use the `HadamardEmbedder` class to generate the embedding of each couple of nodes contained in the training set. Those values will be used as feature vectors to perform the training of our model.

In this example, we used the `HadamardEmbedder` algorithm, but in general, other embedding algorithms can be used, such as the ones described in *Chapter 3, Unsupervised Graph Learning*.

The previous step needs to also be performed for the test set, with the following code:

```
edges_embs = HadamardEmbedder(keyed_vectors=model.wv)
 test_embeddings = [edges_embs[str(x[0]),str(x[1])] for x in
samples_test]
```

The only difference here is given by the `samples_test` array used to compute the edge embeddings. Indeed, in this case, we use the data generated for the test set. Moreover, it should be noted that the `node2vec` algorithm was not recomputed for the test set. Indeed, given the stochastic nature of `node2vec`, it is not possible to ensure that the two learned embeddings are "comparable" and therefore `node2vec` embeddings will change between runs.

Everything is set now. We can finally train—using the `train_embeddings` feature space and the `train_labels` label assignment—an ML algorithm to solve the label prediction problem, as follows:

```
from sklearn.ensemble import RandomForestClassifier
rf = RandomForestClassifier(n_estimators=1000)
 rf.fit(train_embeddings, labels_train);
```

In this example, we used a simple `RandomForestClassifier` class, but every ML algorithm can be used to solve this task. We can then apply the trained model on the `test_embeddings` feature space in order to quantify the quality of the classification, as shown in the following code block:

```
from sklearn import metrics

y_pred = rf.predict(test_embeddings)
 print('Precision:', metrics.precision_score(labels_test, y_
pred))
 print('Recall:', metrics.recall_score(labels_test, y_pred))
 print('F1-Score:', metrics.f1_score(labels_test, y_pred))
```

As a result, we get the following output:

```
Precision: 0.8557114228456913
Recall: 0.8102466793168881
F1-Score: 0.8323586744639375
```

As we already mentioned, the methods we just described are just a general schema; each piece of the pipeline—such as the train/test split, the node/edge embedding, and the ML algorithm—can be changed according to the specific problem we are facing.

This method is particularly useful when dealing with link prediction in temporal graphs. In this case, information relating to an edge obtained at timepoint t used to train a model can be applied in order to predict edges at timepoint $t + 1$.

In this section, we introduced the label prediction problem. We enriched our explanation by providing a description, with several examples, of different techniques used to find a solution to the link prediction problem. We showed that different ways to tackle the problem are available, from simple index-based techniques to more complex embedding-based techniques. However, the scientific literature is full of algorithms to solve the link prediction task, and there are different algorithms to solve this problem. In the paper *Review on Learning and Extracting Graph Features for Link Prediction* (`https://arxiv.org/pdf/1901.03425.pdf`), a good overview of different techniques used to solve the link prediction problem is available. In the next section, we will investigate the community detection problem.

Detecting meaningful structures such as communities

One common problem data scientists face when dealing with networks is how to identify clusters and communities within a graph. This often arises when graphs are derived from social networks and communities are known to exist. However, the underlying algorithms and methods can also be used in other contexts, representing another option to perform clustering and segmentation. For example, these methods can effectively be used in text mining to identify emerging topics and to cluster documents that refer to single events/topics. A community detection task consists of partitioning a graph such that nodes belonging to the same community are tightly connected with each other and are weakly connected with nodes from other communities. There exist several strategies to identify communities. In general, we can define them as belonging to one of two categories, outlined as follows:

- **Non-overlapping** community detection algorithms that provide a one-to-one association between nodes and communities, thus with no overlapping nodes between communities
- **Overlapping** community detection algorithms that allow a node to be included in more than one community—for instance, reflecting the natural tendencies of social networks to develop overlapping communities (for example, friends from school, neighbors, playmates, people being in the same football team, and so on), or in biology, where a single protein can be involved in more than one process and bioreaction

In the following section, we will review some of the most used techniques in the context of community detection.

Embedding-based community detection

One first class of methods that allow us to partition nodes into communities can be simply obtained by applying standard shallow clustering techniques on the node embeddings, computed using the methods described in *Chapter 3, Unsupervised Graph Learning*. The embedding methods in fact allow us to project nodes into a vector space where a distance measure that represents a similarity between nodes can be defined. As we have shown in *Chapter 3, Unsupervised Graph Learning*, embedding algorithms are very effective in separating nodes with similar neighborhood and/or connectivity properties. Then, standard clustering techniques can be used, such as distance-based clustering (K-means), connectivity clustering (hierarchical clustering), distribution clustering (Gaussian mixture), and density-based clustering (**Density-Based Spatial Clustering of Applications with Noise (DBSCAN)**). Depending on the algorithm, these techniques may both provide a single-association community detection or a soft cluster assignment. We will showcase how they would work on a simple barbell graph. We start by creating a simple barbell graph using the `networkx` utility function, as follows:

```
import networkx as nx
G = nx.barbell_graph(m1=10, m2=4)
```

We can then first get the reduced dense node representation using one of the embedding algorithms we have seen previously (for instance, `HOPE`), shown as follows:

```
from gem.embedding.hope import HOPE
gf = HOPE(d=4, beta=0.01)
gf.learn_embedding(G)
embeddings = gf.get_embedding()
```

We can finally run a clustering algorithm on the resulting vector representation provided by the node embeddings, like this:

```
from sklearn.mixture import GaussianMixture
gm = GaussianMixture(n_components=3, random_state=0)
labels = gm.fit_predict(embeddings)
```

We can plot the network with the computed communities highlighted in different colors, like this:

```
colors = ["blue", "green", "red"]
nx.draw_spring(G, node_color=[colors[label] for label in
labels])
```

By doing so, you should obtain the output shown in the following screenshot:

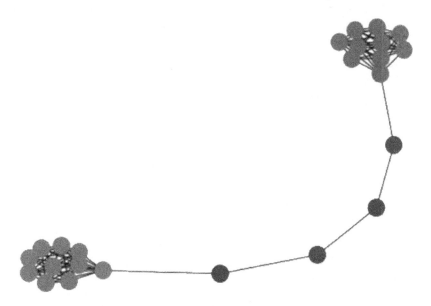

Figure 5.2 – Barbell graph where the community detection algorithm has been applied using embedding-based methods

The two clusters, as well as the connecting nodes, have been correctly grouped into three different communities, reflecting the internal structure of the graph.

Spectral methods and matrix factorization

Another way to achieve a graph partition is to process the adjacency matrix or the Laplacian matrix that represents the connectivity properties of the graph. For instance, spectral clustering can be obtained by applying standard clustering algorithms on the eigenvectors of the Laplacian matrix. In some sense, spectral clustering can also be seen as a special case of an embedding-based community detection algorithm where the embedding technique is so-called spectral embedding, obtained by considering the first k-eigenvectors of the Laplacian matrix. By considering different definitions of the Laplacian as well as different similarity matrices, variations to this method can be obtained. A convenient implementation of this method can be found within the communities Python library and can be used on the adjacency matrix representation easily obtained from a networkx graph, as illustrated in the following code snippet:

```
from communities.algorithms import spectral_clustering
adj=np.array(nx.adjacency_matrix(G).todense())
communities = spectral_clustering(adj, k=2)
```

Moreover, the adjacency matrix (or the Laplacian) can also be decomposed using matrix factorization techniques other than the **singular value decomposition** (**SVD**) technique—such as **non-negative matrix factorization** (**NMF**)—that allow similar descriptions, as illustrated in the following code snippet:

```
from sklearn.decomposition import NMF
nmf = NMF(n_components=2)
 score = nmf.fit_transform(adj)
communities = [set(np.where(score [:,ith]>0)[0])
                     for ith in range(2)]
```

The threshold for belonging to the community was set in this example to 0, although other values can also be used to retain only the community cores. Note that these methods are overlapping community detection algorithms, and nodes might belong to more than one community.

Probability models

Community detection methods can also be derived from fitting the parameters of generative probabilistic graph models. Examples of generative models were already described in *Chapter 1, Getting Started with Graphs in Python*. However, they did not assume the presence of any underlying community, unlike the so-called **stochastic block model** (**SBM**). In fact, this model is based on the assumption that nodes can be partitioned into K disjoint communities and each community has a defined probability of being connected to another. For a network of n nodes and K communities, the generative model is thus parametrized by the following:

- **Membership matrix**: M, which is a $n \times K$ matrix and represents the probability a given node belongs to a certain class k

- **Probability matrix**: B, which is $K \times K$ matrix and represents the edge probability between a node belonging to community i and one node belonging to community j

The adjacency matrix is then generated by the following formula:

$$a_{ij} = \begin{cases} Bernoulli\,(B_{(g_i, g_j)}) & if\ i < j \\ 0 & if\ i = 0 \\ a_{ji} & if\ i > j \end{cases}$$

Here, g_i and g_j represent the community, and they can be obtained by sampling from a multinomial distribution of probabilities M_i and M_j.

In the SBM, we can basically invert the formulation and reduce the community detection problem to posterior estimation of the membership matrix M from the matrix A, via maximum likelihood estimation. A version of this approach has recently been used together with randomized spectral clustering in order to perform community detection in very large graphs. Note that the SBM model in the limit of the constant probability matrix (that is, $B_{ij} = p$) corresponds to the Erdős-Rényi model. These models have the advantage of also describing a relation between communities, identifying community-community relationships.

Cost function minimization

Another possible way to detect communities within a graph is to optimize a given cost function that represents a graph structure and penalizes edges across communities versus edges within communities. This basically consists of building a measure for the quality of a community (as we will see shortly, its modularity) and then optimizing the node association to communities in order to maximize the overall quality of the partitioning.

In the context of a binary associative community structure, the community association can be described by a dichotomic variable s_i with values -1 or 1, depending on whether the node belongs to one of the two communities. In this setting, we can define the following quantity that can indeed be used to effectively represent the cost associated with having a link between two nodes of different communities:

$$\sum_{i,j \, \epsilon \, E} A_{ij}(1 - s_i s_j)$$

Indeed, when two connected nodes, $A_{ij} > 0$ belong to a different community $s_i s_j = -1$, the contribution provided by the edge is positive. On the other hand, the contribution is 0, both when two nodes are not connected ($A_{ij} = 0$) and when two connected nodes belong to the same community ($s_i s_j = 0$). Therefore, the problem is to find the best community assignment (s_i and s_j) in order to minimize the preceding function. This method, however, applies only to binary community detection and is therefore rather limited in its application.

Another very popular algorithm belonging to this class is the Louvain method, which takes its name from the university where it was invented. This algorithm aims to maximize the modularity, defined as follows:

$$Q = \frac{1}{2m} \sum_{i,j \, \epsilon \, E} (A_{ij} - \frac{k_i k_j}{2m}) \, \delta(c_i, c_j)$$

Here, m represents the number of edges, k_i and k_j represent the degree of the i-th and j-th node respectively, and $\delta(c_i, c_j)$ is the Kronecker delta function, which is 1 when c_i and c_j have the same value and 0 otherwise. The modularity basically represents a measure of how much better the community identification performs as compared to randomly rewiring the nodes and thus creating a random network that has the same number of edges and degree distribution.

To maximize this modularity efficiently, the Louvain methods iteratively compute the following steps:

1. **Modularity optimization**: Nodes are swept iteratively, and for each node we compute the change of modularity Q there would be if the node were to be assigned to each community of its neighbors. Once all the ΔQ values are computed, the node is assigned to the community that provides the largest increase. If there is no increase obtained by placing the node in any other community than the one it is in, the node remains in its original community. This optimization process continues until no changes are induced.

2. **Node aggregation**: In the second step, we build a new network by grouping all the nodes in the same community and connecting the communities using edges that result from the sum of all edges across the two communities. Edges within communities are accounted for as well by means of self-loops that have weights resulting from the sum of all edge weights belonging to the community.

A Louvain implementation can already be found in the `communities` library, as can be seen in the following code snippet:

```
from communities.algorithms import louvain_method
communities = louvain_method(adj)
```

Another method to maximize the modularity is the Girvan-Newman algorithm, which is based on iteratively removing edges that have the highest betweenness centrality (and thus connect two separate clusters of nodes) to create connected component communities. Here is the code related to this:

```
from communities.algorithms import girvan_newman
communities = girvan_newman(adj, n=2)
```

> **Note**
>
> The latter algorithm needs to compute the betweenness centrality of all edges to remove the edges. Such computations may be very expensive in large graphs. The Girvan-Newman algorithm in fact scales as $n \cdot m^2$, where m is the number of edges and n is the number of nodes, and should not be used when dealing with large datasets.

Detecting graph similarities and graph matching

Learning a quantitative measure of the *similarity* among graphs is considered a key problem. Indeed, it is a critical step for network analysis and can also facilitate many ML problems, such as classification, clustering, and ranking. Many clustering algorithms, for example, use the concept of similarity for determining if an object should or should not be a member of a group.

In the graph domain, finding an effective similarity measure constitutes a crucial problem for many applications. Consider, for instance, the *role* of a node inside a graph. This node might be very important for spreading information across a network or guaranteeing network robustness: for example, it could be the center of a star graph or it could be a member of a clique. In this scenario, it would be very useful to have a powerful method for comparing nodes according to their roles. For example, you might be interested in searching for individuals showing similar roles or presenting similar unusual and anomalous behaviors. You might also use it for searching similar subgraphs or to determine network compatibility for *knowledge transfer*. For example, if you find a method for increasing the robustness of a network and you know that such a network is very similar to another one, you may apply the same solution that worked well for the first network directly to the second one:

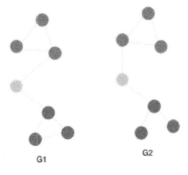

Figure 5.3 – Example of differences between two graphs

Several metrics can be used for measuring the similarity (distance) between two objects. Some examples include the *Euclidean distance, Manhattan distance, cosine similarity,* and so on. However, these metrics might fail to capture the specific characteristics of the data being studied, especially on non-Euclidean structures such as graphs. Take a look at *Figure 5.3*: how "distant" are **G1** and **G2**? They look pretty similar. But what if the missing connection in the red community of **G2** causes a severe loss of information? Do they still look similar?

Several algorithmic approaches and heuristics have been proposed, based on mathematical concepts such as *graph isomorphisms, edit distance,* and *common subgraphs* (we suggest reading `https://link.springer.com/article/10.1007/s10044-012-0284-8` for a detailed review). Many of these approaches are currently used in practical applications, even if they often require exponentially high computational time to provide a solution to **NP-complete** problems in general (where **NP** stands for **nondeterministic polynomial time**). Therefore, it is essential to find or learn a metric for measuring the similarity of data points involved in the specific task. Here is where ML comes to our aid.

Many algorithms among the ones we have already seen in *Chapter 3, Unsupervised Graph Learning,* and *Chapter 4, Supervised Graph Learning* might be useful for learning an effective similarity metric. According to the way they are used, a precise taxonomy can be defined. Here, we provide a simple overview of graph similarity techniques. A more comprehensive list can be found in the paper *Deep Graph Similarity Learning: A Survey* (`https://arxiv.org/pdf/1912.11615.pdf`). They can be essentially divided into three main categories, even if sophisticated combinations can also be developed. **Graph embedding-based methods** use embedding techniques to obtain an embedded representation of the graphs and exploit such a representation to learn the similarity function; **graph kernel-based methods** define the similarity between graphs by measuring the similarity of their constituting substructures; **graph neural network-based methods** use **graph neural networks** (**GNNs**) to jointly learn an embedded representation and a similarity function. Let's see all of them in more detail.

Graph embedding-based methods

Such techniques seek to apply graph embedding techniques to obtain node-level or graph-level representations and further use the representations for similarity learning. For example, *DeepWalk* and *Node2Vec* can be used to extract meaningful embedding that can then be used to define a similarity function or to predict similarity scores. For example, in Tixier et al. (2015), `node2vec` was used for encoding node embeddings. Then, **two-dimensional** (**2D**) histograms obtained from those node embeddings were passed to a classical 2D **convolutional neural network** (**CNN**) architecture designed for images. Such a simple yet powerful approach enabled good results to be derived from many benchmark datasets.

Graph kernel-based methods

Graph kernel-based methods have generated a lot of interest in terms of capturing the similarity between graphs. These approaches compute the similarity between two graphs as a function of the similarities between some of their substructures. Different graph kernels exist based on the substructures they use, which include random walks, shortest paths, and subgraphs. As an example, a method called **Deep Graph Kernels (DGK)** (Yanardag et al., 2015) decomposes graphs into substructures that are viewed as "words". Then, **natural language processing** (**NLP**) approaches such as **continuous bag of words** (**CBOW**) and **skip-gram** are used to learn latent representations of the substructures. This way, the kernel between two graphs is defined based on the similarity of the substructure space.

GNN-based methods

With the emergence of **deep learning** (**DL**) techniques, GNNs have become a powerful new tool for learning representations on graphs. Such powerful models can be easily adapted to various tasks, including graph similarity learning. Furthermore, they present a key advantage with respect to other traditional graph embedding approaches. Indeed, while the latter generally learn the representation in an isolated stage, in this kind of approach, the representation learning and the target learning task are conducted jointly. Therefore, the GNN deep models can better leverage the graph features for the specific learning task. We have already seen an example of similarity learning using GNNs in *Chapter 3, Unsupervised Graph Learning*, where a two-branch network was trained to estimate the proximity distance between two graphs.

Applications

Similarity learning on graphs has already achieved promising results in many domains. Important applications may be found in chemistry and bioinformatics—for example, for finding the chemical compounds that are most similar to a query compound, as illustrated on the left-hand side of the following diagram. In neuroscience, similarity learning methods have started to be applied to measure the similarity of brain networks among multiple subjects, allowing the novel clinical investigation of brain diseases:

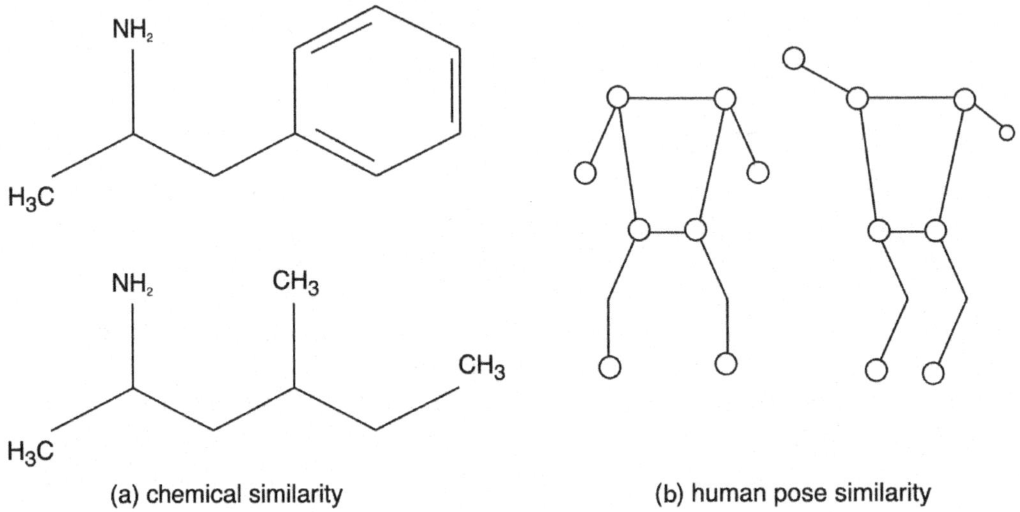

(a) chemical similarity   (b) human pose similarity

Figure 5.4 – Example of how graphs can be useful for representing various objects: (a) differences between two chemical compounds; (b) differences between two human poses

Graph similarity learning has also been explored in computer security, where novel approaches have been proposed for the detection of vulnerabilities in software systems as well as hardware security problems. Recently, a trend for applying such solutions to solve computer vision problems has been observed. Once the challenging problem of converting images into graph data has been solved, interesting solutions can indeed be proposed for human action recognition in video sequences and object matching in scenes, among other areas (as shown on the right-hand side of *Figure 5.4*).

Summary

In this chapter, we have learned how graph-based ML techniques can be used to solve many different problems.

In particular, we have seen that the same algorithm (or a slightly modified version of it) can be adapted to solve apparently very different tasks such as link prediction, community detection, and graph similarity learning. We have also seen that each problem has its own peculiarities, which have been exploited by researchers in order to design more sophisticated solutions.

In the next chapter, we will explore real-life problems that have been solved using ML.

Section 3 – Advanced Applications of Graph Machine Learning

In this section, the reader will acquire a more practical knowledge of the methods outlined in the previous chapters by applying them to real-world use cases and learn how to scale out the approaches to structured and unstructured datasets.

This section comprises the following chapters:

- *Chapter 6, Social Network Graphs*
- *Chapter 7, Text Analytics and Natural Language Processing Using Graphs*
- *Chapter 8, Graphs Analysis for Credit Card Transactions*
- *Chapter 9, Building a Data-Driven Graph-Powered Application*
- *Chapter 10, Novel Trends on Graphs*

6
Social Network Graphs

The growth of social networking sites has been one of the most active trends in digital media over the years. Since the late 1990s, when the first social applications were published, they have attracted billions of active users worldwide, many of whom have integrated digital social interactions into their daily lives. New ways of communication are being driven by social networks such as Facebook, Twitter, and Instagram, among others. Users can share ideas, post updates and feedback, or engage in activities and events while sharing their broader interests on social networking sites.

Besides, social networks constitute a huge source of information for studying user behaviors, interpreting interaction among people, and predicting their interests. Structuring them as graphs, where a vertex corresponds to a person and an edge represents the connection between them, enables a powerful tool to extract useful knowledge.

However, understanding the dynamics that drive the evolution of a social network is a complex problem due to a large number of variable parameters.

In this chapter, we will talk about how we can analyze the Facebook social network using graph theory and how we can solve useful problems such as link prediction and community detection using machine learning.

The following topics will be covered in this chapter:

- Overview of the dataset
- Network topology and community detection
- Embedding for supervised and unsupervised tasks

Technical requirements

We will be using *Jupyter* notebooks with *Python* 3.8 for all of our exercises. The following is a list of the Python libraries that need to be installed for this chapter using `pip`. For example, run `pip install networkx==2.5` on the command line:

```
Jupyter==1.0.0
networkx==2.5
scikit-learn==0.24.0
numpy==1.19.2
node2vec==0.3.3
tensorflow==2.4.1
stellargraph==1.2.1
communities==2.2.0
git+https://github.com/palash1992/GEM.git
```

In the rest of this chapter, if not clearly stated, we will refer to nx, pd, and np as results of the following Python commands: `import networkx as nx`, `import pandas as pd`, and `import numpy as np`.

All code files relevant to this chapter are available at `https://github.com/PacktPublishing/Graph-Machine-Learning/tree/main/Chapter06`.

Overview of the dataset

We will be using the **Social circles SNAP Facebook public dataset**, from Stanford University (`https://snap.stanford.edu/data/ego-Facebook.html`).

The dataset was created by collecting Facebook user information from survey participants. Ego networks were created from 10 users. Each user was asked to identify all the **circles** (list of friends) to which their friends belong. On average, each user identified 19 circles in their **ego networks**, where each circle has on average 22 friends.

For each user, the following information was collected:

- **Edges**: An edge exists if two users are friends on Facebook.
- **Node features**: Features we labeled 1 if the user has this property in their profile and 0 otherwise. Features have been anonymized since the names of the features would reveal private data.

The 10 ego networks were then unified in a single graph that we are going to study.

Dataset download

The dataset can be retrieved using the following URL: https://snap.stanford. edu/data/ego-Facebook.html. In particular, three files can be downloaded: facebook.tar.gz, facebook_combined.txt.gz, and readme-Ego.txt. Let's inspect each file separately:

- facebook.tar.gz: This is an archive containing four files for each **ego user** (40 files in total). Each file is named nodeId.extension where nodeId is the node ID of the ego user and extension is either edges, circles, feat, egofeat, or featnames. The following provides more details:

  a. nodeId.edges: This contains a list of edges for the network of the nodeId node.

  b. nodeId.circles: This contains several lines (one for each circle). Each line consists of a name (the circle name) followed by a series of node IDs.

  c. nodeId.feat: This contains the features (0 if nodeId has the feature, 1 otherwise) for each node in the ego network.

  d. nodeId.egofeat: This contains the features for the ego user.

  e. nodeId.featname: This contains the names of the features.

- facebook_combined.txt.gz: This is an archive containing a single file, facebook_combined.txt, which is a list of edges from all the ego networks combined.

- readme-Ego.txt: This contains a description for the previously mentioned files.

Take a look at those files by yourself. It is strongly suggested to explore and become as comfortable as possible with the dataset before starting any machine learning task.

Loading the dataset using networkx

The first step of our analysis will be loading the aggregated ego networks using networkx. As we have seen in previous chapters, networkx is powerful for graph analysis and, given the size of the datasets, will be the perfect tool for the analysis that we will be doing in this chapter. However, for larger social network graphs with billions of nodes and edges, more specific tools might be required for loading and processing them. We will cover the tools and technologies used for scaling out the analysis in *Chapter 9, Building a Data-Driven Graph-Powered Application.*

As we have seen, the combined ego network is represented as a list of edges. We can create an undirected graph from a list of edges using networkx as follows:

```
G = nx.read_edgelist("facebook_combined.txt", create_using=nx.
Graph(), nodetype=int)
```

Let's print some basic information about the graph:

```
print(nx.info(G))
```

The output should be as follows:

```
Name:
Type: Graph
Number of nodes: 4039
Number of edges: 88234
Average degree:   43.6910
```

As we can see, the aggregated network contains 4039 nodes and 88234 edges. This is a fairly connected network with a number of edges more than 20 times the number of nodes. Indeed, several clusters should be present in the aggregated networks (likely the small worlds of each ego user).

Drawing the network will also help in better understanding what we are going to analyze. We can draw the graph using networkx as follows:

```
nx.draw_networkx(G, pos=spring_pos, with_labels=False, node_
size=35)
```

The output should be as follows:

Figure 6.1 – The aggregated Facebook ego network

We can observe the presence of highly interconnected hubs. This is interesting from a social network analysis point of view since they might be the result of underlying social mechanisms that can be further investigated for better understanding the structure of an individual's relationships with respect to their world.

Before continuing our analysis, let's save the IDs of the ego user nodes inside the network. We can retrieve them from the files contained in the `facebook.tar.gz` archive.

First, unpack the archive. The extracted folder will be named `facebook`. Let's run the following Python code for retrieving the IDs by taking the first part of each filename:

```
ego_nodes = set([int(name.split('.')[0]) for name in
os.listdir("facebook/")])
```

We are now ready for analyzing the graph. In particular, in the next section, we will better understand the structure of the graph by inspecting its properties. This will help us to have a clearer idea of its topology and its relevant characteristics.

Network topology and community detection

Understanding the topology of the network as well as the role of its nodes is a crucial step in the analysis of a social network. It is important to keep in mind that, in this context, nodes are actually users, each with their own interests, habits, and behaviors. Such knowledge will be extremely useful when performing predictions and/or finding insights.

We will be using `networkx` to compute most of the useful metrics we have seen in *Chapter 1, Getting Started with Graphs*. We will try to give them an interpretation to collect insight into the graph. Let's begin as usual, by importing the required libraries and defining some variables that we will use throughout the code:

```
import os
import math
import numpy as np
import networkx as nx
import matplotlib.pyplot as plt
default_edge_color = 'gray'
default_node_color = '#407cc9'
enhanced_node_color = '#f5b042'
enhanced_edge_color = '#cc2f04'
```

We can now proceed to the analysis.

Topology overview

As we have already seen before, our combined network has 4,039 nodes and more than 80,000 edges. The next metric we will compute is assortativity. It will reveal information about the tendency of users to be connected with users with a similar degree. We can do that as follows:

```
assortativity = nx.degree_pearson_correlation_coefficient(G)
```

The output should be as follows:

```
0.06357722918564912
```

Here we can observe a positive assortativity, likely showing that well-connected individuals associate with other well-connected individuals (as we have seen in *Chapter 1, Getting Started with Graphs*). This is expected since inside each circle users might tend to be highly connected to each other.

Transitivity could also help at better understanding how individuals are connected. Recall transitivity indicates the mean probability that two people with a common friend are themselves friends:

```
t = nx.transitivity(G)
```

The output should be as follows:

```
0.5191742775433075
```

Here we have the probability of around 50% that two friends can or cannot have common friends.

The observation is also confirmed by computing the average clustering coefficient. Indeed, it can be considered as an alternative definition of transitivity:

```
aC = nx.average_clustering(G)
```

The output should be as follows:

```
0.6055467186200876
```

Notice that the clustering coefficient tends to be higher than transitivity. Indeed, by definition, it puts more weight on vertices with a low degree, since they have a limited number of possible pairs of neighbors (the denominator of the local clustering coefficient).

Node centrality

Once we have a clearer idea of what the overall topology looks like, we can proceed by investigating the importance of each individual inside the network. As we have seen in *Chapter 1*, *Getting Started with Graphs*, the first definition of importance can be given by means of the betweenness centrality metric. It measures how many shortest paths pass through a given node, giving an idea of how *central* that node is for the spreading of information inside the network. We can compute it using the following:

```
bC = nx.betweenness_centrality(G)
np.mean(list(bC.values()))
```

The output should be as follows:

```
0.0006669573568730229
```

The average betweenness centrality is pretty low, which is understandable given the large amount of non-bridging nodes inside the network. However, we could collect better insight by visual inspection of the graph. In particular, we will draw the combined ego network by enhancing nodes with the highest betweenness centrality. Let's define a proper function for this:

```
def draw_metric(G, dct, spring_pos):
    top = 10
    max_nodes =  sorted(dct.items(), key=lambda v: -v[1])[:top]
```

```
    max_keys = [key for key,_ in max_nodes]
    max_vals = [val*300 for _, val in max_nodes]
    plt.axis("off")
    nx.draw_networkx(G,
                     pos=spring_pos,
                     cmap='Blues',
                     edge_color=default_edge_color,
                     node_color=default_node_color,
                     node_size=3,
                     alpha=0.4,
                     with_labels=False)

    nx.draw_networkx_nodes(G,
                           pos=spring_pos,
                           nodelist=max_keys,
                           node_color=enhanced_edge_color,
                           node_size=max_vals)
```

Now let's invoke it as follows:

```
    draw_metric(G,bC,spring_pos)
```

The output should be as follows:

Figure 6.2 – Betweenness centrality

Let's also inspect the degree centrality of each node. Since this metric is related to the number of neighbors of a node, we will have a clearer idea of how well the nodes are connected to each other:

```
deg_C = nx.degree_centrality(G)
 np.mean(list(deg_C.values()))
 draw_metric(G,deg_C,spring_pos)
```

The output should be as follows:

```
0.010819963503439287
```

Here is a representation of the degree centrality:

Figure 6.3 – Degree centrality

Finally, let's also have a look at the closeness centrality. This will help us understand how close nodes are to each other in terms of the shortest path:

```
clos_C = nx.closeness_centrality(G)
 np.mean(list(clos_C.values()))
 draw_metric(G,clos_C,spring_pos)
```

The output should be as follows:

```
0.2761677635668376
```

Here is a representation of the closeness centrality:

Figure 6.4 – Closeness centrality

From the centrality analysis, it is interesting to observe that each central node seems to be part of a sort of community (this is reasonable, since the central nodes might correspond to the ego nodes of the network). It is also interesting to notice the presence of a bunch of highly interconnected nodes (especially from the closeness centrality analysis). Let's thus identify these communities in the next part of our analysis.

Community detection

Since we are performing social network analysis, it is worth exploring one of the most interesting graph structures for social networks: communities. If you use Facebook, it is very likely that your friends reflect different aspects of your life: friends from an educational environment (high school, college, and so on), friends from your weekly football match, friends you have met at parties, and so on.

An interesting aspect of social network analysis is to automatically identify such groups. This can be done automatically, inferring them from topological properties, or semi-automatically, exploiting some prior insight.

One good criterion is to try to minimize intra-community edges (edges connecting members of different communities) while maximizing inter-community edges (connecting members within the same community).

We can do that in `networkx` as follows:

```
import community
parts = community.best_partition(G)
  values = [parts.get(node) for node in G.nodes()]
n_sizes = [5]*len(G.nodes())
```

```
plt.axis("off")
```
```
nx.draw_networkx(G, pos=spring_pos, cmap=plt.get_cmap("Blues"),
edge_color=default_edge_color, node_color=values, node_size=n_
sizes, with_labels=False)
```

The output should be as follows:

Figure 6.5 – Detected communities using networkx

In this context, it is also interesting to investigate whether the ego users occupy some roles inside the detected communities. Let's enhance the size and color of the ego user nodes as follows:

```
for node in ego_nodes:
    n_sizes[node] = 250
```
```
nodes = nx.draw_networkx_nodes(G,spring_pos,ego_nodes,node_
color=[parts.get(node) for node in ego_nodes])
```
```
nodes.set_edgecolor(enhanced_node_color)
```

The output should be as follows:

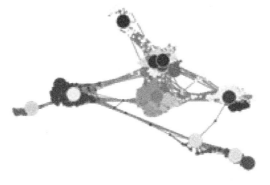

Figure 6.6 – Detected communities using networkx with the ego users node size enhanced

It is interesting to notice that some ego users belong to the same community. It is possible that ego users are actual friends on Facebook, and therefore their ego networks are partially shared.

We have now completed our basic understanding of the graph structure. We now know that some important nodes can be identified inside the network. We have also seen the presence of well-defined communities to which those nodes belong. Keep in mind these observations while performing the next part of the analysis, which is applying machine learning methods for supervised and unsupervised tasks.

Embedding for supervised and unsupervised tasks

Social media represents, nowadays, one of the most interesting and rich sources of information. Every day, thousands of new connections arise, new users join communities, and billions of posts are shared. Graphs mathematically represent all those interactions, helping to make order of all such spontaneous and unstructured traffic.

When dealing with social graphs, there are many interesting problems that can be addressed using machine learning. Under the correct settings, it is possible to extract useful insights from this huge amount of data, for improving your marketing strategy, identifying users with dangerous behaviors (for example, terrorist networks), and predicting the likelihood that a user will read your new post.

Specifically, link prediction is one of the most interesting and important research topics in this field. Depending on what a *connection* in your social graph represents, by predicting future edges, you will be able to predict your next suggested friend, the next suggested movie, and which product you are likely to buy.

As we have already seen in *Chapter 5, Problems with Machine Learning on Graphs*, the link prediction task aims at forecasting the likelihood of a future connection between two nodes and it can be solved using several machine learning algorithms.

In the next examples, we will be applying supervised and unsupervised machine learning graph embedding algorithms for predicting future connections on the SNAP Facebook social graph. Furthermore, we will evaluate the contribution of node features in the prediction task.

Task preparation

In order to perform the link prediction task, it is necessary to prepare our dataset. The problem will be treated as a supervised task. Pairs of nodes will be provided to each algorithm as input, while the target will be binary, that is, *connected* if the two nodes are actually connected in the network, and *not connected* otherwise.

Since we aim to cast this problem as a supervised learning task, we need to create a training and testing dataset. We will therefore create two new subgraphs with the same numbers of nodes but different numbers of edges (as some edges will be removed and treated as positive samples for training/testing the algorithm).

The `stellargraph` library provides a useful tool for splitting the data and creating training and test reduced subgraphs. This process is similar to the one we have already seen in *Chapter 5, Problems with Machine Learning on Graphs*:

```
from sklearn.model_selection import train_test_split
from stellargraph.data import EdgeSplitter
from stellargraph import StellarGraph
edgeSplitter = EdgeSplitter(G)
graph_test, samples_test, labels_test = edgeSplitter.train_
test_split(p=0.1, method="global", seed=24)
edgeSplitter = EdgeSplitter(graph_test, G)
 graph_train, samples_train, labels_train = edgeSplitter.train_
test_split(p=0.1, method="global", seed=24)
```

We are using the `EdgeSplitter` class to extract a fraction (p=10%) of all the edges in `G`, as well as the same number of negative edges, in order to obtain a reduced graph, `graph_test`. The `train_test_split` method also returns a list of node pairs, `samples_test` (where each pair corresponds to an existing or not existing edge in the graph), and a list of binary targets (`labels_test`) of the same length of the `samples_test` list. Then, from such a reduced graph, we are repeating the operation to obtain another reduced graph, `graph_train`, as well as the corresponding `samples_train` and `labels_train` lists.

We will be comparing three different methods for predicting missing edges:

- **Method 1**: node2vec will be used to learn a node embedding without supervision. The learned embedding will be used as input for a supervised classification algorithm to determine whether the input pair is actually connected.

- **Method 2**: The graph neural network-based algorithm GraphSAGE will be used to jointly learn the embedding and perform the classification task.

- **Method 3**: Hand-crafted features will be extracted from the graph and used as inputs for a supervised classifier, together with the nodes' IDs.

Let's analyze them in more detail.

node2vec-based link prediction

The herein proposed method is carried out in several steps:

1. We use node2vec to generate node embeddings without supervision from the training graph. This can be done using the node2vec Python implementation, as we have already seen in *Chapter 5, Problems with Machine Learning on Graphs*:

```
from node2vec import Node2Vec
node2vec = Node2Vec(graph_train)
model = node2vec.fit()
```

2. Then, we use HadamardEmbedder for generating an embedding for each pair of embedded nodes. Such feature vectors will be used as input to train the classifier:

```
from node2vec.edges import HadamardEmbedder

edges_embs = HadamardEmbedder(keyed_vectors=model.wv)
 train_embeddings = [edges_embs[str(x[0]),str(x[1])] for
x in samples_train]
```

3. It's time for training our supervised classifier. We will be using the RandomForest classifier, a powerful decision tree-based ensemble algorithm:

```
from sklearn.ensemble import RandomForestClassifier
from sklearn import metrics
rf = RandomForestClassifier(n_estimators=10)
 rf.fit(train_embeddings, labels_train);
```

4. Finally, let's apply the trained model for creating the embedding of the test set:

```
edges_embs = HadamardEmbedder(keyed_vectors=model.wv)
test_embeddings = [edges_embs[str(x[0]),str(x[1])] for x
in samples_test]
```

5. Now we are ready to perform the prediction on the test set using our trained model:

```
y_pred = rf.predict(test_embeddings)
print('Precision:', metrics.precision_score(labels_test,
y_pred))
print('Recall:', metrics.recall_score(labels_test, y_
pred))
print('F1-Score:', metrics.f1_score(labels_test, y_pred))
```

6. The output should be as follows:

```
Precision: 0.9701333333333333
Recall: 0.9162573983125551
F1-Score: 0.9424260086781945
```

Not bad at all! We can observe that the node2vec-based embedding already provides a powerful representation for actually predicting links on the combined Facebook ego network.

GraphSAGE-based link prediction

Next, we will use GraphSAGE for learning node embeddings and classifying edges. We will build a two-layer GraphSAGE architecture that, given labeled pairs of nodes, outputs a pair of node embeddings. Then, a fully connected neural network will be used to process these embeddings and produce link predictions. Notice that the GraphSAGE model and the fully connected network will be concatenated and trained end to end so that the embeddings learning stage is influenced by the predictions.

Featureless approach

Before starting, we may recall from *Chapters 4, Supervised Graph Learning*, and *Chapter 5, Problems with Machine Learning on Graphs*, that GraphSAGE needs node descriptors (features). Such features may or may not be available in your dataset. Let's begin our analysis by not considering available node features. In this case, a common approach is to assign to each node a one-hot feature vector of length $|V|$ (the number of nodes in the graph), where only the cell corresponding to the given node is 1, while the remaining cells are 0.

This can be done in Python and `networkx` as follows:

```python
eye = np.eye(graph_train.number_of_nodes())
fake_features = {n:eye[n] for n in G.nodes()}
nx.set_node_attributes(graph_train, fake_features, "fake")
eye = np.eye(graph_test.number_of_nodes())
fake_features = {n:eye[n] for n in G.nodes()}
nx.set_node_attributes(graph_test, fake_features, "fake")
```

In the preceding code snippet, we did the following:

1. We created an identity matrix of size $|V|$. Each row of the matrix is the one-hot vector we need for each node in the graph.

2. Then, we created a Python dictionary where, for each `node ID` (used as the key), we assign the corresponding row of the previously created identity matrix.

3. Finally, the dictionary was passed to the `networkx` `set_node_attributes` function to assign the "fake" features to each node in the `networkx` graph.

Notice that the process is repeated for both the training and test graph.

The next step will be defining the generator that will be used to feed the model. We will be using the `stellargraph` `GraphSAGELinkGenerator` for this, which essentially provides the model with pairs of nodes as input:

```python
from stellargraph.mapper import GraphSAGELinkGenerator
batch_size = 64
num_samples = [4, 4]
# convert graph_train and graph_test for stellargraph
sg_graph_train = StellarGraph.from_networkx(graph_train, node_features="fake")
sg_graph_test = StellarGraph.from_networkx(graph_test, node_features="fake")
train_gen = GraphSAGELinkGenerator(sg_graph_train, batch_size, num_samples)
train_flow = train_gen.flow(samples_train, labels_train, shuffle=True, seed=24)
test_gen = GraphSAGELinkGenerator(sg_graph_test, batch_size, num_samples)
test_flow = test_gen.flow(samples_test, labels_test, seed=24)
```

Note that we also need to define `batch_size` (number of inputs per minibatch) and the number of first- and second-hop neighbor samples that GraphSAGE should consider.

Finally, we are ready to create the model:

```
from stellargraph.layer import GraphSAGE, link_classification
from tensorflow import keras
layer_sizes = [20, 20]
graphsage = GraphSAGE(layer_sizes=layer_sizes, generator=train_
gen, bias=True, dropout=0.3)
x_inp, x_out = graphsage.in_out_tensors()
# define the link classifier
prediction = link_classification(output_dim=1, output_
act="sigmoid", edge_embedding_method="ip")(x_out)
model = keras.Model(inputs=x_inp, outputs=prediction)
model.compile(
    optimizer=keras.optimizers.Adam(lr=1e-3),
    loss=keras.losses.mse,
    metrics=["acc"],
)
```

In the preceding snippet, we are creating a GraphSAGE model with two hidden layers of size 20, each with a bias term and a dropout layer for reducing overfitting. Then, the output of the GraphSAGE part of the module is concatenated with a `link_classification` layer that takes pairs of node embeddings (output of GraphSAGE), uses binary operators (inner product; `ip` in our case) to produce edge embeddings, and finally passes them through a fully connected neural network for classification.

The model is optimized via the Adam optimizer (learning rate = `1e-3`) using the mean squared error as a loss function.

Let's train the model for 10 epochs:

```
epochs = 10
history = model.fit(train_flow, epochs=epochs, validation_
data=test_flow)
```

The output should be as follows:

```
Epoch 18/20
loss: 0.4921 - acc: 0.8476 - val_loss: 0.5251 - val_acc: 0.7884
Epoch 19/20
loss: 0.4935 - acc: 0.8446 - val_loss: 0.5247 - val_acc: 0.7922
Epoch 20/20
loss: 0.4922 - acc: 0.8476 - val_loss: 0.5242 - val_acc: 0.7913
```

Once trained, let's compute the performance metrics over the test set:

```
from sklearn import metrics
y_pred = np.round(model.predict(train_flow)).flatten()
print('Precision:', metrics.precision_score(labels_train, y_
pred))
print('Recall:', metrics.recall_score(labels_train, y_pred))
print('F1-Score:', metrics.f1_score(labels_train, y_pred))
```

The output should be as follows:

```
Precision: 0.7156476303969199
Recall: 0.983125550938169
F1-Score: 0.8283289124668435
```

As we can observe, performances are lower than the ones obtained in the node2vec-based approach. However, we are not considering real node features yet, which could represent a great source of information. Let's do that in the following test.

Introducing node features

The process of extracting node features for the combined ego network is quite verbose. This is because, as we have explained in the first part of the chapter, each ego network is described using several files, as well as all the feature names and values. We have written useful functions for parsing all the ego network in order to extract the node features. You can find their implementation in the Python notebook provided in the GitHub repository. Here, let's just briefly summarize how they work:

- The load_features function parses each ego network and creates two dictionaries:

    a. feature_index, which maps numeric indices to feature names

    b. inverted_feature_indexes, which maps names to numeric indices

- The `parse_nodes` function receives the combined ego network G and the ego nodes' IDs. Then, each ego node in the network is assigned with the corresponding features previously loaded using the `load_features` function.

Let's invoke them in order to load a feature vector for each node in the combined ego network:

```
load_features()
parse_nodes(G, ego_nodes)
```

We can easily check the result by printing the information of one node in the network (for example, the node with ID 0):

```
print(G.nodes[0])
```

The output should be as follows:

```
{'features': array([1., 1., 1., ..., 0., 0., 0.])}
```

As we can observe, the node has a dictionary containing a key named `features`. The corresponding value is the feature vector assigned to this node.

We are now ready to repeat the same steps used before for training the GraphSAGE model, this time using `features` as the key when converting the `networkx` graph to the `StellarGraph` format:

```
sg_graph_train = StellarGraph.from_networkx(graph_train, node_
features="features")
sg_graph_test = StellarGraph.from_networkx(graph_test, node_
features="features")
```

Finally, as we have done before, we create the generators, compile the model, and train it for 10 epochs:

```
train_gen = GraphSAGELinkGenerator(sg_graph_train, batch_size,
num_samples)
train_flow = train_gen.flow(samples_train, labels_train,
shuffle=True, seed=24)
test_gen = GraphSAGELinkGenerator(sg_graph_test, batch_size,
num_samples)
test_flow = test_gen.flow(samples_test, labels_test, seed=24)
layer_sizes = [20, 20]
```

```
graphsage = GraphSAGE(layer_sizes=layer_sizes, generator=train_
gen, bias=True, dropout=0.3)
```

```
x_inp, x_out = graphsage.in_out_tensors()
```

```
prediction = link_classification(output_dim=1, output_
act="sigmoid", edge_embedding_method="ip")(x_out)
```

```
model = keras.Model(inputs=x_inp, outputs=prediction)
```

```
model.compile(
    optimizer=keras.optimizers.Adam(lr=1e-3),
    loss=keras.losses.mse,
    metrics=["acc"],
)
```

```
epochs = 10
```

```
history = model.fit(train_flow, epochs=epochs, validation_
data=test_flow)
```

Notice that we are using the same hyperparameters (including the number of layers, batch size, and learning rate) as well as the random seed, to ensure a fair comparison between the models.

The output should be as follows:

```
Epoch 18/20
loss: 0.1337 - acc: 0.9564 - val_loss: 0.1872 - val_acc: 0.9387
Epoch 19/20
loss: 0.1324 - acc: 0.9560 - val_loss: 0.1880 - val_acc: 0.9340
Epoch 20/20
loss: 0.1310 - acc: 0.9585 - val_loss: 0.1869 - val_acc: 0.9365
```

Let's evaluate the model performance:

```
from sklearn import metrics
y_pred = np.round(model.predict(train_flow)).flatten()
print('Precision:', metrics.precision_score(labels_train, y_
pred))
print('Recall:', metrics.recall_score(labels_train, y_pred))
print('F1-Score:', metrics.f1_score(labels_train, y_pred))
```

We can check the output:

```
Precision: 0.7895418326693228
Recall: 0.9982369978592117
F1-Score: 0.8817084700517213
```

As we can see, the introduction of real node features has brought a good improvement, even if the best performances are still the ones achieved using the node2vec approach.

Finally, we will evaluate a shallow embedding approach where hand-crafted features will be used for training a supervised classifier.

Hand-crafted features for link prediction

As we have already seen in *Chapter 4*, *Supervised Graph Learning*, shallow embedding methods represent a simple yet powerful approach for dealing with supervised tasks. Basically, for each input edge, we will compute a set of metrics that will be given as input to a classifier.

In this example, for each input edge represented as a pair of nodes (u,v), four metrics will be considered, namely the following:

- **Shortest path**: The length of the shortest path between u and v. If u and v are directly connected through an edge, this edge will be removed before computing the shortest path. The value 0 will be used if u is not reachable from v.

- **The Jaccard coefficient**: Given a pair of nodes (u,v), it is defined as the intersection over a union of the set of neighbors of u and v. Formally, let $s(u)$ be the set of neighbors of the node u and $s(v)$ be the set of neighbors of the node v:

$$j(u, v) = \frac{s(u) \cap s(v)}{s(u) \cup s(v)}$$

- **The u centrality**: The degree centrality computed for node v.
- **The v centrality**: The degree centrality computed for node u.
- **The u community**: The community ID assigned to node u using the Louvain heuristic.
- **The v community**: The community ID assigned to node v using the Louvain heuristic.

We have written a useful function for computing these metrics using Python and `networkx`. You can find the implementation in the Python notebook provided in the GitHub repository.

Let's compute the features for each edge in the training and the test set:

```
feat_train = get_hc_features(graph_train, samples_train,
labels_train)
```
```
feat_test = get_hc_features(graph_test, samples_test, labels_
test)
```

In the proposed shallow approach, these features will be directly used as input for a Random Forest classifier. We will use its scikit-learn implementation as follows:

```
from sklearn.ensemble import RandomForestClassifier
from sklearn import metrics
rf = RandomForestClassifier(n_estimators=10)
rf.fit(feat_train, labels_train);
```

The preceding lines automatically instantiate and train a RandomForest classifier using the edge features we have computed before. We are now ready to compute the performance as follows:

```
y_pred = rf.predict(feat_test)
print('Precision:', metrics.precision_score(labels_test, y_
pred))
 print('Recall:', metrics.recall_score(labels_test, y_pred))
print('F1-Score:', metrics.f1_score(labels_test, y_pred))
```

The output will be as follows:

```
Precision: 0.9636952636282395
Recall: 0.9777853337866939
F1-Score: 0.970891701828411
```

Surprisingly, the shallow method based on hand-crafted features performs better than the others.

Summary of results

In the preceding examples, we have trained three algorithms on learning, with and without supervision, useful embeddings for link prediction. In the following table, we summarize the results:

Algorithm	Embedding	Node Features	Precision	Recall	F1-Score
node2vec	Unsupervised	No	0.97	0.92	0.94
GraphSAGE	Supervised	Yes	0.72	0.98	0.83
GraphSAGE	Supervised	No	0.79	1.00	0.88
Shallow	manual	No	0.96	0.98	0.97

Table 6.1 – Summary of the results achieved for the link prediction task

As shown in *Table 6.1*, the node2vec-based method is already able to achieve a high level of performance without supervision and per-node information. Such high results might be related to the particular structure of the combined ego network. Due to the high sub-modularity of the network (since it is composed of several ego networks), predicting whether two users will be connected or not might be highly related to the way the two candidate nodes are connected inside the network. For example, there might be a systematic situation in which two users, both connected to several users in the same ego network, have a high chance of being connected as well. On the other hand, two users belonging to different ego networks, or *very far* from each other, are likely to not be connected, making the prediction task easier. This is also confirmed by the high results achieved using the shallow method.

Such a situation might be confusing, instead, for more complicated algorithms like GraphSAGE, especially when node features are involved. For example, two users might share similar interests, making them very similar. However, they might belong to different ego networks, where the corresponding ego users live in two very different parts of the world. So, similar users, which in principle should be connected, are not. However, it is also possible that such algorithms are predicting something further in the future. Recall that the combined ego network is a timestamp of a particular situation in a given period of time. Who knows how it might have evolved right now!

Interpreting machine learning algorithms is probably the most interesting challenge of machine learning itself. For this reason, we should always interpret results with care. Our suggestion is always to dig into the dataset and try to give an explanation of your results.

Finally, it is important to remark that each of the algorithms was not tuned for the purpose of this demonstration. Different results can be obtained by properly tuning each hyperparameter and we highly suggest you try to do this.

Summary

In this chapter, we have seen how machine learning can be useful for solving practical machine learning tasks on social network graphs. Furthermore, we have seen how future connections can be predicted on the SNAP Facebook combined ego network.

We reviewed graph analysis concepts and used graph-derived metrics to collect insight on the social graph. Then, we benchmarked several machine learning algorithms on the link prediction task, evaluating their performance and trying to give them interpretations.

In the next chapter, we will focus on how similar approaches can be used to analyze a corpus of documents using text analytics and natural language processing.

7
Text Analytics and Natural Language Processing Using Graphs

Nowadays, a vast amount of information is available in the form of text in terms of natural written language. The very same book you are reading right now is one such example. The news you read every morning, the tweets or the Facebook posts you sent/read earlier, the reports you write for a school assignment, the emails we write continuously – these are all examples of information we exchange via written documents and text. It is undoubtedly the most common way of indirect interaction, as opposed to direct interaction such as talking or gesticulating. It is, therefore, crucial to be able to leverage such kinds of information and extract insights from documents and texts.

The vast amount of information present nowadays in this form has determined the great development and recent advances in the field of **natural language processing** (NLP).

In this chapter, we will show you how to process natural language texts and review some basic models that allow us to structure text information. Using the information that's been extracted from a corpus of documents, we will show you how to create networks that can be analyzed using some of the techniques we have seen in previous chapters. In particular, using a tagged corpus we will show you how to develop both supervised (classification models to classify documents in pre-determined topics) and unsupervised (community detection to discover new topics) algorithms.

The chapter covers the following topics:

- Providing a quick overview of a dataset
- Understanding the main concepts and tools used in NLP
- Creating graphs from a corpus of documents
- Building a document topic classifier

Technical requirements

We will be using *Python 3.8* for all our exercises. The following is a list of Python libraries that you must install for this chapter using pip. To do this, run, for example, `pip install networkx==2.4` on the command line and so on:

```
networkx==2.4
scikit-learn==0.24.0
stellargraph==1.2.1
spacy==3.0.3
pandas==1.1.3
numpy==1.19.2
node2vec==0.3.3
Keras==2.0.2
tensorflow==2.4.1
communities==2.2.0
gensim==3.8.3
matplotlib==3.3.4
nltk==3.5
fasttext==0.9.2
```

All the code files relevant to this chapter are available at `https://github.com/PacktPublishing/Graph-Machine-Learning/tree/main/Chapter07`.

Providing a quick overview of a dataset

To show you how to process a corpus of documents with the aim of extracting relevant information, we will be using a dataset derived from a well-known benchmark in the field of NLP: the so-called **Reuters-21578**. The original dataset includes a set of 21,578 news articles that were published in the financial Reuters newswire in 1987, which were assembled and indexed in categories. The original dataset has a very skewed distribution, with some categories appearing only in the training set or in the test set. For this reason, we will use a modified version, known as ** ApteMod**, also referred to as *Reuters-21578 Distribution 1.0*, that has a smaller skew distribution and consistent labels between the training and test datasets.

Even though these articles are a bit outdated, the dataset has been used in a plethora of papers on NLP and still represents a dataset that's often used for benchmarking algorithms.

Indeed, Reuters-21578 contains enough documents for interesting post-processing and insights. A corpus with a larger number of documents can easily be found nowadays (see, for instance, `https://github.com/niderhoff/nlp-datasets` for an overview of the most common ones), but they may require larger storage and computational power so that they can be processed. In *Chapter 9, Building a Data-Driven, Graph-Powered Application*, we will show you some of the tools and libraries that can be used to scale out your application and analysis.

Each document of the Reuters-21578 dataset is provided with a set of labels that represent its content. This makes it a perfect benchmark for testing both supervised and unsupervised algorithms. The Reuters-21578 dataset can easily be downloaded using the `nltk` library (which is a very useful library for post-processing documents):

```python
from nltk.corpus import reuters
corpus = pd.DataFrame([
    {"id": _id,
     "text": reuters.raw(_id).replace("\n", ""),
     "label": reuters.categories(_id)}
    for _id in reuters.fileids()
])
```

As you will see from inspecting the `corpus` DataFrame, the IDs are in the form `training/{ID}` and `test/{ID}`, which makes it clear which documents should be used for training and for testing. To start, let's list all the topics and see how many documents there are per topic using the following code:

```
from collections import Counter
Counter([label for document_labels in corpus["label"] for label
in document_labels]).most_common()
```

The Reuters-21578 dataset includes 90 different topics with a significant degree of unbalance between classes, with almost 37% of the documents in the `most common` category and only 0.01% in each of the five least common categories. As you can see from inspecting the text, some of the documents have some newline characters embedded, which can easily be removed in the first text cleaning stage:

```
corpus["clean_text"] = corpus["text"].apply(
    lambda x: x.replace("\n", "")
)
```

Now that we have loaded the data in memory, we can start analyzing it. In the next subsection, we will show you some of the main tools that can be used for dealing with unstructured text data. They will help you extract structured information so that it can be used with ease.

Understanding the main concepts and tools used in NLP

When processing documents, the first analytical step is certainly to infer the document language. Most analytical engines that are used in NLP tasks are, in fact, trained on documents in a specific language and should only be used for such a language. Some attempts to build cross-language models (see, for instance, multi-lingual embeddings such as https://fasttext.cc/docs/en/aligned-vectors.html and https://github.com/google-research/bert/blob/master/multilingual.md) have recently gained increasing popularity, although they still represent a small portion of NLP models. Therefore, it is very common to first infer the language so that you can use the correct downstream analytical NLP pipeline.

You can use different methods to infer the language. One very simple yet effective approach relies on looking for the most common words of a language (the so-called `stopwords`, such as `the`, `and`, `be`, `to`, `of`, and so on) and building a score based on their frequencies. Its precision, however, tends to be limited to short text and does not make use of the word's positioning and context. On the other hand, Python has many libraries that use more elaborated logic, allowing us to infer the language in a more precise manner. Some such libraries are `fasttext`, `polyglot`, and `langdetect`, to name just a few.

As an example, we will use `fasttext` in the following code, which can be integrated with very few lines and provides support for more than 150 languages. The language can be inferred for all documents using the following snippet:

```
from langdetect import detect
import numpy as np
def getLanguage(text: str):
    try:
        return langdetect.detect(text)
    except:
        return np.nan
corpus["language"] = corpus["text"].apply(langdetect.detect)
```

As you will see in the output, there seem to be documents in languages other than English. Indeed, these documents are often either very short or have a strange structure, which means they're not actual news articles. When documents represent text that a human would read and label as news, the model is generally rather precise and accurate.

Now that we have inferred the language, we can continue with the language-dependent steps of the analytical pipeline. For the following tasks, we will be using spaCy, which is an extremely powerful library that allows us to embed state-of-the-art NLP models with very few lines of code. After installing the library with `pip install spaCy`, language-specific models can be integrated by simply installing them using the spaCy download utility. For instance, the following command can be used to download and install the English model:

```
python -m spacy download en_core_web_sm
```

Now, we should have the language models for English ready to use. Let's see which information it can provide. Using spaCy is extremely simple and, using just one line of code, can embed the computation as a very rich set of information. Let's start by applying the model to one of the documents in the Reuters corpus:

> **SUBROTO SAYS INDONESIA SUPPORTS TIN PACT EXTENSION**
>
> Mines and Energy Minister Subroto confirmed Indonesian support for an extension of the sixth **International Tin Agreement (ITA)**, but said a new pact was not necessary. Asked by Reuters to clarify his statement on Monday in which he said the pact should be allowed to lapse, Subroto said Indonesia was ready to back extension of the ITA. "We can support extension of the sixth agreement," he said. "But a seventh accord we believe to be unnecessary." The sixth ITA will expire at the end of June unless a two-thirds majority of members vote for an extension.

spacy can easily be applied just by loading the model and applying it to the text:

```
nlp = spacy.load('en_core_web_md')
parsed = nlp(text)
```

The parsed object, which is returned by spacy, has several fields due to many models being combined into a single pipeline. These provide a different level of text structuring. Let's examine them one by one:

- **Text segmentation and tokenization**: This is a process that aims to split a document into its periods, sentences, and single words (or tokens). This step is generally very important for all subsequent analyses and usually leverages punctuation, black spaces, and newlines characters to infer the best document segmentation. The segmentation engine provided in spacy generally works fairly well. However, please note that, depending on the context, a bit of model tuning or rule modification might be necessary. For instance, when you're dealing with short texts that contain slang, emoticons, links, and hashtags, a better choice for text segmentation and tokenization may be TweetTokenizer, which is included in the nltk library. Depending on the context, we encourage you to explore other possible segmentations.

In the document returned by `spacy`, the sentence segmentation can be found in the `sents` attribute of the `parsed` object. Each sentence can be iterated over its token by simply using the following code:

```
for sent in parsed.sents:
    for token in sent:
        print(token)
```

Each token is a spaCy `Span` object that has attributes that specify the type of token and further characterization that's introduced by the other models.

- **Part-of**-Speech Tagger: Once the text has been divided into its single words (also referred to as tokens), the next step is to associate each token with a **Part-of-Speech (PoS)** tag; that is, its grammatical type. The inferred tags are usually nouns, verbs, auxiliary verbs, adjectives, and so on. The engines that are used for PoS tagging are usually models that have been trained to classify tokens based on a large, labeled corpus, where each token has an associated PoS tag. Being trained on actual data, they learn to recognize the common pattern within a language; for instance, the word "the" (which is a determinative article, `DET`) is usually followed by a noun, and so on. When using spaCy, the information about PoS tagging is usually stored in the `label_` attribute of the `Span` object. The types of tags that are available can be found at `https://spacy.io/models/en`. Conversely, you can get a human-readable value for a given type using the `spacy.explain` function.

- **Named Entity Recognition (NER)**: This analytical step is generally a statistical model that is trained to recognize the type of nouns that appear within the text. Some common examples of entities are Organization, Person, Geographic Location and Addresses, Products, Numbers, and Currencies. Given the context (the surrounding words), as well as the prepositions that are used, the model infers the most probable type of the entity, if any. As in other steps of the NLP pipeline, these models are also usually trained using a large, tagged dataset that they learn common patterns and structures from. In spaCy, the information about the document entities is usually stored in the `ents` attribute of the `parsed` object. spaCy also provides some utilities to nicely visualize the entities in a text using the `displacy` module:

```
displacy.render(parsed, style='ent', jupyter=True)
```

This results in the following output:

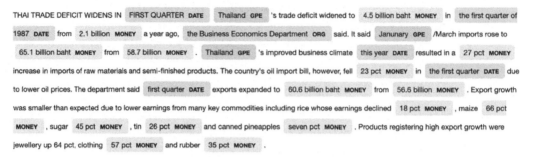

Figure 7.1 – Example of the spaCy output for the NER engine

- **Dependency parser**: The dependency parser is an extremely powerful engine that infers the relationships between tokens within a sentence. It basically allows you to build a syntactic tree of how words are related to each other. The root token (the one all the other tokens depend on) is usually the main verb of the sentence, that relates the subject and the object. Subjects and objects can in turn relate to other syntactic tokens, such as possessive pronouns, adjectives and/or articles. Besides, verbs can relate, beside subject and object, also to propositions, as well as other subordinate predicates. Let's look at a simple example that's been taken from the spaCy website: *Autonomous cars shift insurance liability towards manufacturers.*

  The following diagram shows the dependency tree for this example. Here, we can see that the main verb (or root), "shift," is related, via the subject-object relationship, to "cars" (subject) and "liability" (object). It also sustains the "towards" preposition. In the same way, the remaining nouns/adjectives ("Autonomous," "insurance," and "manufacturers") are related to either the subject, the object, or the preposition. Thus, spacy can be used to build a syntactic tree that can be navigated to identify relationships between the tokens. As we will see shortly, this information can be crucial when building knowledge graphs:

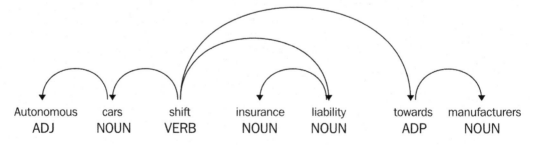

Figure 7.2 – Example of a syntactic dependency tree provided by spaCy

- **Lemmatizer**: Finally, the very last step of the analytical pipeline is the so-called lemmatizer, which allows us to reduce words to a common root to provide a cleaner version of it, thus reducing the morphological variation of words. Take, for instance, the verb *to be*. It can have many morphological variations, such as "is," "are," and "was," all of which are different, valid forms. Now, consider the difference between "car" and "cars." In most cases, we are not interested in these small differences that are introduced by morphology. The lemmatizer helps reduce tokens to their common, stable forms so that they can be processed easily. Usually, the lemmatizer is based on a set of rules that associate particular words (along with conjugations, plurals, inflections) with a common root form. More elaborated implementations may also use the context and the *PoS* tagging information to be more robust against homonyms. **Stemmers** are sometimes used in place of the lemmatizer. Instead of associating words with a common root form, stemmers usually removed the last part of the word to deal with inflectional and derivational variance. Stemmers are usually a bit simpler and are generally based on a set of rules that remove a certain pattern, rather than considering lexica and syntactic information. In spaCy, the lemmatized version of a token can be found in the Span object via the `lemma_` attribute.

As shown in the preceding diagram, spaCy pipelines can be easily integrated to process the entire corpus and store the results in our `corpus` DataFrame:

```
nlp = spacy.load('en_core_web_md')
sample_corpus["parsed"] = sample_corpus["clean_text"]\
    .apply(nlp)
```

This DataFrame represents the structured information of the documents. This will be the base of all our subsequent analysis. In the next section, we will show you how to build graphs while using such information.

Creating graphs from a corpus of documents

In this section, we will use the information we extracted in the previous section using the different text engines to build networks that relate the different information. In particular, we will focus on two kinds of graphs:

- **Knowledge-based graphs**, where we will use the semantic meaning of sentences to infer relationships between the different entities.

- **Bipartite graphs**, where we will be connecting the documents to the entities that appear in the text. We will then project the bipartite graph into a homogeneous graph, which will be made up of either document or entity nodes only.

Knowledge graphs

Knowledge graphs are very interesting as they not only relate entities but also provide a direction and a meaning to the relationship. For instance, let's take a look at the following relationship:

I (->) buy (->) a book

This is substantially different from the following relationship:

I (->) sell (->) a book

Besides the kind of relationship (buying or selling), it is also important to have a direction, where the subject and object are not treated symmetrically, but where there is a difference between who is performing the action and who is the target of such an action.

So, to create a knowledge graph, we need a function that can identify the **Subject-Verb-Object** (**SVO**) triplet for each sentence. This function can then be applied to all the sentences in the corpus; then, all the triplets can be aggregated to generate the corresponding graph.

The SVO extractor can be implemented on top of the enrichment provided by spaCy models. Indeed, the tagging provided by the dependency tree parser can be very helpful for separating main sentences and their subordinates, as well as identifying the SOV triplets. The business logic may need to consider a few special cases (such as conjunctions, negations, and preposition handling), but this can be encoded with a set of rules. Moreover, these rules may also change, depending on the specific use case, with slight variations to be tuned by the user. A base implementation of such rules can be found at https://github.com/NSchrading/intro-spacy-nlp/blob/master/subject_object_extraction.py. These have been slightly adopted for our scope and are included in the GitHub repository provided with this book. Using this helper function, we can compute all the triplets in the corpus and store them in our `corpus` DataFrame:

```python
from subject_object_extraction import findSVOs
corpus["triplets"] = corpus["parsed"].apply(
    lambda x: findSVOs(x, output="obj")
)
edge_list = pd.DataFrame([
    {
        "id": _id,
        "source": source.lemma_.lower(),
        "target": target.lemma_.lower(),
```

```
        "edge": edge.lemma_.lower()
    }
    for _id, triplets in corpus["triplets"].iteritems()
    for (source, (edge, neg), target) in triplets
])
```

The type of the connection (determined by the sentence's main predicate) is stored in the edge column. The first 10 most common relationships can be shown using the following command:

```
edges["edge"].value_counts().head(10)
```

The most common edge types correspond to very basic predicates. Indeed, together with very general verbs (such as be, have, tell, and give), we can also find predicates that are more related to a financial context (such as buy, sell, and make). Using all these edges, we can now create our knowledge-based graph using the networkx utility function:

```
G = nx.from_pandas_edgelist(
    edges, "source", "target",
    edge_attr=True, create_using=nx.MultiDiGraph()
)
```

By filtering the edge DataFrame and creating a subnetwork using this information, we can analyze specific relationship types, such as the lend edge:

```
G=nx.from_pandas_edgelist(
    edges[edges["edge"]=="lend"], "source", "target",
    edge_attr=True, create_using=nx.MultiDiGraph()
)
```

The following diagram shows the subgraph based on the *lend* relationships. As we can see, it already provides interesting economical insights, such as the economic relationships between countries, such as Venezuela-Ecuador and US-Sudan:

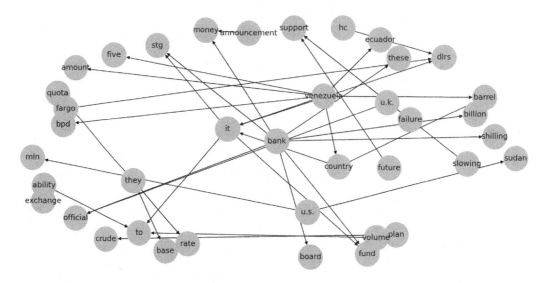

Figure 7.3 – Example of a portion of the knowledge graph for the edges related the lending relationships

You can play around with the preceding code by filtering the graph based on other relationships. We definitely encourage you to do so, in order to unveil further interesting insights from the knowledge graphs we just created. In the next section, we will show you another method that allows us to encode the information that's been extracted from the text into a graph structure. In doing so, we will also make use of a particular type of graph that we introduced in *Chapter 1, Bipartite Graphs*.

Bipartite document/entity graphs

Knowledge graphs can unveil and query aggregated information over entities. However, other graph representations are also possible and can be useful in other situations. For example, when you want to cluster documents semantically, the knowledge graph may not be the best data structure to use and analyze. Knowledge graphs are also not very effective at finding indirect relationships, such as identifying competitors, similar products, and so on, that do not often occur in the same sentence, but that often occur in the same document.

To address these limitations, we will encode the information present in the document in the form of a **bipartite graph**. For each document, we will extract the entities that are most relevant and connect a node, representing the document, with all the nodes representing the relevant entities in such a document. Each node may have multiple relationships: by definition, each document connects multiple entities. By contract, an entity can be referenced in multiple documents. As we will see, cross-referencing can be used to create a measure of similarity between entities and documents. This similarity can also be used for projecting the bipartite graph into one particular set of nodes – either the document nodes or the entity nodes.

To this aim, to build our bipartite graph, we need to extract the relevant entities of a document. The term *relevant entity* is clearly fuzzy and broad. In the current context, we will consider a relevant entity to be either a named entity (such as an organization, person, or location recognized by the NER engine) or a keyword; that is, a word (or a composition of words) that identifies and generally describes the document and its content. For instance, the suitable keywords for this book may be "graph," "network," "machine learning," "supervised model," and "unsupervised model." Many algorithms exist that extract keywords from a document. One very simple way to do this is based on the so-called TF-IDF score, which is based on building a score for each token (or group of tokens, often referred to as *grams*) that is proportional to the word count in the document (the **Term Frequency**, or **TF**) and to the inverse of the frequency of that word in a given corpus (the **Inverse Document Frequency**, or **IDF**):

$$\frac{c_{i,j}}{\sum c_{i,j}} \cdot log \frac{N}{1 + D_i}$$

Here, $c_{i,j}$ represents the count of word i in document j, N represents the number of documents in the corpus, and D_i is the document where the word i appears. Therefore, the TF-IDF score promotes words that are repeated many times in the document, penalizing words that are common and therefore might not be very representative for a document. There are also more sophisticated algorithms.

One method that is quite powerful and worth mentioning in the context of this book is indeed **TextRank**, since it is also based on a graph representation of the document. TextRank creates a network where the nodes are the single token and where the edges between them are created when tokens are within a certain window. After creating such a network, PageRank is used to compute the centrality for each token, which it does by providing a score that allows ranking within the document based on the centrality score. The most central nodes (up to a certain ratio, generally between 5% and 20% of the document size) are identified as candidate keywords. When two candidate keywords occur close to each other, they get aggregated into composite keywords, made up of multiple tokens. Implementations of TextRank are available in many NLP packages. One such package is `gensim`, which can be used in a straightforward manner:

```
from gensim.summarization import keywords
text = corpus["clean_text"][0]
 keywords(text, words=10, split=True, scores=True,
           pos_filter=('NN', 'JJ'), lemmatize=True)
```

This produces the following output:

```
[('trading', 0.4615130639538529),
 ('said', 0.3159855693494515),
 ('export', 0.2691553824958079),
 ('import', 0.17462010006456888),
 ('japanese electronics', 0.1360932626379031),

 ('industry', 0.1286043740379779),
 ('minister', 0.12229815662000462),
 ('japan', 0.11434500812642447),
 ('year', 0.10483992409352465)]
```

Here, the score represents the centrality, which represents the importance of a given token. As you can see, some composite tokens may also occur, such as `japanese electronics`. Keyword extraction can be implemented to compute the keywords for the entire corpus, thus storing the information in our `corpus` DataFrame:

```
corpus["keywords"] = corpus["clean_text"].apply(
    lambda text: keywords(
        text, words=10, split=True, scores=True,
        pos_filter=('NN', 'JJ'), lemmatize=True)
)
```

Besides the keywords, to build the bipartite graph, we also need to parse the named entities that were extracted by the NER engine, and then encode the information in a similar data format as the one that was used for the keywords. This can be done using a few utility functions:

```python
def extractEntities(ents, minValue=1,
                    typeFilters=["GPE", "ORG", "PERSON"]):
    entities = pd.DataFrame([
        {
            "lemma": e.lemma_,
            "lower": e.lemma_.lower(),
            "type": e.label_
        } for e in ents if hasattr(e, "label_")
    ])
    if len(entities)==0:
        return pd.DataFrame()
    g = entities.groupby(["type", "lower"])
    summary = pd.concat({
        "alias": g.apply(lambda x: x["lemma"].unique()),
        "count": g["lower"].count()
    }, axis=1)
    return summary[summary["count"]>1]\
            .loc[pd.IndexSlice[typeFilters, :, :]]


def getOrEmpty(parsed, _type):
    try:
        return list(parsed.loc[_type]["count"]\
            .sort_values(ascending=False).to_dict().items())
    except:
        return []
def toField(ents):
    typeFilters=["GPE", "ORG", "PERSON"]
    parsed = extractEntities(ents, 1, typeFilters)
    return pd.Series({_type: getOrEmpty(parsed, _type)
                    for _type in typeFilters})
```

With these functions, parsing the `spacy` tags can be done with the following code:

```
entities = corpus["parsed"].apply(lambda x: toField(x.ents))
```

The `entities` DataFrame can easily be merged with the `corpus` DataFrame using the `pd.concat` function, thus placing all the information in a single data structure:

```
merged = pd.concat([corpus, entities], axis=1)
```

Now that we have all the ingredients for our bipartite graph, we can create the edge list by looping over all the documents-entity or document-keyword pairs:

```
edges = pd.DataFrame([
    {"source": _id, "target": keyword, "weight": score, "type":
_type}
    for _id, row in merged.iterrows()
    for _type in ["keywords", "GPE", "ORG", "PERSON"]
    for (keyword, score) in row[_type]
])
```

Once the edge list has been created, we can produce the bipartite graph using `networkx` APIs:

```
G = nx.Graph()
G.add_nodes_from(edges["source"].unique(), bipartite=0)
G.add_nodes_from(edges["target"].unique(), bipartite=1)
G.add_edges_from([
    (row["source"], row["target"])
    for _, row in edges.iterrows()
])
```

Now, we can look at an overview of our graph by using `nx.info`:

```
Type: Graph
Number of nodes: 25752
Number of edges: 100311
Average degree:    7.7905
```

In the next subsection, we will project the bipartite graph in either of the two sets of nodes: entities or documents. This will allow us to explore the difference between the two graphs and cluster both the terms and documents using the unsupervised techniques described in *Chapter 4, Supervised Graph Learning*. Then, we will return to the bipartite graph to show an example of supervised classification, which we'll do by leveraging the network information of the bipartite graphs.

Entity-entity graph

We will start by projecting our graph into the set of entity nodes. `networkx` provides a special submodule for dealing with bipartite graphs, `networkx.algorithms.bipartite`, where a number of algorithms have already been implemented. In particular, the `networkx.algorithms.bipartite.projection` submodule provides a number of utility functions to project bipartite graphs on a subset of nodes. Before performing projection, we must extract the nodes relative to a particular set (either documents or entities) using the "bipartite" property we created when we generated the graph:

```
document_nodes = {n
                for n, d in G.nodes(data=True)
                if d["bipartite"] == 0}
entity_nodes = {n
                for n, d in G.nodes(data=True)
                if d["bipartite"] == 1}
```

The graph projection basically creates a new graph with the set of selected nodes. Edges are places between the nodes based on whether two nodes have neighbors in common. The basic `projected_graph` function creates such a network with unweighted edges. However, it is usually more informative to have edges weighted based on the number of common neighbors. The `projection` module provides different functions based on how the weights are computed. In the next section, we will use `overlap_weighted_projected_graph`, where the edge weight is computed using the Jaccard similarity based on common neighbors. However, we encourage you to also explore the other options that, depending on your use case and context, may best suit your aims.

Be aware of dimensions – filtering the graph

There is another point of caution you should be aware of when dealing with projections: the dimension of the projected graph. In certain cases, like the one we are considering here, projection may create an extremely large number of edges, which makes the graph hard to analyze. In our use case, following the logic we used to create our network, a document node is connected to at least 10 keywords, plus a few entities. In the resulting entity-entity graph, all these entities will be connected to each other as they share at least one common neighbor (the document that contains them). Therefore, we will only be generating around $15 \cdot {}^{14}/_2 \approx 100$ edges for one document. If we multiply this number for the number of documents, $\sim 10^5$, we will end up with several edges that, despite the small use case, already become almost intractable, since there's a few million edges. Although this surely represents a conservative upper bound (as some of the co-occurrence between entities will be common in many documents and therefore not repeated), it provides an order of magnitude of the complexity that you might expect. Therefore, we encourage you to proceed with caution before projecting your bipartite graph, depending on the topology of the underlying network and the size of your graph. One trick to reduce this complexity and make the projection feasible is to only consider entity nodes that have a certain degree. Most of the complexity arises from the presence of entities that appear only once or a few times, but still generate *cliques* within the graph. Such entities are not very informative for capturing patterns and providing insights. Besides, they are possibly strongly affected by statistical variability. On the other hand, we should focus on strong correlations that are supported by larger occurrences and provide more reliable statistical results.

Therefore, we will only consider entity nodes with a certain degree. To this aim, we will generate the filtered bipartite subgraph, which excludes nodes with low degree values, namely smaller than 5:

```
nodes_with_low_degree = {n
    for n, d in nx.degree(G, nbunch=entity_nodes) if d<5}
subGraph = G.subgraph(set(G.nodes) - nodes_with_low_degree)
```

This subgraph can now be projected without generating a graph with an excessive number of edges:

```
entityGraph = overlap_weighted_projected_graph(
    subGraph,
    {n for n in subGraph.nodes() if n in entity_nodes}
)
```

We can check the dimension of the graph with the `networkx` function of `nx.info`:

```
Number of nodes: 2386
Number of edges: 120198
Average degree: 100.7527
```

Despite the filters we've applied, the number of edges and the average node degree are still quite large. The following graph shows the distribution of the degree and of the edge weights, where we can observe one peak in the degree distribution at fairly low values, with a fat tail toward large degree values. Also, the edge weight shows a similar behavior, with a peak at rather low values and fat right tails. These distributions suggest the presence of several small communities, namely cliques, which are connected to each other via some central nodes:

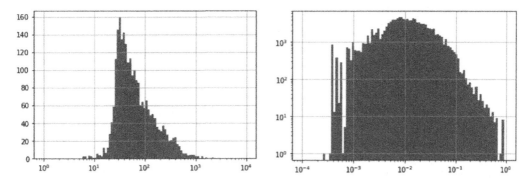

Figure 7.4 – Degree and weight distribution for the entity-entity network

The distribution of the edge weights also suggests that a second filter could be applied. The filter on the entity degree that we applied previously on the bipartite graph allowed us to filter out rare entities that only appeared in a few documents. However, the resulting graph could also be affected by the opposite problem: popular entities may be connected just because they tend to appear often in documents, even if there is not an interesting causal connection between them. Consider the US and Microsoft. They are almost surely connected, as it is extremely likely that there will be at least one or a few documents where they both appear. However, if there is not a strong and causal connection between them, it is very unlikely that the Jaccard similarity will be large. Considering only the edges with the largest weights allows you to focus on the most relevant and possibly stable relationships. The edge weight distribution shown in the preceding graph suggests that a suitable threshold could be `0.05`:

```
filteredEntityGraph = entityGraph.edge_subgraph(
    [edge
    for edge in entityGraph.edges
```

```
        if entityGraph.edges[edge]["weight"]>0.05])
```

Such a threshold reduces the number of edges significantly, making it feasible to analyze the network:

```
Number of nodes: 2265
Number of edges: 8082
Average degree:    7.1364
```

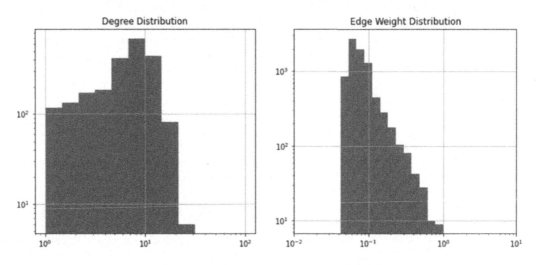

Figure 7.5 – Degree Distribution (Left) and Edge Weight Distribution (Right) for the resulting graph, after filtering based on the edge weight

The preceding diagram shows the distribution of the node degree and edge weights for the filtered graph. The distribution for the edge weights corresponds to the right tail of the distribution shown in *Figure 7.4*. The relationship that the degree distribution has with *Figure 7.4* is less obvious, and it shows the peak for the nodes that have a degree around 10, as opposed to the peak shown in *Figure 7.4*, which was observed in the low range, at around 100.

Analyzing the graph

Using Gephi we can provide an overview of the overall network, which is shown in *Figure 7.6*.

The graph is as follows:

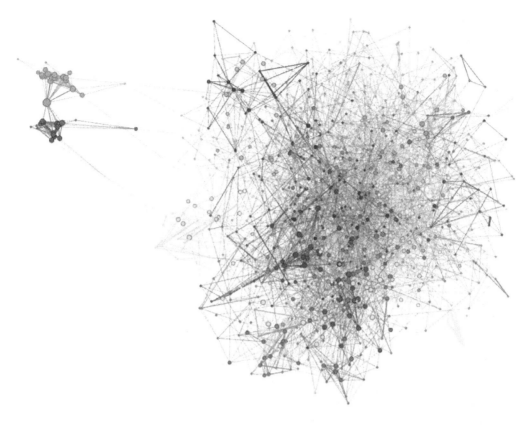

Figure 7.6 – Entity-entity network highlighting the presence of multiple small subcommunities

To obtain some further insights on the topology of the network, we will also compute some global measures, such as the average shortest path, clustering coefficient, and global efficiency. Although the graph has five different connected components, the largest one almost entirely accounts for the whole graph, including 2,254 out of 2,265 nodes:

```
components = nx.connected_components(filteredEntityGraph)
 pd.Series([len(c) for c in components])
```

The global properties of the largest components can be found with the following code:

```
comp = components[0]
global_metrics = pd.Series({
    "shortest_path": nx.average_shortest_path_length(comp),
    "clustering_coefficient": nx.average_clustering(comp),
    "global_efficiency": nx.global_efficiency(comp)
})
```

The shortest path and global efficiency may require a few minutes of computation. This results in the following output:

```
{
    'shortest_path': 4.715073779178782,
    'clustering_coefficient': 0.21156314975836915,
    'global_efficiency': 0.22735551077454275
}
```

Based on the magnitude of these metrics (with a shortest path of about 5 and a clustering coefficient around 0.2), together with the degree distribution shown previously, we can see that the network has multiple communities of a limited size. Other interesting local properties, such as degree, page rank, and betweenness centralities distributions, are shown in the following graph, which shows how all these measures tend to correlate and connect to each other:

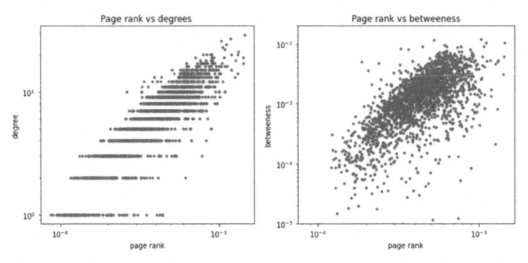

Figure 7.7 – Relationships and distribution between the degree, page rank, and betweenness centrality measures

After providing a description in terms of loca;/global measures, as well as a general visualization of the network, we will apply some of the techniques we have seen in the previous chapters to identify some insights and information within the network. We will do this using the unsupervised techniques described in *Chapter 4, Supervised Graph Learning.*

We will start by using the Louvain community detection algorithms, which, by optimizing their modularity, aim to identify the best partitions of the nodes in disjoint communities:

```
import community
communities = community.best_partition(filteredEntityGraph)
```

Note that the results might vary between runs because of random seeds. However, a similar partition, with a distribution of cluster memberships similar to the one shown in the following graph, should emerge. We generally observe about 30 communities, with the larger ones containing around 130-150 documents.

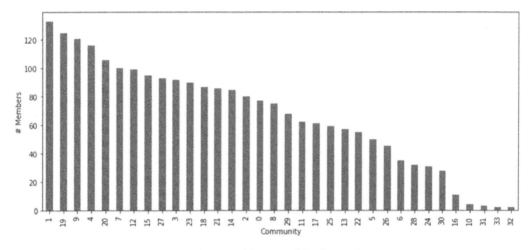

Figure 7.8 – Distribution of the size of the detected communities

Figure 7.9 shows a close-up of one of the communities, where we can identify a particular topic/argument. On the left, beside the entity nodes, we can also see the document nodes, thus uncovering the structure of the related bipartite graph:

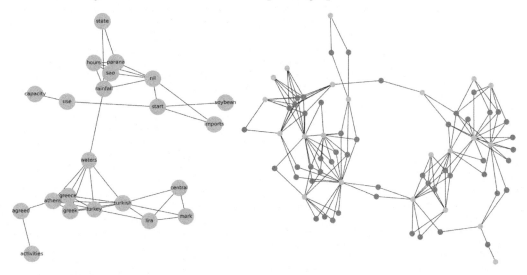

Figure 7.9 – Close-up for one of the communities we've identified

As shown in *Chapter 4, Supervised Graph Learning,* we can extract insightful information about the topology and similarity between entities by using node embeddings. In particular, we can use Node2Vec, which, by feeding a randomly generated walk to a skip-gram model, can project the nodes into a vector space, where close-by nodes are mapped to nearby points:

```
from node2vec import Node2Vec
node2vec = Node2Vec(filteredEntityGraph, dimensions=5)
model = node2vec.fit(window=10)
embeddings = model.wv
```

In the vector space of embeddings, we can apply traditional clustering algorithms, such as *GaussianMixture, K-means,* and *DB-scan.* As we did in the previous chapters, we can also project the embeddings into a 2D plane using t-SNE to visualize clusters and communities. Besides giving us another option to identify clusters/communities within the graph, Node2Vec can also be used to provide similarity between words, as traditionally done by **Word2Vec**. For instance, we can query the Node2Vec embedding model and find the word that's most similar "turkey," which provides semantically similar words:

```
[('turkish', 0.9975333213806152),
```

```
('lira', 0.9903393983840942),
('rubber', 0.9884852170944214),
('statoil', 0.9871745109558105),
('greek', 0.9846569299697876),
('xuto', 0.9830175042152405),
('stanley', 0.9809650182723999),
('conference', 0.9799597263336182),
('released', 0.9793018102645874),
('inra', 0.9775203466415405)]
```

Although these two approaches, Node2Vec and Word2Vec, share some methodological similarities, the two embedding schemes come from different types of information: Word2Vec is built directly from the text and encloses relationships at the sentence level, while Node2Vec encodes a description that acts more at the document level, since it comes from the bipartite entity-document graph.

Document-document graph

Now, let's project the bipartite graph into the set of document nodes to create a document-document network we can analyze. In a similar way to when we created an entity-entity network, we will use the `overlap_weighted_projected_graph` function to obtain a weighted graph that can be filtered to reduce the number of significant edges. Indeed, the topology of the network and the business logic used to build the bipartite graph do not favor clique creation, as we saw for the entity-entity graph: two nodes will only be connected when they share at least one keyword, organization, location, or person. This is certainly possible, but not extremely likely, within groups of 10-15 nodes, as observed for the entities.

As we did previously, we can easily build our network with the following lines:

```
documentGraph = overlap_weighted_projected_graph(
    G,
    document_nodes
)
```

The following graph shows the distribution of the degree and the edge weight. This can help us decide on the value of the threshold to be used to filter out the edges. Interestingly, the node degree distribution shows a clear peak toward large values compared to the degree distribution observed for the entity-entity graph. This suggests the presence of a number of *supernodes* (that is, nodes with rather large degrees) that are highly connected. Also, the edge weight distribution shows the Jaccard index's tendency to attain values close to 1, which are much larger than the ones we observed in the entity-entity graph. These two observations highlight a profound difference between the two networks: whereas the entity-entity graph is characterized by many tightly connected communities (namely cliques), the document-document graph is characterized by a rather tight connection among nodes with a large degree (which constitutes the core) versus a periphery of weakly connected or disconnected nodes:

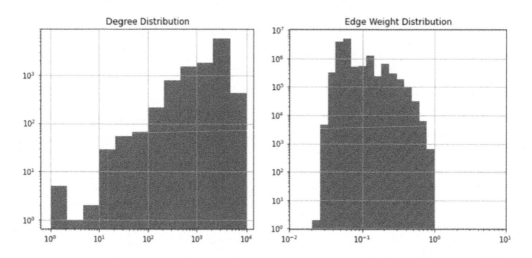

Figure 7.10 – Degree Distribution and Edge Weight Distribution for the projection of the bipartite graph into the document-document network

It can be convenient to store all the edges in a DataFrame so that we can plot them and then use them to filter and, thus, create a subgraph:

```
allEdgesWeights = pd.Series({
    (d[0], d[1]): d[2]["weight"]
    for d in documentGraph.edges(data=True)
})
```

By looking at the preceding diagram, it seems reasonable to set a threshold value of 0.6 for the edge weight, thus allowing us to generate a more tractable network using the edge_subgraph function of networkx:

```
filteredDocumentGraph = documentGraph.edge_subgraph(
    allEdgesWeights[(allEdgesWeights>0.6)].index.tolist()
)
```

The following graph shows the resulting distribution for the degree and for the edge weight for the reduced graph:

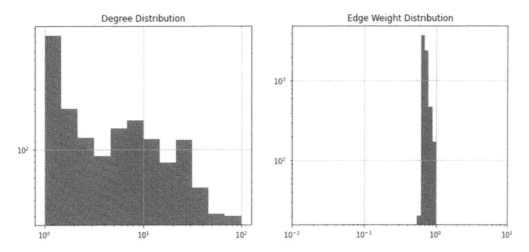

Figure 7.11 – Degree Distribution and Edge Weight Distribution for the document-document filtered network

The substantial difference in topology of the document-document graph with respect to the entity-entity graph can also be clearly seen in the following diagram, which shows a full network visualization. As anticipated by the distributions, the document-document network is characterized by a core network and several weekly connected satellites. These satellites represent all the documents that share none or a few keywords or entity common occurrences. The number of disconnected documents is quite large and accounts for almost 50% of the total:

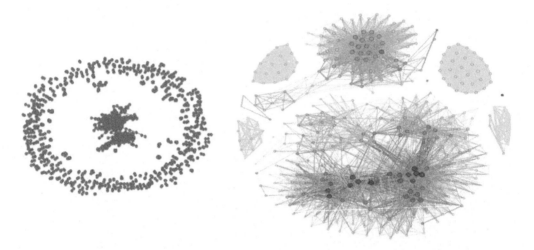

Figure 7.12 – (Left) Representation of the document-document filtered network, highlighting the presence of a core and a periphery. (Right) Close-up of the core, with some subcommunities embedded. The node size is proportional to the node degree

It may be worthwhile extracting the connected components for this network using the following commands:

```
components = pd.Series({
    ith: component
    for ith, component in enumerate(
        nx.connected_components(filteredDocumentGraph)
    )
})
```

In the following graph, we can see the distribution for the connected component sizes. Here, we can clearly see the presence of a few very large clusters (the cores), together with a large number of disconnected or very small components (the periphery or satellites). This structure is strikingly different from the one we observed for the entity-entity graph, where all the nodes were generated by a very large, connected cluster:

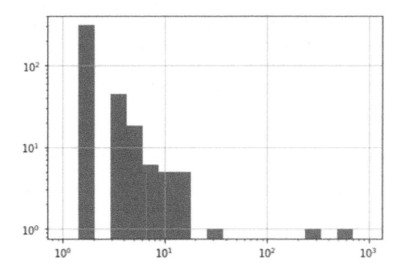

Figure 7.13 – Distribution of the connected component sizes, highlighting the presence of many small-sized communities (representing the periphery) and a few large communities (representing the core)

It can be interesting to investigate the structure of the core components further. We can extract the subgraph composed of the largest components of the network from the full graph with the following code:

```
coreDocumentGraph = nx.subgraph(
    filteredDocumentGraph,
    [node
    for nodes in components[components.apply(len)>8].values
    for node in nodes]
)
```

We can inspect the properties of the core network using nx.info:

```
Type: Graph
Number of nodes: 1050
Number of edges: 7112
Average degree:  13.5467
```

The left panel in *Figure 7.12* shows a Gephi visualization of the core. As we can see, the core is composed of a few communities, along with nodes with fairly large degrees strongly connected to each other.

As we did for the entity-entity network, we can process the network to identify communities embedded in the graph. However, different from what we did previously, the document-document graph now provides a mean for judging the clustering using the document labels. Indeed, we expect documents belonging to the same topic to be close and connected to each other. Moreover, as we will see shortly, this will also allow us to identify similarities among topics.

First, let's start by extracting the candidate communities:

```
import community
communities = pd.Series(
    community.best_partition(filteredDocumentGraph)
)
```

Then, we will extract the topic mixture within each community to see whether there is a homogeneity (all the documents belonging to the same class) or some correlation between topics:

```
from collections import Counter
def getTopicRatio(df):
    return Counter([label
                    for labels in df["label"]
                    for label in labels])

communityTopics = pd.DataFrame.from_dict({
    cid: getTopicRatio(corpus.loc[comm.index])
    for cid, comm in communities.groupby(communities)
}, orient="index")

normalizedCommunityTopics = (
    communityTopics.T / communityTopics.sum(axis=1)
).T
```

`normalizedCommunityTopics` is a DataFrame that, for each community (row in the DataFrame), provides the topic mixture (in percentage) of the different topics (along the column axis). To quantify the heterogeneity of the topic mixture within the clusters/communities, we must compute the Shannon entropy of each community:

$$I_c = -\sum_i \log t_{ci}$$

Here, I_c represents the entropy of the cluster, c, and t_{ci} corresponds to the percentage of topic i in community c. We must compute the empirical Shannon entropy for all communities:

```
normalizedCommunityTopics.apply(
    lambda x: np.sum(-np.log(x)), axis=1)
```

The following graph shows the entropy distribution across all communities. Most communities have zero or very low entropy, thus suggesting that the documents that belong to the same class (label) tend to cluster together:

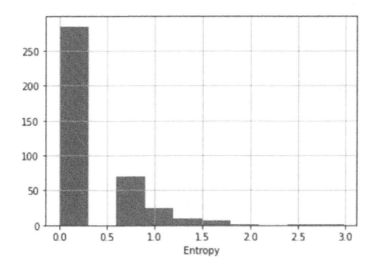

Figure 7.14 – Entropy distribution of the topic mixture in each community

Even if most of the communities show zero or low variability around topics, it is interesting to investigate whether there is a relationship between topics, when communities show some heterogeneity. Namely, we compute the correlation between topic distributions:

```
topicsCorrelation = normalizedCommunityTopics.corr().fillna(0)
```

These can then be represented and visualized using a topic-topic network:

```
topicsCorrelation[topicsCorrelation<0.8]=0
topicsGraph = nx.from_pandas_adjacency(topicsCorrelation)
```

The left-hand side of the following diagram shows the full graph representation for the topics network. As observed for the document-document network, the topic-topic graph shows a structure organized in a periphery of disconnected nodes and a strongly connected core. The right-hand side of the following diagram shows a close-up of the core network. This indicates a correlation that is supported by a semantic meaning, with the topics related to commodities tightly connected to each other:

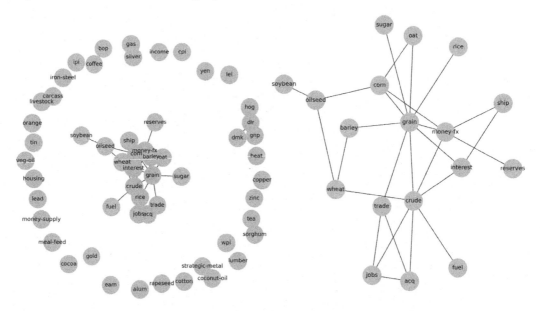

Figure 7.15 – (Left) Topic-topic correlation graph, organized with a periphery-core structure. (Right) Close-up of the core of the network

In this section, we analyzed the different types of networks that arise when analyzing documents and, more generally, text sources. To do so, we used global and local properties to statistically describe the networks, as well as some unsupervised algorithms, which allowed us to unveil some structure within the graph. In the next section, we will show you how to leverage these graph structures when building a machine learning model.

Building a document topic classifier

To show you how to leverage a graph structure, we will focus on using the topological information and the connections between the entities provided by the bipartite entity-document graph to train multi-label classifiers. This will help us predict the document topics. To do this, we will analyze two different approaches:

- **A shallow machine-learning approach,** where we will use the embeddings we extracted from the bipartite network to train *traditional* classifiers, such as a RandomForest classifier.

- **A more integrated and differentiable approach** based on using a graphical neural network that's been applied to heterogeneous graphs (such as the bipartite graph).

Let's consider the first 10 topics, which we have enough documentation on to train and evaluate our models:

```
from collections import Counter
topics = Counter(
    [label
     for document_labels in corpus["label"]
     for label in document_labels]
).most_common(10)
```

The preceding code block produces the following output. This shows the names of the topics, all of which we will focus on in the following analysis:

```
[('earn', 3964), ('acq', 2369), ('money-fx', 717),
('grain', 582), ('crude', 578), ('trade', 485),
('interest', 478), ('ship', 286), ('wheat', 283),
('corn', 237)]
```

When training topic classifiers, we must restrict our focus to only those documents that belong to such labels. The filtered corpus can easily be obtained by using the following code block:

```
topicsList = [topic[0] for topic in topics]
  topicsSet = set(topicsList)
dataset = corpus[corpus["label"].apply(
    lambda x: len(topicsSet.intersection(x))>0
)]
```

Now that we have extracted and structured the dataset, we are ready to start training our topic models and evaluating their performance. In the next section, we will start by creating a simple model using shallow learning methods so that we can increase the complexity of the model by using graph neural networks.

Shallow learning methods

We will start by implementing a shallow approach for the topic classification tasks by leveraging the network's information. We will show you how to do this so that you can customize even further, depending on your use case:

1. First, we will compute the embeddings by using `Node2Vec` on the bipartite graph. Filtered document-document networks are characterized by a periphery with many nodes that are disconnected, so they would not benefit from topological information. On the other hand, the unfiltered document-document network will have many edges, which makes the scalability of the approach an issue. Therefore, using the bipartite graph is crucial in order to efficiently leverage the topological information and the connection between entities and documents:

   ```
   from node2vec import Node2Vec
   node2vec = Node2Vec(G, dimensions=10)
   model = node2vec.fit(window=20)
   embeddings = model.wv
   ```

   Here, the `dimension` embedding, as well as our `window`, which is used for generating the walks, are hyperparameters that must be optimized via cross-validation.

2. To make this computationally efficient, a set of embeddings can be computed beforehand, saved to disk, and then be used in the optimization process. This would work based on the assumption that we are in a *semi-supervised* setting or in a *transductive* task, where we have connection information about the entire dataset, apart from their labels, at training time. Later in this chapter, we will outline another approach, based on graph neural networks, that provides an inductive framework for integrating topology when training classifiers. Let's store the embeddings in a file:

   ```
   pd.DataFrame(embeddings.vectors,
                index=embeddings.index2word
   ).to_pickle(f"graphEmbeddings_{dimension}_{window}.p")
   ```

Here, we can choose and loop different values for `dimension` and `window`. Some possible choices are 10, 20, and 30 for both variables.

3. These embeddings can be integrated into a scikit-learn `transformer` so that they can be used in a grid search cross-validation process:

```python
from sklearn.base import BaseEstimator
class EmbeddingsTransformer(BaseEstimator):

    def __init__(self, embeddings_file):
        self.embeddings_file = embeddings_file

    def fit(self, *args, **kwargs):
        self.embeddings = pd.read_pickle(
            self.embeddings_file)
        return self

    def transform(self, X):
        return self.embeddings.loc[X.index]

    def fit_transform(self, X, y):
        return self.fit().transform(X)
```

4. To build a modeling training pipeline, we will split our corpus into training and test sets:

```python
def train_test_split(corpus):
    indices = [index for index in corpus.index]
    train_idx = [idx
                 for idx in indices
                 if "training/" in idx]
    test_idx = [idx
                for idx in indices
                if "test/" in idx]
    return corpus.loc[train_idx], corpus.loc[test_idx]

train, test = train_test_split(dataset)
```

We will also build functions to conveniently extract features and labels:

```python
def get_features(corpus):
    return corpus["parsed"]
def get_labels(corpus, topicsList=topicsList):
    return corpus["label"].apply(
        lambda labels: pd.Series(
            {label: 1 for label in labels}
        ).reindex(topicsList).fillna(0)
    )[topicsList]
def get_features_and_labels(corpus):
    return get_features(corpus), get_labels(corpus)
features, labels = get_features_and_labels(train)
```

5. Now, we can instantiate the modeling pipeline:

```python
from sklearn.pipeline import Pipeline
from sklearn.ensemble import RandomForestClassifier
from sklearn.multioutput import MultiOutputClassifier
pipeline = Pipeline([
    ("embeddings", EmbeddingsTransformer(
        "my-place-holder")
    ),
    ("model", MultiOutputClassifier(
        RandomForestClassifier())
    )
])
```

6. Let's define the parameter space, as well as the configuration, for the cross-validated grid search:

```
from glob import glob
param_grid = {
    "embeddings__embeddings_file":
glob("graphEmbeddings_*"),
    "model__estimator__n_estimators": [50, 100],
    "model__estimator__max_features": [0.2,0.3, "auto"],
}
grid_search = GridSearchCV(
    pipeline, param_grid=param_grid, cv=5, n_jobs=-1)
```

7. Finally, let's train our topic model by using the `fit` method of the sklearn API:

```
model = grid_search.fit(features, labels)
```

Great! You have just created your topic model, which leverages the graph's information. Once the best model has been identified, we can use this model on the test dataset to evaluate its performance. To do so, we must define the following helper function, which allows us to obtain a set of predictions:

```
def get_predictions(model, features):
    return pd.DataFrame(
        model.predict(features),
        columns=topicsList, index=features.index)
preds = get_predictions(model, get_features(test))
labels = get_labels(test)
```

Using `sklearn` functionalities, we can promptly look at the performance of the trained classifier:

```
from sklearn.metrics import classification_report
print(classification_report(labels, preds))
```

This provides the following output, which shows the overall performance measure that's received by the F1-score. This is around 0.6 – 0.8, depending on how unbalanced classes are accounted for:

	precision	recall	f1-score	support
0	0.97	0.94	0.95	1087

1	0.93	0.74	0.83	719
2	0.79	0.45	0.57	179
3	0.96	0.64	0.77	149
4	0.95	0.59	0.73	189
5	0.95	0.45	0.61	117
6	0.87	0.41	0.56	131
7	0.83	0.21	0.34	89
8	0.69	0.34	0.45	71
9	0.61	0.25	0.35	56
micro avg	0.94	0.72	0.81	2787
macro avg	0.85	0.50	0.62	2787
weighted avg	0.92	0.72	0.79	2787
samples avg	0.76	0.75	0.75	2787

You can play around with the types and hyperparameters of the analytical pipeline, vary the models, and experiment with different values when you're encoding the embeddings. As we mentioned previously, the preceding approach is clearly transductive since it uses an embedding that's been trained on the entire dataset. This is a common situation in semi-supervised tasks, where the labeled information is only present in a small subset of points, and the task is to infer the labels for all the unknown samples. In the next subsection, we will outline how to build an inductive classifier using graph neural networks. These can be used when the test samples are not known at training time.

Graph neural networks

Now, let's describe a neural network-based approach that natively integrates and makes use of the graph structure. Graph neural networks were introduced in *Chapter 3, Unsupervised Graph Learning*, and *Chapter 4, Supervised Graph Learning*. However, here, we will show you how to apply this framework to heterogeneous graphs; that is, graphs where there is more than one type of node. Each node type might have a different set of features and the training might target only one specific node type over the other.

The approach we will show here will make use of `stellargraph` and the `GraphSAGE` algorithms, which we described previously. These methods also support the use of features for each node, instead of just relying on the topology of the graph. If you do not have any node features, the one-hot node representation can be used in its place, as shown in *Chapter 6, Social Network Graphs*. However, here, to make things more general, we will produce a set of node features based on the TF-IDF score (which we saw earlier) for each entity and keyword. Here, we will show you a step-by-step guide that will help you train and evaluate a model, based on graph neural networks, for predicting document topic classification:

1. Let's start by computing the TF-IDF score for each document. `sklearn` already provides some functionalities that allow us to easily compute the TF-IDF scores from a corpus of documents. The `TfidfVectorizer sklearn` class already comes with a `tokenizer` embedded. However, since we already have a tokenized and lemmatized version that we extracted with `spacy`, we can also provide an implementation of a custom tokenizer that leverages on spaCy processing:

```python
def my_spacy_tokenizer(pos_filter=["NOUN", "VERB",
"PROPN"]):
    def tokenizer(doc):
        return [token.lemma_
                for token in doc
                if (pos_filter is None) or
                (token.pos_ in pos_filter)]
    return tokenizer
```

This can be used in `TfidfVectorizer`:

```python
cntVectorizer = TfidfVectorizer(
    analyzer=my_spacy_tokenizer(),
    max_df = 0.25, min_df = 2, max_features = 10000
)
```

To make the approach truly inductive, we will only train the TF-IDF for the training set. This will only be applied to the test set:

```python
trainFeatures, trainLabels = get_features_and_
labels(train)
testFeatures, testLabels = get_features_and_labels(test)


trainedIDF = cntVectorizer.fit_transform(trainFeatures)
testIDF = cntVectorizer.transform(testFeatures)
```

For our convenience, the two TF-IDF representations (for the training and test sets) can now be stacked together into a single data structure representing the features for the document nodes for the whole graph:

```
documentFeatures = pd.concat([trainedIDF, testIDF])
```

2. Beside the feature information for document nodes, we will also build a simple feature vector for entities, based on the one-hot encoding representation of the entity type:

```
entityTypes = {
    entity: ith
    for ith, entity in enumerate(edges["type"].unique())
}
entities = edges\
    .groupby(["target", "type"])["source"]\
    .count()\
    .groupby(level=0).apply(
        lambda s: s.droplevel(0)\
                    .reindex(entityTypes.keys())\
                    .fillna(0))\
    .unstack(level=1)
entityFeatures = (entities.T / entities.sum(axis=1))
```

3. We now have all the information we need to create an instance of a `StellarGraph`. We will do this by merging the information of the node features, both for documents and for entities, with the connections provided by the `edges` DataFrame. We should only filter out some of the edges/nodes so that we only include the documents that belong to the targeted topics:

```
from stellargraph import StellarGraph

_edges = edges[edges["source"].isin(documentFeatures.
index)]
nodes = {«entity»: entityFeatures,
         «document»: documentFeatures}
stellarGraph = StellarGraph(
    nodes, _edges,
    target_column=»target», edge_type_column=»type»
)
```

With that, we have created our `StellarGraph`. We can inspect the network, similar to what we did for `networkx`, with the following command:

```
print(stellarGraph.info())
```

This produces the following overview:

```
StellarGraph: Undirected multigraph
 Nodes: 23998, Edges: 86849


Node types:
  entity: [14964]
    Features: float32 vector, length 6
    Edge types: entity-GPE->document, entity-ORG-
>document, entity-PERSON->document, entity-keywords-
>document
  document: [9034]
    Features: float32 vector, length 10000
    Edge types: document-GPE->entity, document-ORG-
>entity,
  document-PERSON->entity, document-keywords->entity


Edge types:
    document-keywords->entity: [78838]
        Weights: range=[0.0827011, 1], mean=0.258464,
 std=0.0898612
        Features: none
    document-ORG->entity: [4129]
        Weights: range=[2, 22], mean=3.24122, std=2.30508
        Features: none
    document-GPE->entity: [2943]
        Weights: range=[2, 25], mean=3.25926, std=2.07008


        Features: none
    document-PERSON->entity: [939]
        Weights: range=[2, 14], mean=2.97444, std=1.65956
        Features: none
```

The `StellarGraph` description is actually very informative. Besides, `StellarGraph` also natively handles different types of nodes and edges and provides out-of-the-box segmented statistics for each node/edge type.

4. You may have noted that the graph we just created includes both training and test data. To truly test the performance of an inductive approach and avoid information from being linked between the train and test sets, we need to create a subgraph that only contains the data available at training time:

```
targets = labels.reindex(documentFeatures.index).
fillna(0)
  sampled, hold_out = train_test_split(targets)
allNeighbors = np.unique([n
    for node in sampled.index
    for n in stellarGraph.neighbors(node)
])
subgraph = stellarGraph.subgraph(
    set(sampled.index).union(allNeighbors)
)
```

The considered subgraph contains 16,927 nodes and 62,454 edges, compared to the 23,998 nodes and 86,849 edges in the entire graph.

5. Now that we only have the data and the network available at training time, we can build our machine learning model on top of it. To do so, we will split the data into train, validation, and test data. For training, we will only use 10% of the data, which resembles a semi-supervised task:

```
from sklearn.model_selection import train_test_split
train, leftOut = train_test_split(
    sampled,
    train_size=0.1,
    test_size=None,
    random_state=42
)
validation, test = train_test_split(
    leftOut, train_size=0.2, test_size=None, random_
state=100,
)
```

6. Now, we can start to build our graph neural network model using `stellargraph` and the `keras` API. First, we will create a generator able to produce the samples that will feed the neural network. Note that, since we are dealing with a heterogeneous graph, we need a generator that will sample examples from nodes that only belong to specific class. Here, we will be using the `HinSAGENodeGenerator` class, which generalizes the node generator we used for the homogeneous graph into heterogeneous graphs, allowing us to specify the node type we want to target:

```
from stellargraph.mapper import HinSAGENodeGenerator
batch_size = 50
num_samples = [10, 5]
generator = HinSAGENodeGenerator(
    subgraph, batch_size, num_samples,
    head_node_type="document"
)
```

Using this object, we can create a generator for the train and validation datasets:

```
train_gen = generator.flow(train.index, train,
shuffle=True)
 val_gen = generator.flow(validation.index, validation)
```

7. Now, we can create our GraphSAGE model. As we did for the generator, we need to use a model that can handle heterogenous graphs. Here, `HinSAGE` will be used in place of `GraphSAGE`:

```
from stellargraph.layer import HinSAGE
from tensorflow.keras import layers
graphsage_model = HinSAGE(
    layer_sizes=[32, 32], generator=generator,
    bias=True, dropout=0.5
)
x_inp, x_out = graphsage_model.in_out_tensors()
prediction = layers.Dense(
    units=train.shape[1], activation="sigmoid"
)(x_out)
```

Note that in the final dense layer, we use a *sigmoid* activation function instead of a *softmax* activation function, since the problem at hand is a multi-class, multi-label task. Thus, a document may belong to more than one class, and the sigmoid activation function seems a more sensible choice in this context. As usual, we will compile our Keras model:

```
from tensorflow.keras import optimizers, losses, Model
model = Model(inputs=x_inp, outputs=prediction)
model.compile(
    optimizer=optimizers.Adam(lr=0.005),
    loss=losses.binary_crossentropy,
    metrics=["acc"]
)
```

8. Finally, we will train the neural network model:

```
history = model.fit(
    train_gen, epochs=50, validation_data=val_gen,
    verbose=1, shuffle=False
)
```

This results in the following output:

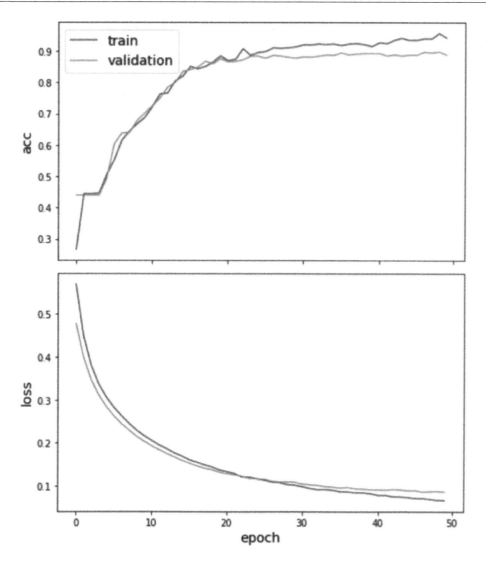

Figure.7.16 – (Top) Train and validation accuracy versus the number of epochs. (Bottom) Binary cross-entropy loss for the training and validation dataset versus the number of epochs

The preceding graph shows the plots of the evolution of the train and validation losses and accuracy versus the number of epochs. As we can see, the train and validation accuracy increase consistently, up to around 30 epochs. Here, the accuracy of the validation set settle to a *plateau*, whereas the training accuracy continues to increase, indicating a tendency for overfitting. Thus, stopping training at around 50 seems a rather legitimate choice.

9. Once the model has been trained, we can test its performance on the test set:

```
test_gen = generator.flow(test.index, test)
 test_metrics = model.evaluate(test_gen)
```

This should provide the following values:

```
loss: 0.0933
accuracy: 0.8795
```

Note that because of the unbalanced label distribution, accuracy may not be the best choice for assessing performances. Besides, a value of 0.5 is generally used for thresholding, so providing label assignment may also be sub-optimal in unbalanced settings.

10. To identify the best threshold to be used to classify the documents, we will compute the prediction over all the test samples:

```
test_predictions = pd.DataFrame(
    model.predict(test_gen), index=test.index,
    columns=test.columns)
test_results = pd.concat({
    "target": test,
    "preds": test_predictions
}, axis=1)
```

Then, we will compute the F1-score with a macro average (where the F1-score for the single classes are averaged) for different threshold choices:

```
thresholds = [0.01,0.05,0.1,0.2,0.3,0.4,0.5]
f1s = {}
for th in thresholds:
    y_true = test_results["target"]
    y_pred = 1.0*(test_results["preds"]>th)
    f1s[th] = f1_score(y_true, y_pred, average="macro")
pd.Series(f1s).plot()
```

As shown in the following graph, a threshold value of 0.2 seems to be the best choice as it achieves the best performance:

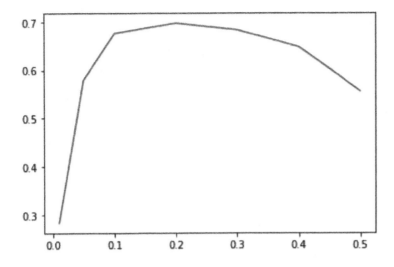

Figure 7.17 – Macro-averaged F1-score versus the threshold used for labeling

11. Using a threshold value of 0.2, we can extract the classification report for the test set:

```
print(classification_report(
    test_results["target"], 1.0*(test_
results["preds"]>0.2))
)
```

This gives us the following output:

	precision	recall	f1-score	support
0	0.92	0.97	0.94	2075
1	0.85	0.96	0.90	1200
2	0.65	0.90	0.75	364
3	0.83	0.95	0.89	305
4	0.86	0.68	0.76	296
5	0.74	0.56	0.63	269
6	0.60	0.80	0.69	245
7	0.62	0.10	0.17	150
8	0.49	0.95	0.65	149
9	0.44	0.88	0.58	129
micro avg	0.80	0.89	0.84	5182
macro avg	0.70	0.78	0.70	5182
weighted avg	0.82	0.89	0.84	5182
samples avg	0.83	0.90	0.85	5182

12. At this point, we have trained a graph neural network model and assessed its performance. Now, let's apply this model to a set of unobserved data – the data that we left out at the very beginning – and represent the true test data in an inductive setting. To do this, we need to instantiate a new generator:

```
generator = HinSAGENodeGenerator(
    stellarGraph, batch_size, num_samples,
    head_node_type="document")
```

Note that the graph we've taken as an input from `HinSAGENodeGenerator` is now the entire graph (in place of the filtered one we used previously), which contains both training and test documents. Using this class, we can create a generator that only samples from the test nodes, filtering out the ones that do not belong to one of our main selected topics:

```
hold_out = hold_out[hold_out.sum(axis=1) > 0]
hold_out_gen = generator.flow(hold_out.index, hold_out)
```

13. The model can then be evaluated over these samples, and the labels are predicted using the threshold we identified earlier; that is, 0.2:

```
hold_out_predictions = model.predict(hold_out_gen)
preds = pd.DataFrame(1.0*(hold_out_predictions > 0.2),
                     index = hold_out.index,
                     columns = hold_out.columns)
results = pd.concat(
    {"target": hold_out,"preds": preds}, axis=1
)
```

Finally, we can extract the performance of the inductive test dataset:

```
print(classification_report(
    results["target"], results["preds"])
)
```

This produces the following table:

	precision	recall	f1-score	support
0	0.93	0.99	0.96	1087
1	0.90	0.97	0.93	719
2	0.64	0.92	0.76	179
3	0.82	0.95	0.88	149
4	0.85	0.62	0.72	189

5	0.74	0.50	0.59	117
6	0.60	0.79	0.68	131
7	0.43	0.03	0.06	89
8	0.50	0.96	0.66	71
9	0.39	0.86	0.54	56
micro avg	0.82	0.89	0.85	2787
macro avg	0.68	0.76	0.68	2787
weighted avg	0.83	0.89	0.84	2787
samples avg	0.84	0.90	0.86	2787

Compared to the shallow learning method, we can see that we have achieved a substantial improvement in performance that's between 5-10%.

Summary

In this chapter, you learned how to process unstructured information and how to represent such information by using graphs. Starting from a well-known benchmark dataset, the Reuters-21578 dataset, we applied standard NLP engines to tag and structure textual information. Then, we used these high-level features to create different types of networks: knowledge-based networks, bipartite networks, and projections for a subset of nodes, as well as a network relating the dataset topics. These different graphs have also allowed us to use the tools we presented in previous chapters to extract insights from the network representation.

We used local and global properties to show you how these quantities can represent and describe structurally different types of networks. We then used unsupervised techniques to identify semantic communities and cluster documents that belong to similar subjects/topics. Finally, we used the labeled information provided in a dataset to train supervised multi-class multi-label classifiers, which also leveraged the topology of the network.

Then, we applied supervised techniques to a heterogeneous graph, where two different node types are present: documents and entities. In this setting, we showed you how to implement both transductive and inductive approaches by using shallow learning and graph neural networks, respectively.

In the next chapter, we will look at another domain where graph analytics can be efficiently used to extract insights and/or create machine learning models that leverage network topology: transactional data. The next use case will also allow you to generalize the bipartite graph concepts that were introduced in this chapter to another level: tripartite graphs.

8
Graph Analysis for Credit Card Transactions

Analysis of financial data is one of the most common and important domains in big data and data analysis. Indeed, due to the increasing number of mobile devices and the introduction of a standard platform for online payment, the amount of transactional data that banks are producing and consuming is increasing exponentially.

As a consequence, new tools and techniques are needed to exploit as much as we can from this huge amount of information in order to better understand customers' behavior and support data-driven decisions in business processes. Data can also be used to build better mechanisms to improve security in the online payment process. Indeed, as online payment systems are becoming increasingly popular due to e-commerce platforms, at the same time, cases of fraud are also increasing. An example of a fraudulent transaction is a transaction performed with a stolen credit card. Indeed, in this case, the fraudulent transactions will be different from the transactions made by the original owner of the credit card.

However, building automatic procedures to detect fraudulent transactions could be a complex problem due to the large number of variables involved.

In this chapter, we will describe how we can represent credit card transaction data as a graph in order to automatically detect fraudulent transactions using machine learning algorithms. We will start processing the dataset by applying some of the techniques and algorithms we described in previous chapters to build a fraud detection algorithm.

The following topics will be covered in this chapter:

- Generating a graph from credit card transactions

- Extraction of properties and communities from the graph

- Application of supervised and unsupervised machine learning algorithms to fraud classification

Technical requirements

We will be using *Jupyter* notebooks with *Python* 3.8 for all of our exercises. The following is a list of Python libraries that will be installed for this chapter using `pip`. For example, run `pip install networkx==2.5` on the command line:

```
Jupyter==1.0.0
networkx==2.5
scikit-learn==0.24.0
pandas==1.1.3
node2vec==0.3.3
numpy==1.19.2
communities==2.2.0
```

In the rest of this book, unless clearly stated to the contrary, we will refer to nx as the results of the Python `import networkx as nx` command.

All code files relevant to this chapter are available at `https://github.com/PacktPublishing/Graph-Machine-Learning/tree/main/Chapter08`.

Overview of the dataset

The dataset used in this chapter is the *Credit Card Transactions Fraud Detection Dataset* available on *Kaggle* at the following URL: `https://www.kaggle.com/kartik2112/fraud-detection?select=fraudTrain.csv`.

The dataset is made up of simulated credit card transactions containing legitimate and fraudulent transactions for the period January 1, 2019 – December 31, 2020. It includes the credit cards of 1,000 customers performing transactions with a pool of 800 merchants. The dataset was generated using *Sparkov Data Generation*. More information about the generation algorithm is available at the following URL: `https://github.com/namebrandon/Sparkov_Data_Generation`.

For each transaction, the dataset contains 23 different features. In the following table, we will show only the information that will be used in this chapter:

Column Name	Column Description	Type
Index	Unique Identifier for each row	Integer
cc_num	Credit Card Number of Customer	String
merchant	Merchant name	String
amt	Number of transactions (in dollars)	Double
is_fraud	Target variable. It is 0 if it is a genuine transaction, 1 for a fraudulent transaction	Binary

Table 8.1 – List of variables used in the dataset

For the purposes of our analysis, we will use the `fraudTrain.csv` file. As already suggested, take a look at the dataset by yourself. It is strongly suggested to explore and become as comfortable as possible with the dataset before starting any machine learning task. We also suggest that you investigate two other datasets that will not be covered in this chapter. The first one is the Czech Bank's Financial Analysis dataset, available at `https://github.com/Kusainov/czech-banking-fin-analysis`. This dataset came from an actual Czech bank in 1999, for the period covering 1993 – 1998. The data pertaining to clients and their accounts consists of directed relations. Unfortunately, there are no labels on the transactions, making it impossible to train a fraud detection engine using machine learning techniques. The second dataset is the paysim1 dataset, available at `https://www.kaggle.com/ntnu-testimon/paysim1`. This dataset comprises simulated mobile money transactions based on a sample of real transactions extracted from one month of financial logs from a mobile money service implemented in an African country. The original logs were provided by a multinational company, which is the provider of the mobile financial service and is currently running in more than 14 countries across the globe. This dataset also contains labels on fraudulent/genuine transactions.

Loading the dataset and graph building using networkx

The first step of our analysis will be to load the dataset and build a graph. Since the dataset represents a simple list of transactions, we need to perform several operations to build the final credit card transaction graph. The dataset is a simple CSV file; we can use `pandas` to load the data as follows:

```
import pandas as pd
df = df[df["is_fraud"]==0].sample(frac=0.20, random_state=42).
append(df[df["is_fraud"] == 1])
```

In order to help the reader deal with the dataset, we selected 20% of the genuine transactions and all of the fraudulent transactions. As a result, from a total of 1,296,675 transactions, we will only use 265,342 transactions. Moreover, we can also investigate the number of fraudulent and genuine transactions in our dataset as follows:

```
df["is_fraud"].value_counts()
```

By way of a result, we get the following:

```
0       257834
1         7506
```

In other words, from a total of 265,342 transactions, only 7506 (2.83 %) are fraudulent transactions, while the others are genuine.

The dataset can be represented as a graph using the `networkx` library. Before starting with the technical description, we will start by specifying how the graph is built from the data. We used two different approaches to build the graph, namely, the bipartite and tripartite approaches, as described in the paper *APATE: A Novel Approach for Automated Credit Card Transaction Fraud Detection Using Network-Based Extensions*, available at `https://www.scinapse.io/papers/614715210`.

For the **bipartite approach**, we build a weighted bipartite graph $G = (V, E, \omega)$ where $V = V_c \cup V_m$, where each node $c \in V_c$ represents a customer, and each node $m \in V_m$ represents a merchant. An edge (v_c, v_m) is created if a transaction exists from the customer, v_c, to the merchant, v_m. Finally, to each edge of the graph, we assign an (always positive) weight representing the amount (in US dollars) of the transaction. In our formalization, we allow both directed and undirected graphs.

Since the dataset represents temporal transactions, multiple interactions can happen between a customer and a merchant. In both our formalizations, we decided to collapse all that information in a single graph. In other words, if multiple transactions are present between a customer and a merchant, we will build a single edge between the two nodes with its weight given by the sum of all the transaction amounts. A graphical representation of the direct bipartite graph is visible in *Figure 8.1*:

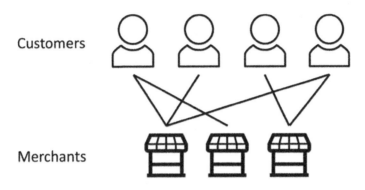

Customers

Merchants

Figure 8.1 – Bipartite graph generated from the input dataset

The bipartite graph we defined can be built using the following code:

```
def build_graph_bipartite(df_input, graph_type=nx.Graph()):
    df = df_input.copy()
    mapping = {x:node_id for node_id,x in enumerate(set(df["cc_
num"].values.tolist() + df["merchant"].values.tolist()))}
    df["from"] = df["cc_num"].apply(lambda x: mapping[x])
    df["to"] = df["merchant"].apply(lambda x: mapping[x])
    df = df[['from', 'to', "amt", "is_fraud"]].groupby(['from',
'to']).agg({"is_fraud": "sum", "amt": "sum"}).reset_index()
    df["is_fraud"] = df["is_fraud"].apply(lambda x: 1 if x>0
else 0)
    G = nx.from_edgelist(df[["from", "to"]].values, create_
using=graph_type)
    nx.set_edge_attributes(G, {(int(x["from"]),
```

```
int(x["to"])):x["is_fraud"] for idx, x in df[["from","to","is_
fraud"]].iterrows()}, "label")
    nx.set_edge_attributes(G,{(int(x["from"]),
int(x["to"])):x["amt"] for idx, x in df[["from","to","amt"]].
iterrows()}, "weight")
    return G
```

The code is quite simple. To build the bipartite credit card transaction graph, we use different `networkx` functions. To go more in depth, the operations we performed in the code are as follows:

1.   We built a map to assign a `node_id` to each merchant or customer.

2.   Multiple transactions are aggregated in a single transaction.

3.   The `networkx` function, `nx.from_edgelist`, is used to build the networkx graph.

4.   Two attributes, namely, `weight` and `label`, are assigned to each edge. The former represents the total number of transactions between the two nodes, whereas the latter indicates whether the transaction is genuine or fraudulent.

As we can also see from the code, we can select whether we want to build a directed or an undirected graph. We can build an undirected graph by calling the following function:

```
G_bu = build_graph_bipartite(df, nx.Graph(name="Bipartite
Undirect"))))
```

We can instead build a direct graph by calling the following function:

```
G_bd = build_graph_bipartite(df, nx.DiGraph(name="Bipartite
Direct"))))
```

The only difference is given by the second parameter we pass in the constructor.

The **tripartite approach** is an extension of the previous one, also allowing the transactions to be represented as a vertex. If, on the one hand, this approach drastically increases network complexity, on the other hand, it allows extra node embeddings to be built for merchants and cardholders and every transaction. Formally for this approach, we build a weighted tripartite graph, $G = (V, E, \omega)$, where $V = V_t \cup V_c \cup V_m$, where each node $c \in V_c$ represents a customer, each node $m \in V_m$ represents a merchant, and each node $t \in V_t$ is a transaction. Two edges (v_c, v_t) and (v_t, v_m) are created for each transaction, v_t, from customer v_c to the merchant v_m.

Finally, to each edge of the graph, we assign an (always positive) weight representing the amount (in US dollars) of the transaction. Since, in this case, we create a node for each transaction, we do not need to aggregate multiple transactions from a customer to a merchant. Moreover, as for the other approach, in our formalization, we allow both directed and undirected graphs. A graphical representation of the direct bipartite graph is visible in *Figure 8.2*:

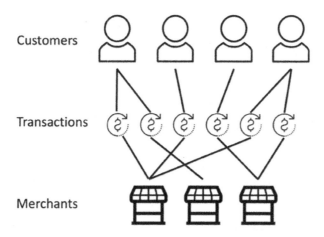

Figure 8.2 – Tripartite graph generated from the input dataset

The tripartite graph we defined can be built using the following code:

```
def build_graph_tripartite(df_input, graph_type=nx.Graph()):
    df = df_input.copy()
    mapping = {x:node_id for node_id,x in enumerate(set(df.
index.values.tolist() + df["cc_num"].values.tolist() +
df["merchant"].values.tolist()))}
    df["in_node"] = df["cc_num"].apply(lambda x: mapping[x])
    df["out_node"] = df["merchant"].apply(lambda x: mapping[x])
    G = nx.from_edgelist([(x["in_node"], mapping[idx]) for idx,
x in df.iterrows()] + [(x["out_node"], mapping[idx]) for idx, x
in df.iterrows()], create_using=graph_type)
    nx.set_edge_attributes(G,{(x["in_node"],
mapping[idx]):x["is_fraud"] for idx, x in df.iterrows()},
"label")
    nx.set_edge_attributes(G,{(x["out_node"],
mapping[idx]):x["is_fraud"] for idx, x in df.iterrows()},
"label")
    nx.set_edge_attributes(G,{(x["in_node"],
mapping[idx]):x["amt"] for idx, x in df.iterrows()}, "weight")
    nx.set_edge_attributes(G,{(x["out_node"],
mapping[idx]):x["amt"] for idx, x in df.iterrows()}, "weight")
    return G
```

The code is quite simple. To build the tripartite credit card transaction graph, we use different networkx functions. To go more in depth, the operations we performed in the code are as follows:

1. We built a map to assign a node_id to each merchant, customer, and transaction.

2. The networkx function, nx.from_edgelist, is used to build the networkx graph,

3. Two attributes, namely, weight and label, are assigned to each edge. The former represents the total number of transactions between the two nodes, whereas the latter indicates whether the transaction is genuine or fraudulent.

As we can also see from the code, we can select whether we want to build a directed or an undirected graph. We can build an undirected graph by calling the following function:

```
G_tu = build_graph_tripartite(df, nx.Graph(name="Tripartite
Undirect"))
```

We can instead build a direct graph by calling the following function:

```
G_td = build_graph_tripartite(df, nx.DiGraph(name="Tripartite
Direct"))
```

The only difference is given by the second parameter we pass in the constructor.

In the formalized graph representation that we introduced, the real transactions are represented as edges. According to this structure for both bipartite and tripartite graphs, the classification of fraudulent/genuine transactions is described as an edge classification task. In this task, the goal is to assign to a given edge a label (0 for genuine, 1 for fraudulent) describing whether the transaction the edge represents is fraudulent or genuine.

In the rest of this chapter, we use for our analysis both bipartite and tripartite undirected graphs, denoted by the Python variables G_bu and G_tu, respectively. We will leave it to you, as an exercise, an extension of the analyses proposed in this chapter to direct graphs.

We begin our analysis with a simple check to validate whether our graph is a real bipartite graph using the following line:

```
from networkx.algorithms import bipartite
all([bipartite.is_bipartite(G) for G in [G_bu,G_tu]]
```

As result, we get True. This check gives us the certainty that the two graphs are actually bipartite/tripartite graphs.

Moreover, using the following command, we can get some basic statistics:

```
for G in [G_bu, G_tu]:
  print(nx.info(G))
```

By way of a result, we get the following:

```
Name: Bipartite Undirect
Type: Graph
Number of nodes: 1676
Number of edges: 201725
Average degree: 240.7220
Name: Tripartite Undirect
Type: Graph
```

```
Number of nodes: 267016
Number of edges: 530680
Average degree:   3.9749
```

As we can see, the two graphs differ in both, the number of nodes and the number of edges. The bipartite undirected graph has 1,676, equal to the number of customers plus the number of merchants with a high number of edges (201,725). The tripartite undirected graph has 267,016, equal to the number of customers plus the number of merchants plus all the transactions.

In this graph, the number of nodes, as expected, is higher (530,680) compared to the bipartite graph. The interesting difference in this comparison is given by the average degree of the two graphs. Indeed, the average degree of the bipartite graph is higher compared to the tripartite graph, as expected. Indeed, since, in the tripartite graph, the connections are "split" by the presence of the transaction nodes, the average degree is lower.

In the next section, we will describe how we can now use the transaction graphs generated to perform a more complete statistical analysis.

Network topology and community detection

In this section, we are going to analyze some graph metrics to have a clear picture of the general structure of the graph. We will be using networkx to compute most of the useful metrics we have seen in *Chapter 1*, *Getting Started with Graphs*. We will try to interpret the metrics to gain insights into the graph.

Network topology

A good starting point for our analysis is the extraction of simple graph metrics to have a general understanding of the main properties of bipartite and tripartite transaction graphs.

We start by looking at the distribution of the degree for both bipartite and tripartite graphs using the following code:

```python
for G in [G_bu, G_tu]:
  plt.figure(figsize=(10,10))
  degrees = pd.Series({k: v for k, v in nx.degree(G)})
  degrees.plot.hist()
  plt.yscale("log")
```

By way of a result, we get the plot in the following diagram:

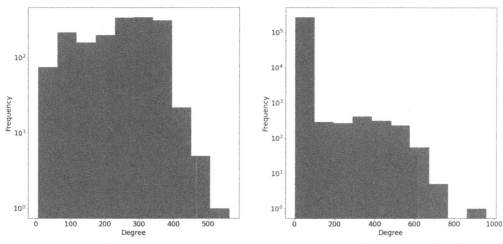

Bipartite nodes degree distribution   **Tripartite nodes degree distribution**

Figure 8.3 – Degree distribution for bipartite (left) and tripartite (right) graphs

From *Figure 8.3*, it is possible to see how the distribution of nodes reflects the average degree we previously saw. In greater detail, the bipartite graph has a more variegate distribution, with a peak of around 300. For the tripartite graph, the distribution has a big peak for degree 2, while the other part of the tripartite degree distribution is similar to the bipartite distribution. These distributions completely reflect the differences in how the two graphs were defined. Indeed, if bipartite graphs are made by connections from the customer to the merchant, in the tripartite graph, all the connections pass through the transaction nodes. Those nodes are the majority in the graph, and they all have a degree of 2 (an edge from a custom and an edge to a merchant). As a consequence, the frequency in the bin representing degree 2 is equal to the number of transaction nodes.

We will continue our investigation by analyzing the `edges weight` distribution:

1. We begin by computing the quantile distribution:

```
for G in [G_bu, G_tu]:
    allEdgesWeights = pd.Series({(d[0], d[1]): d[2]
["weight"] for d in G.edges(data=True)})
    np.quantile(allEdgesWeights.values, [0.10,0.50,0.70,0.9])
```

2. By way of a result, we get the following:

```
array([   5.03 ,    58.25 ,    98.44 ,  215.656])
  array([   4.21,    48.51,    76.4 ,  147.1 ])
```

3. Using the same command as before, we can also plot (in log scale) the distribution of edges weight, cut to the 90ᵗʰ percentile. The result is visible in the following diagram:

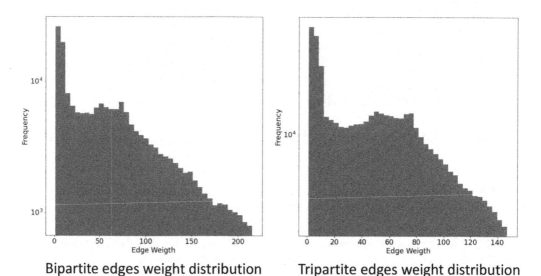

Bipartite edges weight distribution   Tripartite edges weight distribution

Figure 8.4 – Edge weight distribution for bipartite (left) and tripartite (right) graphs

We can see how, due to the aggregation of the transaction having the same customer and merchant, the distribution of the bipartite graph is shifted to the right (high values) compared to the tripartite graph, where edge weights were not computed, aggregating multiple transactions.

4. We will now investigate the betweenness centrality metric. It measures how many shortest paths pass through a given node, giving an idea of how *central* that node is for the spreading of information inside the network. We can compute the distribution of node centrality by using the following command:

```
for G in [G_bu, G_tu]:
    plt.figure(figsize=(10,10))
    bc_distr = pd.Series(nx.betweenness_centrality(G))
```

```
bc_distr.plot.hist()
plt.yscale("log")
```

5. As result, we get the following distributions:

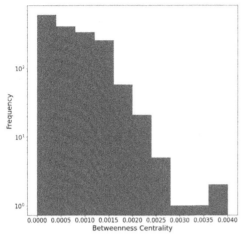

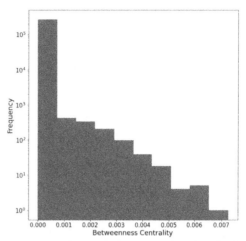

Bipartite betweenness centrality distribution   **Tripartite betweenness centrality distribution**

Figure 8.5 – Betweenness centrality distribution for bipartite (left) and tripartite (right) graphs

As expected, for both graphs, the betweenness centrality is low. This can be understood due to the large number of non-bridging nodes inside the network. Similar to what we saw for the degree distribution, the distribution of betweenness centrality values is different in the two graphs. Indeed, if the bipartite graph has a more variegate distribution with a mean of 0.00072, in the tripartite graph, the transaction nodes are the ones that mainly move the distribution values and lower the mean to 1.38e-05. Also, in this case, we can see that the distribution for the tripartite graph has a big peak, representing the transaction nodes, and the rest of the distribution is quite similar to the bipartite distribution.

6. We can finally compute the assortativity of the two graphs using the following code:

```
for G in [G_bu, G_tu]:
    print(nx.degree_pearson_correlation_coefficient(G))
```

7. By way of a result, we get the following:

```
-0.1377432041049189
-0.8079472914876812
```

Here, we can observe how both graphs have a negative assortativity, likely showing that well-connected individuals associate with poor-connected individuals. For the bipartite graph, the value is low (-0.14), since customers who have a low degree are only connected with merchants who have high degrees due to the high number of incoming transactions. The assortativity is even lower (-0.81) for the tripartite graph. This behavior is expected due to the presence of the transaction nodes. Indeed, those nodes always have a degree of 2, and they are linked to customers and merchants represented by highly connected nodes.

Community detection

Another interesting analysis we can perform is community detection. This analysis can help to identify specific fraudulent patterns:

1. The code to perform community extraction is as follows:

    ```
    import community
    for G in [G_bu, G_tu]:
        parts = community.best_partition(G, random_state=42,
    weight='weight')
        communities = pd.Series(parts)    print(communities.
    value_counts().sort_values(ascending=False))
    ```

    In this code, we simply use the `community` library to extract the communities in the input graph. We then print the communities detected by the algorithms, sorted according to the number of nodes contained.

2. For the bipartite graph, we obtain the following output:

5	546
0	335
7	139
2	136
4	123
3	111

8	83
9	59
10	57
6	48
11	26
1	13

3. For the tripartite graph, we obtain the following output:

11	4828		
3	4493		
26	4313		
94	4115		
8	4036		
	... 47	1160	
103	1132		
95	954		
85	845		
102	561		

4. Due to a large number of nodes in the tripartite graph, we found 106 communities (we reported just a subset of them), while, for the bipartite graph, only 12 communities were found. As consequence, to have a clear picture, for the tripartite graph, it is better to plot the distribution of the nodes contained in the different communities using the following command:

```
communities.value_counts().plot.hist(bins=20)
```

5. By way of a result, we get the following:

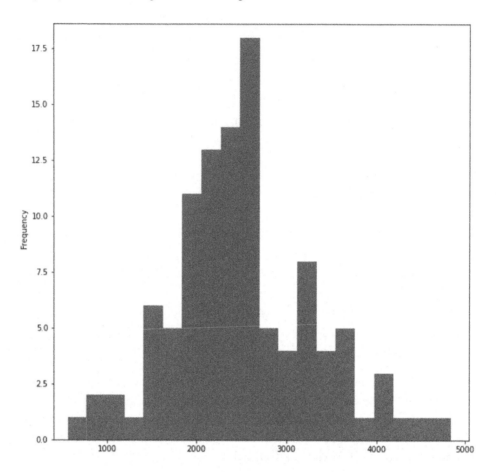

Figure 8.6 – Distribution of communities' node size

From the diagram, it is possible to see how the peak is reached around 2,500. This means that more than 30 large communities have more than 2,000 nodes. From the plot, it is also possible to see that a few communities have fewer than 1,000 nodes and more than 3,000 nodes.

6. For each set of communities detected by the algorithm, we can compute the percentage of fraudulent transactions. The goal of this analysis is to identify specific sub-graphs where there is a high concentration of fraudulent transactions:

```
graphs = []
d = {}
for x in communities.unique():
```

```
        tmp = nx.subgraph(G, communities[communities==x].
    index)
        fraud_edges = sum(nx.get_edge_attributes(tmp,
    "label").values())
        ratio = 0 if fraud_edges == 0 else (fraud_edges/tmp.
    number_of_edges())*100
        d[x] = ratio
        graphs += [tmp]
    print(pd.Series(d).sort_values(ascending=False))
```

7. The code simply generates a node-induced subgraph by using the nodes contained in a specific community. The graph is used to compute the percentage of fraudulent transactions as a ratio of the number of fraudulent edges over the number of all the edges in the graph. We can also plot a node-induced subgraph detected by the community detection algorithm by using the following code:

```
gId = 10
spring_pos = nx.spring_layout(graphs[gId])
 edge_colors = ["r" if x == 1 else "g" for x in nx.get_
edge_attributes(graphs[gId], 'label').values()]
nx.draw_networkx(graphs[gId], pos=spring_pos, node_
color=default_node_color, edge_color=edge_colors, with_
labels=False, node_size=15)
```

Given a particular community index, gId, the code extracts the node-induced subgraph, using the node available in the gId community index, and plots the graph obtained.

8. By running the two algorithms on the bipartite graph, we will obtain the following:

9	26.905830
10	25.482625
6	22.751323
2	21.993834
11	21.333333
3	20.470263
8	18.072289
4	16.218905
7	6.588580
0	4.963345

5	1.304983
1	0.000000

9. For each community, we have the percentage of its fraudulent edges. To have a better description of the subgraph, we can plot community 10 by executing the previous line of code using gId=10. As a result, we get the following:

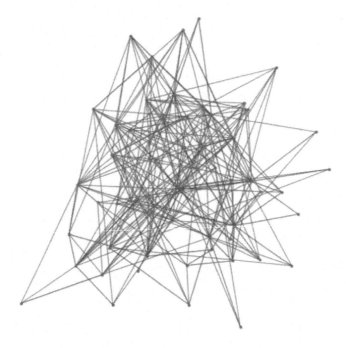

Figure 8.7 – Induced subgraph of community 10 for the bipartite graph

10. The image of the induced subgraph allows us to better understand whether specific patterns are visible in the data. Running the same algorithms on the tripartite graph, we obtain the following output:

6	6.857728
94	6.551151
8	5.966981
1	5.870918
89	5.760271
	. . .
102	0.889680
72	0.836013

85	0.708383
60	0.503461
46	0.205170

11. Due to the large number of communities, we can plot the distribution of the fraudulent over genuine ratio with the following command:

```
pd.Series(d).plot.hist(bins=20)
```

12. By way of a result, we get the following:

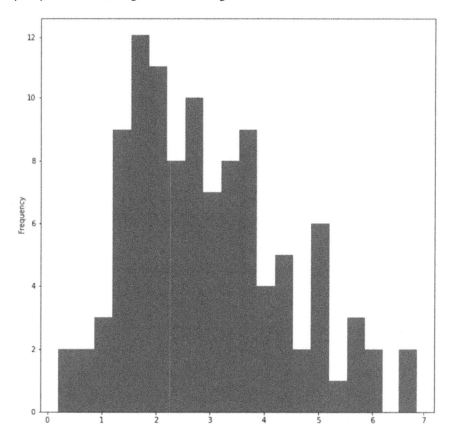

Figure 8.8 – Distribution of communities' fraudulent/genuine edge ratio

From the diagram, we can observe that a large part of the distribution is around communities having a ratio of between 2 and 4. There are a few communities with a low ratio (<1) and with a high ratio (>5).

13. Also, for the tripartite graph, we can plot community 6 (with a ratio of 6.86), made by 1,935 nodes, by executing the previous line of code using `gId=6`:

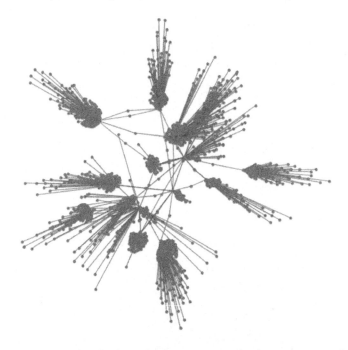

Figure 8.9 – Induced subgraph of community 6 for the tripartite graph

As for the bipartite use case, in this image, we can see an interesting pattern that could be used to perform a deeper exploration of some important graph sub-regions.

In this section, we perform some explorative tasks to better understand the graphs and their properties. We also gave an example describing how a community detection algorithm can be used to spot patterns in the data. In the next section, we will describe how machine learning can be used to automatically detect fraudulent transactions.

Embedding for supervised and unsupervised fraud detection

In this section, we will describe how the bipartite and tripartite graphs described previously can be used by graph machine learning algorithms to build automatic procedures for fraud detection using supervised and unsupervised approaches. As we already discussed at the beginning of this chapter, transactions are represented by edges, and we then want to classify each edge in the correct class: fraudulent or genuine.

The pipeline we will use to perform the classification task is the following:

- A sampling procedure for the imbalanced task
- The use of an unsupervised embedding algorithm to create a feature vector for each edge
- The application of supervised and unsupervised machine learning algorithms to the feature space defined in the previous point

Supervised approach to fraudulent transaction identification

Since our dataset is strongly imbalanced, with fraudulent transactions representing 2.83% of total transactions, we need to apply some techniques to deal with unbalanced data. In this use case, we will apply a simple random undersampling strategy. Going into more depth, we will take a subsample of the majority class (genuine transactions) to match the number of samples of the minority class (fraudulent transactions). This is just one of the many techniques available in literature. It is also possible to use outlier detection algorithms, such as isolation forest, to detect fraudulent transactions as outliers in the data. We leave it to you, as an exercise, to extend the analyses using other techniques to deal with imbalanced data, such as random oversampling or using cost-sensitive classifiers for the classification task. Specific techniques for node and edge sampling that can be directly applied to the graph will be described in *Chapter 10, Novel Trends on Graphs*:

1. The code we use for random undersampling is as follows:

```
from sklearn.utils import resample
df_majority = df[df.is_fraud==0]
df_minority = df[df.is_fraud==1]
df_maj_dowsampled = resample(df_majority, n_
samples=len(df_minority), random_state=42)
df_downsampled = pd.concat([df_minority, df_maj_
dowsampled])
G_down = build_graph_bipartite(df_downsampled,
nx.Graph())
```

2. The code is straightforward. We applied the `resample` function of the `sklearn` package to filter the `downsample` function of the original data frame. We then build a graph using the function defined at the beginning of the chapter. To create the tripartite graph, the `build_graph_tripartite` function should be used. As the next step, we split the dataset into training and validation with a ratio of 80/20:

```
from sklearn.model_selection import train_test_split
train_edges, val_edges, train_labels, val_labels = train_
test_split(list(range(len(G_down.edges))), list(nx.
get_edge_attributes(G_down, "label").values()), test_
size=0.20, random_state=42)
  edgs = list(G_down.edges)
train_graph = G_down.edge_subgraph([edgs[x] for x in
train_edges]).copy()
train_graph.add_nodes_from(list(set(G_down.nodes) -
set(train_graph.nodes)))
```

As before, also in this case, the code is straightforward since we simply apply the `train_test_split` function of the `sklearn` package.

3. We can now build the feature space using the `Node2Vec` algorithm as follows:

```
from node2vec import Node2Vec
node2vec = Node2Vec(train_graph, weight_key='weight')
  model = node2vec_train.fit(window=10)
```

The `node2vec` results are used to build, as described in *Chapter 3, Unsupervised Graph Learning*, the edge embedding that will generate the final feature space used by the classifier.

4. The code to perform this task is the following:

```
from sklearn import metrics
from sklearn.ensemble import RandomForestClassifier
from node2vec.edges import HadamardEmbedder,
AverageEmbedder, WeightedL1Embedder, WeightedL2Embedder
classes = [HadamardEmbedder, AverageEmbedder,
WeightedL1Embedder, WeightedL2Embedder]
for cl in classes:
    embeddings = cl(keyed_vectors=model.wv)
    train_embeddings = [embeddings[str(edgs[x][0]),
str(edgs[x][1])] for x in train_edges]
```

```
    val_embeddings = [embeddings[str(edgs[x][0]),
str(edgs[x][1])] for x in val_edges]
    rf = RandomForestClassifier(n_estimators=1000,
random_state=42)
    rf.fit(train_embeddings, train_labels)
    y_pred = rf.predict(val_embeddings)
    print(cl)
    print('Precision:', metrics.precision_score(val_
labels, y_pred))
    print('Recall:', metrics.recall_score(val_labels, y_
pred))
    print('F1-Score:', metrics.f1_score(val_labels, y_
pred))
```

Different steps are performed compared to the previous code:

1. For each `Edge2Vec` algorithm, the previously computed `Node2Vec` algorithm is used to generate the feature space.

2. A `RandomForestClassifier` from the `sklearn` Python library is trained on the feature set generated in the previous step.

3. Different performance metrics, namely, precision, recall, and F1-score, are computed on the validation test.

We can apply the code we previously described to both bipartite and tripartite graphs to solve the fraud detection task. In the following table, we report the performances for the bipartite graph:

EMBEDDING ALGORITHM	PRECISION	RECALL	F1-SCORE
HADAMARD EMBEDDER	0.73	0.76	0.75
AVERAGE EMBEDDER	0.71	0.79	0.75
WEIGHTED L1 EMBEDDER	0.64	0.78	0.70
WEIGHTED L2 EMBEDDER	0.63	0.78	0.70

Table 8.2 – Supervised fraud edge classification performances for a bipartite graph

In the following table, we report the performances for the tripartite graph:

EMBEDDING ALGORITHM	PRECISION	RECALL	F1-SCORE
HADAMARD EMBEDDER	0.89	0.29	0.44
AVERAGE EMBEDDER	0.74	0.45	0.48
WEIGHTED L1 EMBEDDER	0.66	0.46	0.55
WEIGHTED L2 EMBEDDER	0.66	0.47	0.55

Table 8.3 – Supervised fraud edge classification performances for a tripartite graph

In *Table 8.2* and *Table 8.3*, we reported the classification performances obtained using bipartite and tripartite graphs. As we can see from the results, the two methods, in terms of F1-score, precision, and recall, show significant differences. Since, for both graph types, Hadamard and average edge embedding algorithms give the most interesting results, we are going to focus our attention on those two. Going into more detail, the tripartite graph has a better precision compared to the bipartite graph (0.89 and 0.74 for the tripartite graph versus 0.73 and 0.71 for the bipartite graph).

In contrast, the bipartite graph has a better recall compared to the tripartite graph (0.76 and 0.79 for the bipartite graph versus 0.29 and 0.45 for the tripartite graph). We can therefore conclude that in this specific case, the use of a bipartite graph could be a better choice since it achieves high performances in terms of F1 with a smaller graph (in terms of nodes and edges) compared to the tripartite graph.

Unsupervised approach to fraudulent transaction identification

The same approach can also be applied in unsupervised tasks using k-means. The main difference is that the generated feature space will not undergo a train-validation split. Indeed, in the following code, we will compute the Node2Vec algorithm on the entire graph generated following the downsampling procedure:

```
nod2vec_unsup = Node2Vec(G_down, weight_key='weight')
unsup_vals = nod2vec_unsup.fit(window=10)
```

As previously defined for the supervised analysis, when building the node feature vectors, we can use different `Egde2Vec` algorithms to run the k-means algorithm as follows:

```python
from sklearn.cluster import KMeans
classes = [HadamardEmbedder, AverageEmbedder,
WeightedL1Embedder, WeightedL2Embedder]
 true_labels = [x for x in nx.get_edge_attributes(G_down,
"label").values()]
for cl in classes:
    embedding_edge = cl(keyed_vectors=unsup_vals.wv)
    embedding = [embedding_edge[str(x[0]), str(x[1])] for x in
G_down.edges()]
    kmeans = KMeans(2, random_state=42).fit(embedding)
    nmi = metrics.adjusted_mutual_info_score(true_labels,
kmeans.labels_)
    ho = metrics.homogeneity_score(true_labels, kmeans.labels_)
    co = metrics.completeness_score(true_labels, kmeans.labels_
    vmeasure = metrics.v_measure_score(true_labels, kmeans.
labels_)
    print(cl)
    print('NMI:', nmi)
    print('Homogeneity:', ho)
    print('Completeness:', co)
    print('V-Measure:', vmeasure)
```

Different steps are performed in the previous code:

1. For each `Edge2Vec` algorithm, the previously computed `Node2Vec` algorithm on train and validation sets is used to generate the feature space.

2. A `KMeans` clustering algorithm from the `sklearn` Python library is fitted on the feature set generated in the previous step.

3. Different performance metrics, namely, adjusted **mutual information** (**MNI**), homogeneity, completeness, and v-measure scores.

We can apply the code described previously to both bipartite and tripartite graphs to solve the fraud detection task using the unsupervised algorithm. In the following table, we report the performances for the bipartite graph:

EMBEDDING ALGORITHM	MNI	HOMOGENEITY	COMPLETENESS	V-MEASURE
HADAMARD EMBEDDER	0.34	0.33	0.36	0.34
AVERAGE EMBEDDER	0.07	0.07	0.07	0.07
WEIGHTED L1 EMBEDDER	0.06	0.06	0.06	0.06
WEIGHTED L2 EMBEDDER	0.05	0.05	0.05	0.05

Table 8.4 – Unsupervised fraud edge classification performances for the bipartite graph

In the following table, we report the performances for the tripartite graph:

EMBEDDING ALGORITHM	MNI	HOMOGENEITY	COMPLETENESS	V-MEASURE
HADAMARD EMBEDDER	0.44	0.44	0.45	0.44
AVERAGE EMBEDDER	0.06	0.06	0.06	0.06
WEIGHTED L1 EMBEDDER	0.001	0.001	0.00	0.06
WEIGHTED L2 EMBEDDER	0.0004	0.0004	0.0004	0.0004

Table 8.5 – Unsupervised fraud edge classification performances for the tripartite graph

In *Table 8.4* and *Table 8.5*, we reported the classification performances obtained using bipartite and tripartite graphs with the application of an unsupervised algorithm. As we can see from the results, the two methods show significant differences. It is also worth noticing that, in this case, the performances obtained with the Hadamard embedding algorithm clearly outperform all other approaches.

As shown by *Table 8.4* and *Table 8.5*, also for this task, the performances obtained with the tripartite graph outstrip those obtained with the bipartite graph. In the unsupervised case, we can see how the introduction of the transaction nodes improves overall performance. We can assert, that, in the unsupervised setting, for this specific use case and using as a reference the results obtained in *Table 8.4* and *Table 8.5*, use of the tripartite graph could be a better choice since it enables the attainment of superior performances compared with the bipartite graph.

Summary

In this chapter, we described how a classical fraud detection task can be described as a graph problem and how the techniques described in the previous chapter can be used to tackle the problem. Going into more detail, we introduced the dataset we used and described the procedure to transform the transactional data into two types of graph, namely, bipartite and tripartite undirected graphs. We then computed local (along with their distributions) and global metrics for both graphs, comparing the results.

Moreover, a community detection algorithm was applied to the graphs in order to spot and plot specific regions of the transaction graph where the density of fraudulent transactions is higher compared to the other communities.

Finally, we solved the fraud detection problem using supervised and unsupervised algorithms, comparing the performances of the bipartite and tripartite graphs. As the first step, since the problem was unbalanced with a higher presence of genuine transactions, we performed simple downsampling. We then applied different Edge2Vec algorithms in combination with a random forest, for the supervised task, and k-means for an unsupervised task, achieving good classification performances.

This chapter concludes the series of examples that are used to show how graph machine learning algorithms can be applied to problems belonging to different domains, such as social network analysis, text analytics, and credit card transaction analysis.

In the next chapter, we will describe some practical uses for graph databases and graph processing engines that are useful for scaling out the analysis to large graphs.

9
Building a Data-Driven Graph-Powered Application

So far, we have provided you with both theoretical and practical ideas to allow you to design and implement machine learning models that leverage graph structures. Besides designing the algorithm, it is often very important to embed the modeling/analytical pipeline into a robust and reliable end-to-end application. This is especially true in industrial applications, where the end goal is usually to design and implement production systems that support data-driven decisions and/or provide users with timely information. However, creating a data-driven application that resorts to graph representation/modeling is indeed a challenging task that requires a proper design that is a lot more complicated than simply importing `networkx`. This chapter aims to provide you with a general overview of the key concepts and frameworks that are used when building graph-based, scalable, data-driven applications.

We will start by providing an overview of the so-called **Lambda architectures**, which provide a framework to structure scalable applications that require large-scale processing and real-time updates. We will then continue by applying this framework in the context of *graph-powered applications*, that is, applications that leverage graph structures using techniques such as the ones described in this book. We will describe their two main analytical components: **graph processing engines** and **graph querying engines**. We'll present some of the technologies used, both in shared memory machines and distributed memory machines, outlining similarities and differences. The following topics will be covered in this chapter:

- Overview of Lambda architectures

- Lambda architectures for graph-powered applications

- Technologies and examples of graph processing engines

- Graph querying engines and graph databases

Technical requirements

We will be using Python 3.8 for all of our exercises. In the following code block, you can find a list of the Python libraries that need to be installed for this chapter using `pip`. For example, run `pip install networkx==2.5` on the command line, and so on:

```
networkx==2.5
neo4j==4.2.0
gremlinpython==3.4.6
```

All the code files relevant to this chapter are available at `https://github.com/PacktPublishing/Graph-Machine-Learning/tree/main/Chapter09`.

Overview of Lambda architectures

In recent years, great focus has been given to designing scalable architectures that will allow, on the one hand, the *processing of a large amount of data*, and, on the other, *providing answers/alerts/actions in real time, using the latest available information*.

Besides, these systems need to also be able to scale out seamlessly to a larger number of users or a larger amount of data by increasing resources horizontally (adding more servers) or vertically (using servers that are more powerful). **Lambda architecture** is a particular data-processing architecture that is designed to process massive quantities of data and ensure large throughput in a very efficient manner, preserving reduced latency and ensuring fault tolerance and negligible errors.

The Lambda architecture is composed of three different layers:

- **The batch layer**: This layer sits on top of the (possibly distributed and scalable) storage system, and can handle and store all historical data, as well as performing **Online Analytical Processing (OLAP)** computation on the entire dataset. New data is continuously ingested and stored, as it would be traditionally done in data warehouse systems. Large-scale processing is generally achieved via massively parallel jobs, which aim at producing aggregation, structuring, and computation of relevant information. In the context of machine learning, model training that relies on historic information is generally done in this layer, thus producing a trained model to be used either in a batch prediction job or in real-time execution.

- **The speed layer**: This is a low-latency layer that allows the real-time processing of the information to provide timely updates and information. It is generally fed by a streaming process, usually involving fast computation that does not require long computational time or load. It produces an output that is integrated with the data generated by the batch layer in (near) real time, providing support for **Online Transaction Processing (OLTP)** operations. The speed layer might also very well use some outputs of the OLAP computations, such as a trained model. Oftentimes, applications that use machine learning modeling in real time (for example, fraud detection engines used in credit card transactions) embed in their speed layers trained models that provide prompt predictions and trigger real-time alerts of potential fraud. Libraries may operate at an event level (such as Apache Storm) or over mini-batches (such as Spark Streaming), providing, depending on the use case, slightly different requirements for latency, fault tolerance, and computational speed.

- **The serving layer**: The serving layer has the duty of organizing, structuring, and indexing information in order to allow the fast retrieval of data coming from the batch and speed layers. The serving layer thus integrates the outputs of the batch layer with the most updated and real-time information of the speed layer in order to deliver to the user a unified and coherent view of the data. A serving layer can be composed of a persistence layer that integrates both historical aggregation and real-time updates. This component may be based on some kind of database, which can be relational or not, conveniently indexed in order to reduce latency and allow the fast retrieval of relevant data. The information is generally exposed to the user via either a direct connection to the database and is accessible using a specific domain query language, such as SQL, or also via dedicated services, such as RESTful API servers (which in Python can be easily implemented using several frameworks, such as `flask`, `fastapi`, or `turbogear`), which provide the data via specifically designed endpoints:

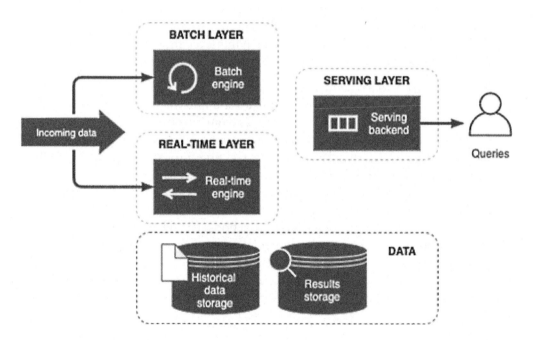

Figure 9.1 – Functional diagram for an application based on Lambda architecture

Lambda architectures have several benefits that have motivated and promoted their use, especially in the context of *big data* applications. In the following bullet points, we list some of the main pros of Lambda architectures:

- **No server management**: As the Lambda architectural design pattern typically abstracts the functional layers and does not require installing, maintaining, or administering any software/infrastructure

- **Flexible scaling**: As the application can be either automatically scaled or scaled by controlling the number of processing units that are used in batch layers (for example, computing nodes) and/or in speed layers (for example, Kafka brokers) separately

- **Automated high availability**: Due to the fact that it represents a serverless design for which we already have built-in availability and fault tolerance

- **Business agility**: Reacts in real time to changing business/market scenarios

Although very powerful and flexible, Lambda architectures come with some limitations mainly due to the presence of two interconnected processing flows: the **batch layer** and the **speed layer**. This may require developers to build and maintain separate code bases for batch and stream processes, resulting in more complexity and code overhead, which may lead to harder debugging, possible misalignment, and bug promotion.

Here, we have provided a short overview of Lambda architectures and their basic building blocks. For more details on how to design scalable architectures and the most commonly used architectural patterns, please refer to the book *Data Lake for Enterprises*, 2017, by Tomcy John and Pankaj Misra.

In the next section, we will show you how to implement a Lambda architecture for graph-powered applications. In particular, we will describe the main components and review the most common technologies.

Lambda architectures for graph-powered applications

When dealing with scalable, graph-powered, data-driven applications, the design of Lambda architectures is also reflected in the separation of functionalities between two crucial components of the analytical pipeline, as shown in *Figure 9.2*:

- The **graph processing engine** executes computations on the graph structure in order to extract features (such as embeddings), compute statistics (such as degree distributions, the number of edges, and cliques), compute metrics and **Key Performance Indicators (KPIs)** (such as centrality measures and clustering coefficients), and identify relevant subgraphs (for example, communities) that often require OLAP.

- The **graph querying engine** allows us to persist network data (usually done via a graph database) and provides fast information retrieval and efficient querying and graph traversal (usually via graph querying languages). All of the information is already persisted in some data storage (that may or may not be in memory) and no further computation is required apart from (possibly) some final aggregation results, for which indexing is crucial to achieving high performance and low latency:

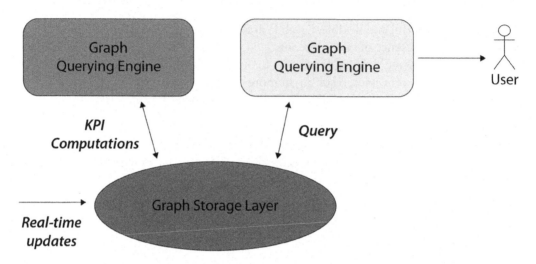

Figure 9.2 – Graph-based architecture, with the main components
also reflected in a Lambda architectural pattern

Graph processing engines sit on top of batch layers and produce outputs that may be stored and indexed in appropriate graph databases. These databases are the backend of graph querying engines, which allow relevant information to be easily and quickly retrieved, representing the operational views used by the serving layer. Depending on the use cases and/or the size of the graph, it often makes sense to run both the graph processing engine and the graph query engine on top of the same infrastructure.

Instead of storing the graph on a low-level storage layer (for example, the filesystem, HDFS, or S3), there are graph database options that could support both OLAP and OLTP. These provide, at the same time, a backend persistence layer where historical information processed by batch layers, together with real-time updates from the speed layer, is stored, and information to be queried efficiently by the serving layer.

As compared to other use cases, this condition is indeed quite peculiar for graph-powered, data-driven applications. Historical data often provides a topology on top of which new, real-time updates and OLAP outputs (KPIs, data aggregations, embeddings, communities, and so on) can be stored. This data structure also represents the information that is later queried by the serving layer that traverses the enriched graph.

Graph processing engines

To select the right technology for a **graph processing engine**, it is crucial to estimate the size in memory of the network compared to the capacity of the target architecture. You can start by using simpler frameworks that allow fast prototyping during the first phases of a project when the goal is to quickly build a **Minimum Viable Product (MVP)**.

Such frameworks can then be substituted by more advanced tools later on when performance and scalability become more crucial. A microservice modular approach and proper structuring of these components will allow the switching of technologies/libraries independently from the rest of the application to target specific issues, which will also guide the choice of the backend stack.

Graph processing engines require information on the whole graphs to be accessed quickly, that is, having all of the graph in memory, and depending on the context, you might or might not need *distributed architectures*. As we saw in *Chapter 1, Getting Started with Graphs*, networkx is a great example of a library to build a graph processing engine when dealing with reasonably small datasets. When datasets get larger, but they can still fit in single servers or shared memory machines, other libraries may help to reduce computational time. As seen in *Chapter 1, Getting Started with Graphs*, using libraries other than networkx where graph algorithms are implemented in more performant languages,
such as C++ or Julia, may dramatically speed up the computation by more than two orders of magnitude.

However, there are cases where datasets grow so much that it is no longer technologically or economically viable to use shared memory machines of increasing capacity (fat nodes). In such cases, it is rather necessary to distribute the data on clusters of tens or hundreds of computing nodes, allowing horizontal scaling. The two most popular frameworks that can support a graph processing engine in these cases are the following:

- **Apache Spark GraphX**, which is the module of the Spark library that deals with graph structures (`https://spark.apache.org/graphx`). It involves a distributed representation of the graph using **Resilient Distributed Datasets (RDDs)** for both vertices and edges. The graph repartition throughout the computing nodes can be done either with an *edge-cut* strategy, which logically corresponds to dividing the nodes among multiple machines, or a *vertex-cut* strategy, which logically corresponds to assigning edges to different machines and allowing vertices to span multiple machines. Although written in Scala, GraphX features wrappers with both R and Python. GraphX already comes with some algorithms implemented, such as *PageRank*, *connected components*, and *triangle counting*. There are also other libraries that can be used on top of GraphX for other algorithms, such as **SparklingGraph**, which implements more centrality measures.

- **Apache Giraph**, which is an iterative graph processing system built for high scalability (`https://giraph.apache.org/`). It was developed, and is currently used, by Facebook to analyze the social graph formed by users and their connections and is built on top of the Hadoop ecosystem for unleashing the potential of structured datasets at a massive scale. Giraph is natively written in Java and, similarly to GraphX, also provides a scalable implementation for some basic graph algorithms, such as *PageRank* and *shortest path*.

When we consider scale-out to a distributed ecosystem, we should always keep in mind that the available choice for algorithms is significantly smaller than in a shared machine context. This is generally due to two reasons:

- First, implementing algorithms in a distributed way is a lot more complex than in a shared machine due to communication among nodes, which also reduces the overall efficiency.

- Secondly, and more importantly, one fundamental mantra of big data analytics is that only algorithms that (nearly) scale linearly with the number of data points should be implemented in order to ensure horizontal scalability of the solution, by increasing the computational nodes as the dataset increases.

In this respect, both Giraph and GraphX allow you to define scalable, vertex-centric, iterative algorithms using standard interfaces based on **Pregel**, which can be seen as a sort of equivalent of iterative map-reduce operations for graphs (actually, iterative map-reduce operations applied to triplet node-edge-node instances). A Pregel computation is composed of a sequence of iterations, each called a **superstep**, each involving a node and its neighbors.

During the superstep, S, a user-defined function is applied for each vertex, V. This function takes the messages sent to V in superstep $S - 1$ as input and modifies the state of V and its outgoing edges. This function represents the mapping stage, which can be easily parallelized. Besides computing the new states of V, the function also sends messages to other vertices connected to V, which will receive this information at superstep $S + 1$. Messages are typically sent along outgoing edges, but a message may be sent to any vertex whose identifier is known. In *Figure 9.3*, we show a sketch of what a Pregel algorithm would look like when computing the maximum value over a network. For further details on this algorithm, please refer to the original paper, *Pregel: A System for Large-Scale Graph Processing*, written by Malewicz et al. in 2010:

Superstep S

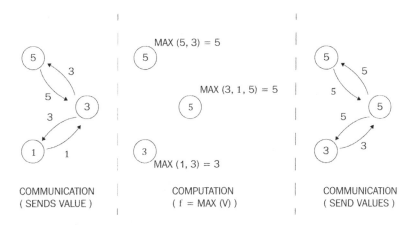

Figure 9.3 – Example of calculating a maximum value over a node property using Pregel

By using Pregel, you can easily implement other algorithms, such as *PageRank* or *connected components*, in a very efficient and general way, or even implement node embeddings' parallel variants (for an example, see *Distributed-Memory Vertex-Centric Network Embedding for Large-Scale Graphs*, Riazi and Norris, 2020).

Graph querying layer

In the last decade, due to the large diffusion of non-structured data, NoSQL databases have started to gain considerable attention and importance. Among them, **graph databases** are indeed extremely powerful to store information based on a relation between entities. Indeed, in many applications, data can naturally be seen as entities, associated with metadata in the form of node properties, connected by edges that also have properties that further describe the relationship between entities.

Examples of graph databases are libraries or tools such as Neo4j, OrientDB, ArangoDB, Amazon Neptune, Cassandra, and JanusGraph (previously named TitanDB). In the following sections, we will briefly describe some of them, together with the languages that allow us to query and traverse the underlying graphs, which are called **graph querying languages**.

Neo4j

At the time of writing, **Neo4J** (`https://neo4j.com/`) is surely the most common graph database around, with a large community supporting its use and adoption. It features two editions:

- *Community Edition*, released under a GPL v3 license, which allows users/developers to openly include Neo4j in their applications
- *Enterprise Edition*, designed for commercial deployments where scale and availability are crucial

Neo4j can scale out to fairly large datasets via **sharding**, that is, distributing data over multiple nodes and parallelizing queries and aggregation over multiple instances of the database. Besides, the Neo4j federation also allows querying smaller separated graphs (sometimes even with a different schema) as if they were one large graph.

Some of Neo4j's strong points are its flexibility (which allows the schema to be evolved) and its user-friendliness. In particular, many operations in Neo4j can be done through its query language, which is very intuitive and easy to learn: **Cypher**. Cypher can just be seen as the counterpart of SQL for graph databases.

Testing out Neo4j and Cypher is extremely easy. You could install the Community Edition (via Docker; see the next section) or play around with an online sandbox version (`https://neo4j.com/sandbox/`).

By using the latter, you can import some built-in datasets, such as the Movie dataset, and start querying it using the Cypher query language. The Movie dataset is made up of 38 movies and 133 people that acted in, directed, wrote, reviewed, and produced them. Both the on-premises version and the online version are equipped with a user-friendly UI that allows the user to query and visualize the data (see *Figure 9.4*). We start by listing 10 actors in the Movie dataset, by simply querying the following:

```
MATCH (p: Person) RETURN p LIMIT 10
```

But let's now leverage the information about relations between data points. We see that one of the actors that appears in the database is Keanu Reeves. We may wonder who all the actors that he has acted with in the listed movies are. This information can be easily retrieved using the following query:

```
MATCH (k: Person {name:"Keanu Reeves"})-[:ACTED_IN]-(m: Movie)-
[:ACTED_IN]-(a: Person) RETURN k, m, a
```

As shown in the following figure, the query intuitively and graphically indicates in its syntax how to traverse the graph by declaring the path we are interested in:

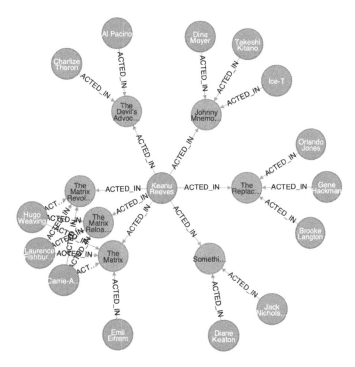

Figure 9.4 – Example of the Neo4j UI with the Cypher query to retrieve the co-actors of Keanu Reeves in the Movie dataset

Besides Cypher, data can also be queried using Gremlin. This will be described shortly as a common interface for graph databases.

Neo4j also provides bindings with several programming languages, such as Python, JavaScript, Java, Go, Spring, and .NET. For Python in particular, there are several libraries that implement connections with Neo4j, such as `neo4j`, `py2neo`, and `neomodel`, of which `neo4j` is the official and supported one and provides direct connections to the database via a binary protocol. Creating a connection to the database and running a query is just a matter of a few lines of code:

```
from neo4j import GraphDatabase
driver = GraphDatabase("bolt://localhost:7687", "my-user", "my-password")
def run_query(tx, query):
    return tx.run(query)
with driver.session() as session:
    session.write_transaction(run_query, query)
```

A query could be any Cypher query, for instance, the one written previously to retrieve the co-actors of Keanu Reeves.

JanusGraph – a graph database to scale out to very large datasets

Neo4j is an extremely great piece of software, unbeatable when you want to get things done quickly, thanks to its intuitive interface and query language. Neo4j is indeed a graph database suitable for production, but especially good in MVPs when agility is crucial. However, as data increases, its scalability based on sharding and breaking down large graphs into smaller subgraphs may not be the best option.

When the volume of the data increases substantially, you should probably start to consider other graph database options. Once again, this should be done only when the use case requirements start to hit the scalability limitation of Neo4j, as needs evolve from the MVP initial requirements.

In such cases, there are several options. Some of them are commercial products, such as Amazon Neptune or Cassandra. However, open source options are also available. Among them, we believe it is worth mentioning **JanusGraph** (https://janusgraph.org/), which is a particularly interesting piece of software. JanusGraph is the evolution of a previously open source project that was called **TitanDB** and is now an official project under the Linux Foundation, also featuring support from top players in the tech landscape, such as IBM, Google, Hortonworks, Amazon, Expero, and Grakn Labs.

JanusGraph is a scalable graph database designed for storing and querying graphs distributed across a multi-machine cluster with hundreds of billions of vertices and edges. As a matter of fact, JanusGraph does not have a storage layer on its own, but it is rather a component, written in Java, that sits on top of other data storage layers, such as the following:

- **Google Cloud Bigtable** (`https://cloud.google.com/bigtable`), which is the cloud version of the proprietary data storage system built on Google File System, designed to scale a massive amount of data distributed across data centers (*Bigtable: A Distributed Storage System for Structured Data*, Fay Chang et al., 2006).

- **Apache HBase** (`https://hbase.apache.org/`), which is a non-relational database that features Bigtable capabilities on top of Hadoop and HDFS, thus ensuring similar scalability and fault tolerance.

- **Apache Cassandra** (`https://cassandra.apache.org/`), which is an open source distributed NoSQL database that allows handling a large amount of data, spanning multiple data centers.

- **ScyllaDB** (`https://www.scylladb.com/`), which is specifically designed for real-time applications, is compatible with Apache Cassandra while achieving significantly higher throughputs and lower latencies.

Thus, JanusGraph inherits all the good features, such as scalability, high availability, and fault tolerance, from scalable solutions, abstracting a graph view on top of them.

With its integration with ScyllaDB, JanusGraph handles extremely fast, scalable, and high-throughput applications. Besides, JanusGraph also integrates indexing layers that can be based on Apache Lucene, Apache Solr, and Elasticsearch in order to allow even faster information retrieval and search functionalities within the graph.

The usage of highly distributed backends together with indexing layers allows JanusGraph to scale to enormous graphs, with hundreds of billions of nodes and edges, efficiently handling the so-called **supernodes**—in other words, nodes that have an extremely large degree, which often arise in real-world applications (remember that a very famous model for real networks is the *Barabasi-Albert* model, based on preferential attachments, which makes hubs naturally emerge within the graph).

In large graphs, supernodes are often potential bottlenecks of the application, especially when the business logic requires traversing the graph passing through them. Having properties that can help with rapidly filtering only the relevant edges during a graph traversal can dramatically speed up the process and achieve better performance.

JanusGraph exposes a standard API to query and traverse the graph via the **Apache TinkerPop** library (`https://tinkerpop.apache.org/`), which is an open source, vendor-agnostic graph computing framework. TinkerPop provides a standard interface for querying and analyzing the underlying graph using the **Gremlin** graph traversal language. All TinkerPop-compatible graph database systems can therefore integrate seamlessly with one another. TinkerPop thus allows you to build "standard" serving layers that do not depend on the backend technology, giving you the freedom to choose/change the appropriate graph technology for your application depending on your actual needs. As a matter of fact, most of the graph databases (even Neo4j as we have seen previously) nowadays feature integration with TinkerPop, making switching between backend graph databases seamless and avoiding any vendor lock-in.

Besides Java connectors, Gremlin also has direct Python bindings thanks to the `gremlinpython` library, which allows Python applications to connect to and traverse graphs. In order to query the graph structure, we first need to connect to the database, using the following:

```python
from gremlin_python.driver.driver_remote_connection import
DriverRemoteConnection
connection = DriverRemoteConnection(
    'ws://localhost:8182/gremlin', 'g'
)
```

Once the connection is created, we can then instantiate `GraphTraversalSource`, which is the basis for all Gremlin traversals, and bind it to the connection we just created:

```python
from gremlin_python.structure.graph import Graph
from gremlin_python.process.graph_traversal import __
graph = Graph()
g = graph.traversal().withRemote(connection)
```

Once `GraphTraversalSource` is instantiated, we can reuse it across the application to query the graph database. Imagine that we have imported the Movie graph database we described previously into JanusGraph; we can re-write the Cypher query we used previously to find all the co-actors of Keanu Reeves using Gremlin:

```python
co_actors = g.V().has('Person', 'name', 'Keanu Reeves').
out("ACTED_IN").in("ACTED_IN").values("name")
```

As can be seen from the preceding code lines, Gremlin is a functional language whereby operators are grouped together to form path-like expressions.

Selecting between Neo4j and GraphX

Neo4j or GraphX? This is a question that often gets asked. However, as we have described briefly, the two pieces of software are not really competitors, but they rather target different needs. Neo4j allows us to store information in a graph-like structure and query the data, whereas GraphX makes it possible to analytically process a graph (especially for large graph dimensions). Although you could also use Neo4j as a processing engine (and indeed the Neo4j ecosystem features a Graph Data Science library, which is an actual processing engine) and GraphX could also be used as an in-memory stored graph, such approaches should be discouraged.

Graph processing engines usually compute KPIs that get stored in the graph database layers (potentially indexed such that querying and sorting become efficient) for later use. Thus, technologies such as GraphX are not competing with graph databases such as Neo4j, and they can very well co-exist within the same application to serve different purposes. As we stressed in the introduction, even in MVPs and at early stages, it is best to separate the two components, the graph processing engine and the graph querying engine, and use appropriate technologies for each of them.

Simple and easy-to-use libraries and tools do exist in both cases and we strongly encourage you to use them wisely in order to build a solid and reliable application that can be scaled out seamlessly.

Summary

In this section, we have provided you with the basic concepts of how to design, implement, and deploy data-driven applications that resort to graph modeling and leverage graph structures. We have highlighted the importance of a modular approach, which is usually the key to seamlessly scaling any data-driven use case from early-stage MVPs to production systems that can handle a large amount of data and large computational performances.

We have outlined the main architectural pattern, which should provide you with a guide when designing the backbone structure of your data-driven applications. We then continued by describing the main components that are the basis of graph-powered applications: *graph processing engines*, *graph databases*, and *graph querying languages*. For each component, we have provided an overview of the most common tools and libraries, with practical examples that will help you to build and implement your solutions. You should thus have by now a good overview of what the main technologies out there are and what they should be used for.

In the next chapter, we will turn to some recent developments and the latest research that trends in machine learning that has been applied to graphs. In particular, we will describe some of the latest techniques (such as generative neural networks) and applications (such as graph theory applied in neuroscience) available in the scientific literature, providing some practical examples and possible applications.

10
Novel Trends on Graphs

In the previous chapters, we described different supervised and unsupervised algorithms that can be used in a wide range of problems concerning graph data structures. However, the scientific literature on graph machine learning is vast and constantly evolving and every month, new algorithms are published. In this chapter, we will provide a high-level description of some new techniques and applications concerning graph machine learning.

This chapter will be divided into two main parts – advanced algorithms and applications. The first part is mainly devoted to describing some interesting new techniques in the graph machine learning domain. You will learn about some data sampling and data augmentation techniques for graphs based on random walk and generative neural networks. Then, you will learn about topological data analysis, a relatively novel tool for analyzing high-dimensional data. In the second part, we will provide you with some interesting applications of graph machine learning in different domains, ranging from biology to geometrical analysis. After reading this chapter, you will be aware of how looking at the relationships between data opened the door to novel intriguing solutions.

Specifically, we will cover the following topics in this chapter:

- Learning about data augmentation for graphs
- Learning about topological data analysis
- Applying graph theory in new domains

Before we get started, let's ensure we have the prerequisites mentioned in the following section.

Technical requirements

We will be using Python 3.6.9 for all our exercises. The following is the list of Python libraries that you must install for this chapter using `pip`. For example, you can run `pip install networkx==2.5` on the command line, and so on:

```
networkx==2.5
littleballoffur==2.1.8
```

All the code files relevant to this chapter are available at URL TO BE DECIDED.

Learning about data augmentation for graphs

In *Chapter 8, Graph Analysis for Credit Card Transactions*, we described how graph machine learning can be used to study and automatically detect fraudulent credit card transactions. While describing the use case, we faced two main obstacles:

- There were too many nodes in the original dataset to handle. As a consequence, the computational cost was too high to be computed. This is why we selected only 20% of the dataset.
- From the original dataset, we saw that less than 1% of the data had been labeled as fraudulent transactions, while the other 99% of the dataset contained genuine transactions. This is why, during the edge classification task, we randomly subsampled the dataset.

The techniques we used to solve these two obstacles, in general, are not optimal. For graph data, more complex and innovative techniques are needed to solve the task. Moreover, when datasets are highly unbalanced, as we mentioned in *Chapter 8*, *Graph Analysis for Credit Card Transactions*, we can solve this using anomaly detection algorithms.

In this section, we will provide a description of some techniques and algorithms we can use to solve the aforementioned problems. We will start by describing the graph sampling problem and we will finish by describing some graph data augmentation techniques. We will share some useful references and Python libraries for both of these.

Sampling strategies

In *Chapter 8*, *Graph Analysis for Credit Card Transactions*, to perform the edge classification task, we started our analysis by sampling only 20% of the whole dataset. Unfortunately, this strategy, in general, it is not an optimal one. Indeed, the subset of nodes that are selected with this simple strategy could generate a subgraph that is not representative of the topology of the whole graph. Due to this, we need to define a strategy for building a subgraph of a given graph by sampling the right nodes. The process of building a (small) subgraph from a given (large) graph by minimizing the loss of *topological* information is known as **graph sampling**.

A good starting point so that we have a full overview of the graph sampling algorithm is available in the paper *Little Ball of Fur: A Python Library for Graph Sampling*, which can be downloaded from the following URL: https://arxiv.org/pdf/2006.04311. pdf. Their Python implementation of using the networkx library is available at the following URL: https://github.com/benedekrozemberczki/littleballoffur. The algorithms that are available in this library can be divided into nodes and edges sampling algorithms. These algorithms sample the nodes and edges in the graph bundling, respectively. As a result, we get a node- or edge-induced subgraph from the original graph. We will leave you to perform the analysis proposed in *Chapter 8*, *Graph Analysis for Credit Card Transactions*, using the different graph sampling strategies available in the littleballoffur Python package.

Exploring data augmentation techniques

Data augmentation is a common technique when we're dealing with unbalanced data. In unbalanced problems, we usually have labeled data from two or more classes. Only a few samples are available for one or more classes in the dataset. A class that contains a few samples is also known as a *minority* class, while a class that contains a large number of samples is known as a *majority* class. For instance, in the use case described in *Chapter 8*, *Graph Analysis for Credit Card Transactions*, we had a clear example of an unbalanced dataset. In the input dataset, only 1% of all the available transactions were marked as fraudulent (the minority class), while the other 99% were genuine transactions (the majority class). When dealing with *classical* datasets, the problem is usually solved using random down or up sampling or using data generation algorithms such as *SMOTE*. However, for graph data, this process may not be as easy since generating new nodes or graphs is not a straightforward process. This is due to the presence of complex topological relations. In the last decade, a large range of data augmentation graph algorithms have been made. Here, we will introduce two of the latest available algorithms, namely *GAug* and *GRAN*.

The GAug algorithm is a node-based data augmentation algorithm. It is described in the paper *Data Augmentation for Graph Neural Networks*, which is available at the following URL: `https://arxiv.org/pdf/2006.06830.pdf`. The Python code for this library is available at the following URL: `https://github.com/zhao-tong/GAug`. This algorithm can be useful for use cases where edge or node classification is needed, as in the use case provided in *Chapter 8*, *Graph Analysis for Credit Card Transactions*, where the nodes belonging to the minority class can be augmented using the algorithm. As an exercise, you can extend on the analysis we proposed in *Chapter 8*, *Graph Analysis for Credit Card Transactions*, using the GAug algorithm.

The GRAN algorithm is a graph-based data augmentation algorithm. It is described in the paper *Efficient Graph Generation with Graph Recurrent Attention Networks*, which is available at the following URL: `https://arxiv.org/pdf/1910.00760.pdf`. The Python code for the library is available at the following URL: `https://github.com/lrjconan/GRAN`. This algorithm is useful for generating new graphs when we're dealing with graph classification/clustering problems. For example, if we're dealing with an unbalanced graph classification problem, it could be useful to create a balance step for the dataset using the GRAN algorithm and then perform the classification task.

Learning about topological data analysis

Topological Data Analysis (TDA) is a rather novel technique that's used to extract features that quantify the *shape of the data*. The idea of this approach is that by observing how datapoints are organized in a certain space, we can reveal some important information about the process that generated it.

The main tool for applying TDA is **persistent homology**. The math behind this method is quite advanced, so let's introduce this concept through an example. Suppose you have a set of data points distributed on a space, and let's suppose you are "observing" them over time. Points are static (they do not move across the space); thus, you will observe those independent points forever. However, let's imagine we can create associations between these data points by connecting them together through some well-defined rules. In particular, let's imagine a sphere expanding from these points through time. Each point will have its own expanding sphere and, once two spheres collide, an "edge" can be placed by these two points. This can be exemplified with the following diagram:

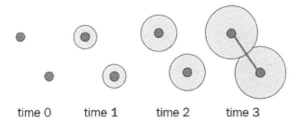

time 0   time 1   time 2   time 3

Figure 10.1 – Example of how relationships between points can be created

The more spheres that collide, the more associations that will be created, and the more edges that will be placed. This happens when multiple spheres intersect more complex geometrical structures such as triangles, tetrahedrons, and so on appear:

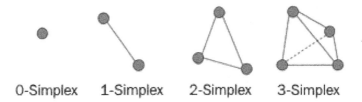

0-Simplex   1-Simplex   2-Simplex   3-Simplex

Figure 10.2 – Example of how connections among points generate geometrical structures

When a new geometrical structure appears, we can note its "*birth*" time. On the other hand, when an existing geometrical structure disappears (for example, it becomes part of a more complex geometrical structure), we can note its "*death*" time. The survival time (time between birth and death) of each geometrical structure that's observed during the simulation can be used as a new feature for analyzing the original dataset.

We can also define the so-called **persistent diagram** by placing each structure's corresponding pair (birth, death) on a two-axis system. Points closer to the diagonal normally reflect noise, whereas points distant from the diagonal represent persisting features. An example of a persistence diagram is as follows. Notice that we described the whole process by using expanding "*spheres*" as an example. In practice, we can change the dimension of this expanding shape (for instance, using 2D circles), thus producing a set of features for each dimension (commonly indicated using the letter H):

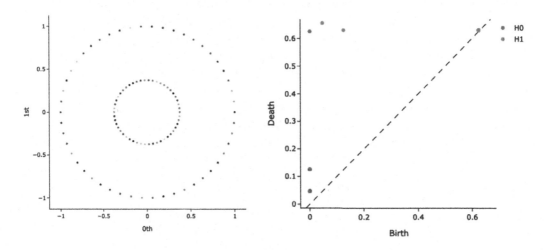

Figure 10.3 – Example of a 2D point cloud (right) and its corresponding persistence diagram (left)

A good Python library for performing topological data analysis is `giotto-tda`, which is available at the following URL: `https://github.com/giotto-ai/giotto-tda`. Using the `giotto-tda` library, it is easy to build the simplicial complex and its relative persistence diagram, as shown in the preceding image.

Topological machine learning

Now that we know the fundamentals behind TDA, let's see how it can be used for machine learning. By providing machine learning algorithms with topological data (such as persistent features), we can capture patterns that might be missed by other traditional approaches.

In the previous section, we saw that persistence diagrams are useful for describing data. Nevertheless, using them to feed machine learning algorithms (such as `RandomForest`) is not a good choice. For instance, different persistent diagrams may have different numbers of points, and basic algebraic operations would not be well defined.

One common way to overcome such a limitation is to transform diagrams into more suitable representations. Embeddings or kernel methods can be used to obtain a "*vectorized*" representation of the diagrams. Moreover, advanced representation methods such as *persistence images*, *persistence landscapes*, and *Betti curves*, among others, have been shown to be very useful in practical applications. Persistent images (*Figure 10.4*), for instance, are bi-dimensional representations of persistence diagrams that can easily be fed into convolutional neural networks.

Several possibilities arise out of this theory, and there is still a connection between the findings and deep learning. Several new ideas are being proposed, making the subject both hot and fascinating:

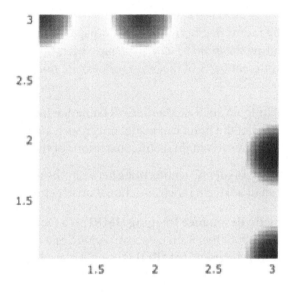

Figure 10.4 – Example of a persistent images

Topological data analysis is a rapidly growing field, especially since it can be combined with machine learning techniques. Several scientific papers are published on this topic every year and we expect novel exciting applications in the near future.

Applying graph theory in new domains

In recent years, due to there being a more solid theoretical understanding of graph machine learning, as well as an increase in available storage space and computational power, we can identify a number of domains in which such learning theories are spreading. With a bit of imagination, you can start looking at the surrounding world as a set of "*nodes*" and "*links*." Our work or study place, the technological devices we use every day, and even our brain can be represented as networks. In this section, we will look at some examples of how graph theory (and graph machine learning) has been applied to, apparently, unrelated domains.

Graph machine learning and neuroscience

The study of the brain by means of graph theory is a prosperous and expanding field. Several ways of representing the *brain as a network* have been investigated, with the aim of understanding how different parts of the brain (nodes) are *functionally* or *structurally* connected to each other.

By means of medical techniques such as **Magnetic Resonance Imaging** (**MRI**), a three-dimensional representation of the brain can be obtained. Such an image can be processed by different kinds of algorithms to obtain distinct partitions of the brain (parcellation).

There are different ways we can define connections between those regions, depending on whether we are interested in analyzing their functional or structural connectivity:

- **Functional Magnetic Resonance Imaging** (**fMRI**) is a technique that's used to measure whether a part of the brain is "active" or not. Specifically, it measures the **blood-oxygen-level-dependent** (**BOLD**) signal of each region (a signal indicating the variation of the level of blood and oxygen at a certain time). Then, the *Pearson correlation* between the BOLD series of two brain regions of interest can be computed. High correlation means that the two parts are "functionally connected," and an edge can be placed between them. An interesting paper on graphically analyzing fMRI data is *Graph-based network analysis of resting-state functional MRI*, which is available at `https://www.frontiersin.org/articles/10.3389/fnsys.2010.00016/full`.

- On the other hand, by using advanced MRI techniques such as **Diffusion Tensor Imaging** (**DTI**), we can also measure the strength of the white matter fiber bundles physically connecting two brain regions of interest. Thus, we can obtain a graph representing the structural connectivity of the brain. A paper where graphs neural networks are used in combination with graphs generated from DTI data is called *Multiple Sclerosis Clinical Profiles via Graph Convolutional Neural Networks* and is available at `https://www.frontiersin.org/articles/10.3389/fnins.2019.00594/full`.

- Functional and structural connectivity can be analyzed using graph theory. There are several studies that enhance significant alterations of such networks related to neurodegenerative diseases, such as Alzheimer's, multiple sclerosis, and Parkinson's, among others.

The final result is a graph describing the connection between the different brain regions, as shown here:

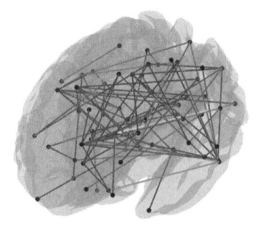

Figure 10.5 – Connection between brain regions as a graph

Here, we can see how different brain regions can be seen as nodes of a graph, while the connections between those regions are edges.

Graph machine learning has been shown to be very useful for this kind of analysis. Different studies have been conducted to automatically diagnose a particular pathology based on the brain network, thus predicting the evolution of the network (for example, identifying potentially vulnerable regions that are likely to be affected by the pathology in the future).

Network neuroscience is a promising field, and, in the future, more and more insight will be collected from those networks so that we can understand pathological alterations and predict a disease's evolution.

Graph theory and chemistry and biology

Graph machine learning can be applied to chemistry. For example, graphs provide a natural method for describing **molecular structures** by treating atoms as the nodes of a graph and bonds as their connections. Such methods have been used to investigate different aspects of chemical systems, including representing reactions, and learning chemical fingerprints (indicating the presence or absence of chemical features or substructures), among others.

Several applications can be also found in biology, where many different elements can be represented as a graph. **Protein-protein interactions** (**PPI**), for example, is one of the most widely studied topics. Here, a graph is constructed, where nodes represent protein and edges represent their interaction. Such a method allows us to exploit the structural information of PPI networks, which has proved to be informative in PPI prediction.

Graph machine learning and computer vision

The rise of deep learning, especially **convolutional neural network** (**CNN**) techniques, has achieved amazing results in computer vision research. For a wide range of tasks, such as image classification, object detection, and semantic segmentation, CNNs can be considered as the state-of-the-art. However, recently, central challenges in computer vision have started to be addressed using graph machine learning techniques – **geometric deep learning** in particular. As we have learned throughout this book, there are fundamental differences between the 2D Euclidean domain in which images are represented and more complex objects such as 3D shapes and point clouds. Restoring the world's 3D geometry from 2D and 3D visual data, scene understanding, stereo matching, and depth estimation are only a few examples of what can be done.

Image classification and scene understanding

Image classification, one of the most widely studied tasks in computer vision, nowadays dominated by CNN-based algorithms, has started to be addressed from a different perspective. Graph neural network models have shown attractive results, especially when huge amounts of labeled data is not available. In particular, there is a trend in combining these models with *zero-shot and few-shot learning techniques*. Here, the goal is to classify classes that the model has never seen during training. For instance, this can be achieved by exploiting the knowledge of how the unseen object is "semantically" related to the seen ones.

Similar approaches have been also used for scene understanding. Using a relational graph between detected objects in a scene provides an interpretable structured representation of the image. This can be used to support high-level reasoning for various tasks, including captioning and visual question answering, among others.

Shape analysis

Differently from images, which are represented by a bi-dimensional grid of pixels, there are several methods for representing 3D shapes, such as *multi-view images, depth maps, voxels, point clouds, meshes,* and *implicit surfaces,* among others. Nevertheless, when applying machine and deep learning algorithms, such representations can be exploited to learn specific geometric features, which can be useful for designing a better analysis.

In this context, geometric deep learning techniques have shown promising results. For instance, GNN techniques have been successfully applied for finding correspondence between deformable shapes, a classical problem that leads to several applications, including texture animation and mapping, as well as scene understanding. For those of you who are interested, some good resources to help you understand this application of graph machine learning are available at `https://arxiv.org/pdf/1611.08097.pdf` and `http://geometricdeeplearning.com/`.

Recommendation systems

Another interesting application of graph machine learning is in recommendation systems, which we can use to predict the "rating" or the "preference" that a user would assign to an item. In *Chapter 6, Social Network Graphs,* we provided an example of how link prediction can be used to build automatic algorithms that provide recommendations to a given user and/or customer. In the paper *Graph Neural Networks in Recommender Systems: A Survey,* available at `https://arxiv.org/pdf/2011.02260.pdf`, the authors provide an extensive survey of graph machine learning that's been applied to build recommendation systems. More specifically, the authors describe different graph machine learning algorithms and their applications.

Summary

In this chapter, we provided a high-level overview of some emerging graph machine learning algorithms and their applications for new domains. At the beginning of this chapter, we described, using the example provided in *Chapter 8, Graph Analysis for Credit Card Transactions,* some sampling and augmentation algorithms for graph data. We provided some Python libraries that can be used to deal with graph sampling and graph data augmentation tasks.

We continued by providing a general description of topological data analysis and how this technique has recently been used in different domains.

Finally, we provided several descriptions of new application domains, such as neuroscience chemistry, and biology. We also described how machine learning algorithms can also be used to solve other tasks, such as image classification, shape analysis, and recommendation systems.

This is it! In this book, we provided an overview of the most important graph machine learning techniques and algorithms. You should now be able to deal with graph data and build machine learning algorithms. We hope that you are now in possession of more tools in your toolkit and that you will use them to develop exciting applications. We also invite you to check the references we provided in this book and to address the challenges we proposed in the different chapters.

The world of graph machine learning is fascinating and rapidly evolving. New research papers are published every day with incredible findings. As usual, a continuous review of the scientific literature is the best way to discover new algorithms, and arXiv (`https://arxiv.org/`) is the best place to search for freely available scientific papers.

`Packt.com`

Subscribe to our online digital library for full access to over 7,000 books and videos, as well as industry leading tools to help you plan your personal development and advance your career. For more information, please visit our website.

Why subscribe?

- Spend less time learning and more time coding with practical eBooks and Videos from over 4,000 industry professionals

- Improve your learning with Skill Plans built especially for you

- Get a free eBook or video every month

- Fully searchable for easy access to vital information

- Copy and paste, print, and bookmark content

Did you know that Packt offers eBook versions of every book published, with PDF and ePub files available? You can upgrade to the eBook version at `packt.com` and as a print book customer, you are entitled to a discount on the eBook copy. Get in touch with us at `customercare@packtpub.com` for more details.

At `www.packt.com`, you can also read a collection of free technical articles, sign up for a range of free newsletters, and receive exclusive discounts and offers on Packt books and eBooks.

Other Books You May Enjoy

If you enjoyed this book, you may be interested in these other books by Packt:

Learn Grafana 7.0

Eric Salituro

ISBN: 978-1-83882-658-1

Explore data science and its various process models

- Find out how to visualize data using Grafana
- Understand how to work with the major components of the Graph panel
- Explore mixed data sources, query inspector, and time interval settings
- Discover advanced dashboard features such as annotations, templating with variables, dashboard linking, and dashboard sharing techniques
- Connect user authentication to Google, GitHub, and a variety of external services
- Find out how Grafana can provide monitoring support for cloud service infrastructures

Interactive Dashboards and Data Apps with Plotly and Dash

Elias Dabbas

ISBN: 978-1-80056-891-4

- Find out how to run a fully interactive and easy-to-use app
- Convert your charts to various formats including images and HTML files
- Use Plotly Express and the grammar of graphics for easily mapping data to various visual attributes
- Create different chart types, such as bar charts, scatter plots, histograms, maps, and more
- Expand your app by creating dynamic pages that generate content based on URLs
- Implement new callbacks to manage charts based on URLs and vice versa

Packt is searching for authors like you

If you're interested in becoming an author for Packt, please visit `authors.packtpub.com` and apply today. We have worked with thousands of developers and tech professionals, just like you, to help them share their insight with the global tech community. You can make a general application, apply for a specific hot topic that we are recruiting an author for, or submit your own idea.

Leave a review - let other readers know what you think

Please share your thoughts on this book with others by leaving a review on the site that you bought it from. If you purchased the book from Amazon, please leave us an honest review on this book's Amazon page. This is vital so that other potential readers can see and use your unbiased opinion to make purchasing decisions, we can understand what our customers think about our products, and our authors can see your feedback on the title that they have worked with Packt to create. It will only take a few minutes of your time, but is valuable to other potential customers, our authors, and Packt. Thank you!

Index

M

N

Made in the USA
Las Vegas, NV
06 March 2022

45154804R00188